"I found myself wanting to read the entire book in one sitting. Nancy captivates me with her simple, down-to-earth, everyday examples of God's amazing grace. She demonstrates that 'Grace is God's invitation to dance with Him' throughout this compilation of grace talks. *Lipstick Grace* is so brilliantly written that I experienced (and I believe you will, too) a greater understanding of God's matchless, endless, all-encompassing love and grace for each of us—in spite of who we are and what we do. Definitely a must-read and share-it-with-your-friends book."

THELMA WELLS
PRESIDENT OF A WOMAN OF GOD MINISTRIES,
WOMEN OF FAITH CONFERENCE SPEAKER,
AUTHOR OF *GOD IS NOT THROUGH WITH ME YET*

"Nancy Kennedy nailed me on the first page! In reading this collection of Nancy's perceptive, amusing, and extremely honest newspaper columns, I felt like I was captured and taken on an enthralling journey—a journey where the ordinary happenings of our lives become filled by the wisest, most unexpected insights. I, too, am always on a search for the perfect lipstick… and I know I'm never going to look at it the same way again."

SHAUNTI FELDHAHN
BESTSELLING AUTHOR OF *FOR WOMEN ONLY*

"Rarely will you find a writer who invites you into her everyday life with such courage, conviction, and transparency as Nancy does. And I know, for me, this is where I need grace the most: in the everyday. You'll laugh out loud one minute, and dab at tears the next. Prepare to be delighted—and changed—with a little *Lipstick Grace*."

CONNIE GRIGSBY
AUTHOR OF *THE POLITICALLY INCORRECT WIFE*
AND *HOW TO GET YOUR HUSBAND TO TALK TO YOU*

Lipstick Grace

NANCY KENNEDY

Multnomah Books

LIPSTICK GRACE
published by Multnomah Books
A division of Random House, Inc.

© 2007 by Nancy Kennedy
International Standard Book Number: 1-59052-767-4

For information:
MULTNOMAH BOOKS
12265 ORACLE BOULEVARD, SUITE 200
COLORADO SPRINGS, COLORADO 80921

Library of Congress Cataloging-in-Publication Data
Kennedy, Nancy, 1954-
Lipstick grace / Nancy Kennedy.
   p. cm.
ISBN 1-59052-767-4
1. Christian women--Religious life. 2. Christian life—Anecdotes. 3. Grace
(Theology)—Miscellanea. I. Title.
BV4527.K4446 2006
242—dc22

                                    2006036583

07 08 09 10 11 12 13 14 15—10 9 8 7 6 5 4 3 2 1 0

This book is dedicated to LK, CK ,Tara, Bod, and Beans.
God is able to make all grace abound to you.

2 CORINTHIANS 9:8

Table *of* Contents

✤ ✤ ✤

✤ ✤ ✤

PUTTING *on* MY LIPSTICK *and* MY DANCING SHOES

*I*N MY DREAMS, I am a dancer, gliding across a polished wooden dance floor in three-quarter time. I'm agile and smooth, my every movement flowing and fluid. I'm lithe and nimble, graceful as a gazelle.

In my dreams, that is.

In real life, I trip over my feet more often than not, even while standing still. The truth is, I can't dance. I got no rhythm. Can't waltz, can't tango. Can't fox-trot, can't jitterbug, can't watusi, can't do-si-do, can't do the electric slide.

I tried line dancing once and kicked some lady in the knee.

I'm woefully lacking in grace. Grace deficient. Grace doesn't come naturally to me.

But I want grace! I want to be graceful. To be full of grace. I want to receive it, give it, live in it, wash in it. I want to immerse myself in grace—amazing, glorious grace.

It's what we all want, whether we know it or not. The problem is that *grace* is a nebulous word, like *faith* and *love*. You can define it ("unmerited favor") but still not understand what it means. Some words are best glimpsed. *Don't tell me about grace—show me what it looks like in everyday life.*

That's what I've attempted to do in *Lipstick Grace: Glimpses of Life, Love, and the Quest for the Perfect Lip Gloss.* I've attempted to show you what grace looks like: saving grace, sufficient grace. Common grace, sanctifying and redeeming grace. Grace that comes through faith in Christ. Grace that draws sinners to the Cross again and again and again.

We can never get enough grace.

If there's such a thing as a favorite theologian, Martin Luther tops my list. A sixteenth-century German monk, Luther stumbled upon the concept of grace while reading the apostle Paul's letter to the Romans: "The just shall live by faith" (Romans 1:17, KJV).

Up until that time, Luther had spent his life trying to atone for his own sins, beating himself and spending hours on his knees confessing his sins, and then agonizing in case he forgot one.

But once the lightbulb went on and he realized that it truly is by grace alone that we are saved and by grace alone that we live, he became one of the greatest grace teachers of all time. *The just shall live by faith, which comes solely by grace.*

As the story goes, someone once said to Luther, "Grace, grace, grace, all you ever talk about is grace."

To which Luther replied, "That's because grace is all there is."

I don't know if that's a true story about Luther—I heard it in a sermon once. If it's not true about Luther's conversation, it's still a true statement about grace.

Grace is all there is.

Grace is God's invitation to dance with Him.

"For God did not send his Son into the world to condemn the world, but to save the world through him" (John 3:17). That all the whosoevers who would believe in Him would not perish, but dance with Him forever.

Apart from grace we are helpless and hopeless. Onlookers and outcasts, in despair and eternally doomed. That's why we who have tasted grace, given to us by the God of grace through faith in His Son, can't stop talking about it. Grace makes blind men see, lame men walk, and dead men get up and dance.

This book is a collection of my glimpses of grace, taken from the past five or so years worth of my weekly column, "Grace Notes," which I write for a Florida daily newspaper, the *Citrus County Chronicle*, where I am on staff as a feature writer. My column also appears in about a dozen newspapers elsewhere.

In my column, and therefore in this book, I have wrestled with my relationships with people and with God and with my own self. I've confessed my sins, questioned my motives and actions and thoughts. I've voiced my doubts as well as my certainty about matters of faith and trust.

I've blathered about petty things like finding the perfect lipstick and have confessed that same pettiness, all the while marveling at the incredible forgiveness, mercy, and grace of our great God.

Grace. It always comes back to grace. It's all that matters. Every moment, every hour, every day.

Grace, grace, grace.

It's all there is—so put on your lipstick and your dancing shoes, and let's dance!

LIPSTICK GRACE

EVERY WEEK I sit down to write all about how much I love Jesus so you will want to be like me, but then I get a pang of conscience and I end up writing the truth. For example, my all-consuming passion these days isn't loving Jesus, but trying to find the perfect lipstick.

Although I want the passion of my life to be Jesus, right now it's not; it's lipstick. Not too red, not too pink, not too brown—and it has to be shiny.

The problem is, I can't find just one satisfactory lip product, so I've had to resort to using a combination of six products: a flesh-colored base, a lip-plumping moisturizing product, a pink liquid lipstick, and—since that's too pink—on top of that, I use a brownish liquid.

Over all of that goes clear, shiny stuff, and then over that goes a setting solution that acts like a lipstick glue. It burns when applied and smells like turpentine, and users are cautioned not to swallow any of it. But it's worth the 140-mile round-trip drive to Orlando and the fifteen dollars I pay for it because it's guaranteed to keep lipstick perfect for hours—as long as you don't eat or drink or smile too broadly.

Of course, my lips will probably fall off by the time I'm sixty, but at least they'll look pink and shiny lying on the ground.

I was telling all of this to a group of Lutheran women recently at their women's retreat. They had invited me to speak to them about the grand passion of my life.

I began by asking them, "What holds you? What captivates your attention and captures your heart? What's the first thing you think about in the morning—and the last thing at night?"

Because we're all proper church ladies, we knew the correct answer was, of course, "Jesus."

I had come to talk to them about Jesus. But something awesome happened after I asked that question. We—the Lutheran women and me, too—put aside the correct answer and started talking about the honest answer, which too often is "not Jesus."

Instead, we talked about lipstick and chocolate and hidden stashes of food. We talked about worrying about our kids, fretting about husbands who don't put away their laundry, and being overly concerned with what people think of us.

Eventually we talked about Jesus, but we had to deal with the "not Jesus" stuff first. The honest stuff. The real stuff that captures our hearts and holds us captive. The stuff from which Jesus wants to set us free.

When we did that, when we risked being honest instead of being correct, when we stopped pretending and got real, something happened.

Grace happened.

I didn't plan it. I don't think any of us can plan grace. Grace just is. God gives it when and where He sees fit.

He saw fit that day.

It was by His grace I was able to confess that my whole life currently revolves around the color of my lips and not Jesus. Grace enabled me to admit that I don't have it all together, that I'm basically a mess, but a mess for whom Jesus died and dearly loves.

When grace happens, messy people are free to admit their struggles to each other and know that they will be accepted. Maybe not always by each other, but definitely by God.

The truth is, I'll never love Jesus the way I should, or even the way others think I do. Something always interferes. If it's not lipstick, then it's watching *Gilmore Girls* or eating waffles and maple syrup or searching for the perfect relationship.

As long as I'm a sinner, I'll continue to chase after all those somethings that lure my affections away from the only One whose love can fill the empty parts inside.

That's why I need grace. And if I ever start to forget, I have a bathroom drawer full of discarded lipsticks to remind me.

BIRDBRAINED EVANGELISM

USED TO THINK I could control the universe. Maybe not the whole universe, but at least my part of it. And maybe not control, but at least help God control it, especially when it came to others coming to faith in Jesus.

When I was a new believer, I was, for the most part, one of those obnoxious Christians most non-Christians run away from. I thought it was my job and mine alone to make everyone around me also believe.

About that time, my husband and I and our then-toddler Alison moved from Maine to California and moved in with my family temporarily while we looked for a place to live.

Back then, Mom had a parrot named George. George had a limited vocabulary, mostly standard parrot phraseology and a few choice swear words, which everyone blamed on my youngest brother.

Convinced that God created George for me to use as an evangelistic tool, I set out to teach him certain surefire, Spirit (I hoped)-filled phrases.

Each morning after everyone left for work, I'd sit down next to George's cage and coach him to say things like "All have sinned" and "Come to Jesus." I sang "Jesus Loves Me" to him, attempted to engage him in theological conversations.

But as hard as I tried, he refused to say anything beyond "Hey, baby!" and "[expletive deleted]".

I planned to feign surprise if my ploy really worked. If someone in my family walked in upon George's uttering something profound like, "Repent and be baptized," I would drop open my mouth, raise my eyebrows, and cry, "Even God's creatures praise Him!"

However, George was a bad bird. Not only wouldn't he cooperate with my attempts to use him to evangelize my family members, but he used to pick fights with people. He especially had it in for my husband.

One night Barry opened George's cage to feed him, and the bird escaped and chased us into the garage, pecking at our legs. We hid from our eighteen-inch foe for what seemed hours until Barry finally confronted him with a rolled-up newspaper in one hand and a bribe of fruit in the other. Eventually George returned to his cage, but not before I decided he wasn't a tool of God after all, but of the devil.

Not long after that, we moved into our own place and George died.

I wasn't sorry either. However, I was sorry—although not until years later—that I had been one of those Christians who takes matters into her own hands and goes to great lengths to coerce and manipulate people into trusting and believing in Jesus.

I hadn't understood that while some people do respond in faith by shotgun methods such as being cornered in an elevator by a zealous Christian wielding a gospel tract or maybe even a bird parroting a force-fed phrase, most don't. Incidents like that usually just reinforce the image of Christians as pushy religious fruitcakes. It's a wonder God uses us to spread the message of the gospel at all.

Sometimes I wish I could crawl inside God's head and think His thoughts. Then I could know why some people believe and some don't. Why some are flat-out antagonistic toward Jesus, why some are mocking, and others agreeably indifferent.

Why some will eventually believe and some never will.

I might not ever know the answers, and that's okay. I do know that I can't save another's soul—that job belongs to God alone—and that no one comes to Jesus unless the Father draws him.

That means I don't have to push and strive, argue or debate. Instead, what God requires of me is to do what's fair, to love kindness and mercy, and to walk humbly with Him. I'm to love my enemies and, with gentleness, courtesy, and respect, be ready to give an answer to anyone who asks about the hope I have in Christ.

The saving of souls belongs to the One who controls the universe.

All things considered, especially with my track record for trying to convert uncooperative, unrepentant, nonevangelical birds, I'm glad it's Him and not me.

FAILURES WANTED

*W*HEN I GET E-MAILS from readers, usually they're kind; sometimes they're challenging. Sometimes someone's pleas for mercy and grace cause me to drop to my knees and pray.

One such came from a woman who had read my book *When He Doesn't Believe*. She confessed that, despite knowing that God's best for a believer is to marry another like-minded Christian, she chose to ignore what she knew was right and married outside the faith. They had been married twenty years, and although her husband is a good man whom she dearly loves, she said their spiritual differences weigh heavy upon her. She grieves for their lack of unity and oneness.

What hit me about her e-mail was her misconception that she had committed an unpardonable sin when she married. She still carried a burden of guilt, feeling like a failure.

"How can God's promises be for me when I knew what I was doing was wrong?" she asked. "I've repented over and over. Yet…"

I love receiving letters like hers because it gives me the opportunity to share good news: Of course God's promises and blessings are yours! For those who confess, there's always forgiveness. For those who are God's, there's grace.

As for failure, join the club. The kingdom of God is full of failures—that's how we enter. It's through our continued failures and God's restoration of us that we experience the greatness of His grace.

I talk often about times when "God shows up," but it's the one time He didn't that will stick forever in my mind. I had been invited to speak at a women's group and accepted the invitation because I wanted the money and craved yet one more time on stage, all eyes upon me.

I had prepared what I thought was an inspirational talk that would have the women snorting Diet Pepsi out their noses from laughter and then crying into their hankies because of my poignancy. By the time I got to the church, I was so full of myself that I thought I could walk on water.

The "act" before me, a guy with a guitar, had been awesome—and hilarious between his songs. I hated him because I knew that I wouldn't be able to top him. However, I was determined to try. Then as I stepped up to the microphone, God stepped out of the room.

Sadly, I didn't even notice at first.

But as every story I told fell flat, as I fumbled and stammered and lost my train of thought, I looked around, searching for His presence, only to find that He had hidden Himself from me.

I wanted to die right then and there.

When I finished, the women applauded politely, but no one bought my books and no one asked me to please come back. I cried all the way home, a miserable failure.

After that, I didn't get another invitation to speak for nearly two years. God had put me in "time-out." However, it wasn't so much to punish me as it was to perfect me.

If it hadn't been for my failure, I might not have come to understand my propensity for building my own kingdom. If I had missed the experience of falling on my face and the humiliation of doing it before an audience, I would have missed the experience of God eventually reaching down to lift me back up.

If I hadn't confessed my sin of pride and arrogance, I never would have known His restorative grace. Instead, I would have assumed that He builds His kingdom with perfect people, not per-fected failures. He is in the process of perfecting His people, one failure at a time.

The Bible is filled with failures, and the common theme throughout is that "Jesus Christ came to save sinners, of whom (insert your name here) is chief" (1 Timothy 1:15). But He not only saves them; He restores them. He perfects them. And as He does, He offers forgiveness. He offers grace. He makes His promises available for all who call Him Lord.

The sign on heaven's gate reads: Only Failures May Enter Here.

MY YEAR *of* LIVING FRIVOLOUSLY

*H*ERE'S ADVICE you can take to the bank: Never tell your car or any major household appliance when you have extra money. Likewise, never let God know that what you'd really like is to be rich. Either way, chances are you'll end up with a handful of bus tokens.

In the children's book *Alexander Who Used to Be Rich Last Sunday*, unlike his brothers, poor Alexander only has bus tokens...until his grandparents give him a dollar on Sunday. Suddenly, Alexander is rich!

However, through a series of frivolous and unwise purchases (gum, a used candle, a deck of cards, "snake rental," and magic tricks), plus losing a bet and being fined by his parents for mouthing off, Alexander goes from being poor to rich and back to poor before the week is up. He ends up with what he started with—bus tokens.

Oh, how I can relate. Like Alexander who used to be rich last Sunday, I'm Nancy who used to be rich last year. Not millionaire rich, but more-money-than-I'd-ever-had-before rich.

I'd signed a book contract at the beginning of the year, offering me a ridiculous amount of money. The check came, and as I put it in the bank and sang "Oh Happy Day," my car leaked fluids and groaned. So I bought a new car. I took a few trips. I went shopping—a lot.

The termite people stopped by for a visit, which always costs. My computer and my cell phone became deathly ill, so I bought new ones.

I went shopping again. The IRS sent me a lovely note requesting a third of my windfall.

I bought a couch. My kids came for Christmas—digital cameras for everyone!

My accountant did my taxes. The IRS decided they wanted more of my riches, and now I'm back to where I started. Not poor, but not rich like I was last year.

I complained to my uncle.

"I'm sorry you're not rich anymore," he said. "Vote Republican!"

I said I wasn't sure that would help. I also said I wasn't surprised either, that I saw it coming. I'd heard chuckling from heaven, as if God was up to something.

Sometimes when I speak to women about the things in our lives that we think we hold but really hold us, I always confess that when it comes to my bank account, I always want more. "Not millions and billions," I say, "but just a smidge more than 'enough.' I want to know that I can get my hair cut *and* my carpets cleaned *and* go out to dinner all in the same week without having to budget or even think about it.

"That's all," I tell them. "Just a smidge more than enough. Just that extra cushion…" Then I pause before revealing the bottom line to my bottom line: "… so I won't have to trust God."

That's when the room gets silent.

So it didn't surprise me that my riches dwindled away. I would have been more surprised if they hadn't. That's why when I realized that, like Alexander, I was back to bus tokens, I didn't fling myself onto my new couch and wail and moan.

Actually, I laughed. I'd had a fun year living frivolously. I had wanted to be rich and was, albeit briefly, but I knew it had to end. God loves me too much for it not to.

I used to clean the house of a wealthy woman who would tell me how she envied me. In her eyes, because I came to work smiling, I was the wealthy one. She didn't smile much. She'd say, "Money just causes trouble."

Lots of people know that the Bible talks about the love of money being the root of all kinds of evil and discontent, but they often overlook the answer to contentment. It's not in vilifying riches or selling everything and living in a cave. Instead, contentment is found in knowing God's promise: "Never will I leave you; never will I forsake you" (Hebrews 13:5).

In that way, even though I don't have lots of extra money anymore and I'm back to budgeting for haircuts, I'm still the richest woman on earth—and not even the IRS can take that away from me.

THE GRACE *of a* MIDDLE SCHOOL GEEK

HEN I WAS in middle school, I had only two preeminent thoughts: Bob Richardson and Scott Kelly. They were my sole reasons for existence, although they both preferred my best friend, Cheryl Peterson. But as cute as they both were, it was Charles Benson, the school geek, who left a lasting, eternal impression on me.

Charles Benson was the kind of kid other kids pushed into the lockers. It wasn't uncommon to see him sprawled on the ground after having tripped over someone's outstretched foot. I can still see his string bean frame and his oily brown hair plastered to his head. He wore his shirts buttoned up to his neck—thirty years before it was fashionable. He wasn't quite right (in my seventh-grade opinion). Today he might be called something politically correct like "mentally challenged." Back then we called him names I'd be ashamed to print here, mostly because I probably called them out the loudest. Charles Benson alternately made my life heaven and hell on earth. I took great delight in tormenting him. He was easy prey. All you had to do was look at him and he'd practically dive into a locker on his own. Still, pushing him was beyond fun.

Even so, Charles Benson also made my life hell. Nothing I or anyone else did to torture him seemed to faze him. He'd just get up and go on. That drove me crazy! What fun is tormenting a geek unless you can watch him crack under the pressure? Not only that, but he used to wear the most annoying slogan button ever created. It said simply: "I'm third."

One day I cornered him in the hallway, and jabbing my finger into his chest, I pointed at his button and demanded, "Charles Benson, what does that mean?"

Without flinching he answered, "Jesus is first, others are second, and I'm third."

Although I wouldn't admit it then, I'll admit it now: His words pierced me through to the core of my being. However, as an ultracool seventh-grader, I jabbed at him some more and said, "That's the stupidest thing I've ever heard." It may have been stupid back then, but his answer haunted me for the next ten years, until Jesus grabbed hold of my heart at age twenty-three.

It's been eons since middle school, but I still think about Charles Benson and his simple message. I was reminded of it again this week when I popped into an FCA (Fellowship of Christian Athletes) meeting at a local middle school. One of the youth pastors talked about kids like Charles Benson and how a kind word or gesture of genuine love can make an eternal difference in their lives.

He challenged the students to reach out to the outcasts at their school and share Christ's love. Give a valentine to someone other kids pick on. Love the unloved. He reminded them that God loved us when we least deserved it and sent His Son to die in our place.

As the kids left the gymnasium, I wondered if anyone would take up the pastor's challenge. I wondered who the outcasts of the school were and if kids pushed them into lockers. I almost started to feel smug and glad that I was never a seventh-grade outcast when a thought crossed my mind: In God's eyes, it wasn't Charles Benson who didn't belong back in junior high, but me!

Apart from Christ, I was the loser. I was the outcast. I was the geek.

Funny isn't it, how we see things differently than God sees them?

I think about Charles Benson a lot. I tried looking him up on the Internet, and once I even sent a letter to a Charles Benson in Canoga Park, California, but I never got a reply. That's okay. Someday when I get to heaven I'll look him up. I want to thank him for reaching out with the love of His Savior to a seventh-grade outcast back at Christopher Columbus Junior High School. And if there are any lockers in heaven…maybe God will let him give me a shove.

Just for fun.

When God Shows Up

I'M LOOKING for God these days. Not that He's lost or hiding. I'm just looking for Him to show up in my life. He does that sometimes, although when He does, it's rarely as you expect. You expect whirlwinds and flashing lights, fanfare and pomp. Maybe a phone call in advance of His coming.

But He doesn't do what you expect. That's because He's God and you're not. Still, He seems to enjoy showing up in the lives of His children.

I remember one visit when I was young in my faith and had signed up for a week at my church's children's summer camp. I wanted to work in the kitchen with the adults, but they put me in a cabin with Elmer's Glue, the staff members' kids who were too young for regular camp. They were called Elmer's Glue because everyone had to stay stuck together all week.

Stuck is right. Whoever made camp assignments didn't realize that I don't do kids. Or maybe God assigned it. Either way, it was the longest week of my life. My only hope was the last night's campfire, the highlight of the entire camp. Everyone had told me, "That's when God shows up." Then, as well as now, I wanted nothing more than to be visited by God. So I set my eyes on that final campfire and endured the week with the Glue.

When Friday night arrived, I couldn't wait to get to the campfire. I didn't want to miss God showing up. I didn't know what it would be like, only that it would be awesome. However, no one came to Elmer's Glue to replace me so I could attend. I considered sneaking off, but one of my charges wet his bunk and woke everyone else up. You could say I was Glued to the cabin.

If self-pity were a virtue, I would've been an exemplary

example of it that night. When everyone finally went back to sleep, I sat on the cabin's front porch and sulked. Then God showed up.

How do you explain it? Once a friend asked, "When God shows up, does He knock first?" I told her that God doesn't have to knock. He just…shows up. One minute you're on a porch step with your chin in the dirt, and the next minute you hear crickets chirp in the woods and watch an owl swoop through the trees and across the brightest moon you've ever seen. Next thing you know, the fresh wind of the Spirit blows over you, lifts your sagging spirit, and a praise song wells up in your soul. You can't explain it, but you know that your Creator has visited you.

A few years ago, a friend's husband left her with two small children to raise. She, too, had been looking for God to show up, but He had been silent. One day, she tried starting her lawn mower, but it wouldn't start. Unable to bear the stress any longer, she screamed toward heaven, "Where are You, God?" As tears streamed down her face, a man on a riding lawn mower came around the corner and offered his help. God hadn't forgotten her. He came just in time.

Sometimes God shows up and the earth quakes and the Red Sea parts. Water turns to wine. Dead men are raised. At other times, He shows up on a tractor lawn mower at your lowest moment and quiets your despair. Sometimes He shows up in a friend's simple gesture of genuine care when your world is in turmoil. A shoulder to cry on. A stupid joke that makes you laugh. Sometimes He just slips in and sits with you on a porch stoop and spoils your pity party.

No matter how He does it, at the right moment He shows up to remind you that if you're His, you've been His since before eternity and that He loves you with an everlasting love. He reminds you that nothing you're facing is out of His control.

So I'm looking for God these days. I don't know when He'll show up or how, only that He will when I need Him most. Not too early, not too late. That's what He does because that's who He is.

THIS OLD HOUSE

WHEN WE LIVED on the Monterey Peninsula in California, my husband was hired to restore a house in San Francisco. It wasn't one of the Victorians the city is famous for, but as houses go, it was old, dating back to the 1920s or '30s. Nearly every weekend he would travel the one hundred miles north and carefully and painstakingly tear down walls and rebuild.

The woman who had owned the house was a friend's aunt. She had lived there for decades with her mentally retarded daughter. When the woman died, the daughter found a case of canisters of talcum powder and emptied them all by shaking them throughout the house, upstairs and down. It was Barry's job to first clean up the mess, then to restore the house.

Occasionally, our daughters and I would go along and help. Even with all of us working, it took months to get rid of all the talcum residue and clean out the closets before Barry could begin restoration.

One particular weekend, our youngest daughter found a small box tucked away in a linen closet. She opened it and, discovering nothing but dust, took it outside to toss in the air. That's when we discovered that it was actually "doggy dust," the cremated remains of dearly departed Scoot.

The remainder of the restoration process was uneventful; nothing tops a preschooler playing with doggy dust and then, as a parent, having to explain it.

When the year was up, the house had been cleaned, disassembled, and put back together with new plumbing and wiring, a new furnace and carpeting, scrubbed cabinets and fixtures, and freshly painted walls.

Before my husband had come to its rescue, the house was dingy, moldy, and cold, not to mention covered with white powder. No one would have wanted to live in it—no one could have, not the way it was. But once my husband was finished, the house was fit for sale, and it sold at a pretty price.

This may sound odd, but whenever I hear the carol "Joy to the World" I think about that house in San Francisco. "No more let sins and sorrows grow, nor thorns infest the ground; He comes to make His blessings flow far as the curse is found," wrote Isaac Watts nearly three hundred years ago.

When I hear that song, it reminds me that I was once much like that old house: unfit, messed up, in disarray and disrepair. Sin does that to a person.

But then Jesus came.

He came and set about cleaning me up and restoring me, which is not always a comfortable process. I remember my husband using a sledgehammer and a crowbar to pry old tile off a shower wall and how swollen and bloodied his hands were when he was done. The process of restoring that old house involved gutting and exposing raw beams and tearing down walls. We hauled away scores of bags of trash and debris.

I also remember how meticulously he worked. He wouldn't say he was finished until he was sure he was finished.

Some say Christmas is about light and peace on earth, joy and goodwill toward men. It is, but it's about so much more. It's really about house remodeling and about the birth of a Carpenter who came to take lives in need of restoration and tear them apart and put them back together better than before.

Jesus has come, and even though His work of redemption through His death on the cross is finished, the tearing apart and putting back together of individual lives isn't. He's still ripping down rotting drywall and exposing secret boxes of dusty remains.

However, He doesn't leave us that way. He has promised to finish everything He starts: to bind broken hearts, mend broken lives, restore broken relationships, especially the relationship between Himself and man. Himself and me—and you, too.

He has come to "make His blessings flow far as the curse is found." And when He's done, those whom He has restored will be better than new, from the inside out, and worth far more than all the houses on all the hills in San Francisco.

Oh, the joy He brings to the world.

INTRUDING LIZARDS *and* ESCAPING BTUS

I DON'T KNOW how to tell my husband this, but we've got an uninvited houseguest. I discovered him (or her) in the bathtub the other day.

It's my own fault that he (she? it?) came into the house. I have a bad habit of leaving the front door open and forgetting about it, "wasting the Btus," which is a mortal sin at my house. (Btus are British Thermal Units and have something to do with the air conditioner and rising electric bills.)

It seems that an open door serves as a welcome sign to renegade lizards.

I'm not one of those squeamish-of-lizards sissy girls. As lizards go, I like them, although not as much as my friend Tara, who knows how to hang them from her earlobes like earrings. I may look, but I won't touch.

Once I saw what I thought was a two-headed, eight-legged

lizard on my front porch. It didn't run away when I opened the door, so I watched it a while. Until I realized it wasn't one lizard, but two, so I shut the door to give them some privacy.

A few weeks or months later I had scads of teeny lizard toddlers scurrying all over, which confirmed what I had seen that lizard couple doing, and I accidentally killed one lizard baby. He (she? it?) moved too fast or I moved too fast, and I clipped it with my bike, the aftermath of which wasn't pretty.

As for my current houseguest, I'm not sure if he (she? it?) is a direct descendent of the pair I saw canoodling on the porch. It doesn't matter; I just want the reptile out of my house!

Outdoors, lizards are lovely; they're God's creatures. But indoors, they're ugly miniature dinosaurs that might scamper across my face as I sleep. Or, because I don't keep a supply of naturally occurring lizard yummies handy and don't even know what they eat, one inside my house will most likely die of starvation and become a petrified lizard carcass in my living room and I'll have to, like, touch the icky thing.

That happened once. A lizard had been hanging from my bedroom curtain for about a month and wouldn't leave. My husband was gone and since I was the man of the house, I poked it with a stick to shoo it away, but it disintegrated into lizard dust all over the carpet, which was unbelievably gross and I was mildly traumatized the rest of the day.

So you would think that I might keep the front door closed. However, if I'm just going to the garage for a minute to get clothes out of the dryer, I'll leave the door open so I won't have to risk dropping clean laundry while fumbling with the door handle.

I keep thinking that just a few minutes won't matter, although it only takes a nanosecond for an intruder to invade. It's a whole lot wiser to keep the door closed and make two or three trips to the garage and back.

By now I hope you know that, although I started this about lizards and escaping Btus, I'm really talking about something else—like keeping the door closed to sin and temptation. For example, I don't buy packages of cookies because I cannot eat one or two like a normal person; I will eat them all, all at once. I don't open the door to that inevitability.

Likewise, I don't carry my J. C. Penney credit card with me. I throw out catalogs that come in the mail. I don't dwell on past hurts or let my anger simmer until it becomes bitter resentment.

The Bible warns against letting the devil get a foothold, and my husband keeps warning me that one of these days I'm going to squish a lizard in the middle of the night and it will be my own fault and that I should keep the door closed.

He's right. The Bible's right, too.

Lizards and sin. They sneak in so easily.

BAPTISMS *and* HOLY TATTOOS

E HAD A BAPTISM at church last week, and that made me think about my tattoo.

More about that later.

At my church, we baptize babies and kids and adults. We baptize by having water poured on our heads. Actually, it's more like scooped. The pastor scoops water from a bowl and pours it over the person's head and says, "I baptize you in the name of the Father and of the Son and of the Holy Spirit."

When it's a baby or a kid being baptized, the pastor says, "Joshua (or Megan or Fritz), child of the covenant, I baptize you in the name…"

"Child of the covenant," refers to the covenant God makes with His people to set apart their children for special care.

The church where I was baptized was a dunking church. I climbed into a big tank of water, and the pastor bent me over backwards and I went under the water. My oldest daughter was baptized in a swimming pool. My youngest, as a "child of the covenant," was "scooped."

Most churches that dunk believe baptism is for adults or older children who come to faith in Christ. They baptize as an outward sign of the inward goings on, the heart change that's taken place. It signifies new life and being washed and identifying with Jesus.

My church believes that as well, even though we scoop rather than dunk. But we baptize babies, too, and that's an awesome thing to participate in. I almost wrote "an awesome thing to watch," but as a church member, it goes beyond that.

Last week, a mom and dad brought their two little girls in matching yellow dresses for baptism. The pastor explained that parents bring children not because they think a scoop of water on their heads will make them acceptable to God, but as a way of saying, "Our children need to be washed."

We as a church—we who have been washed—participate by agreeing to help these parents as they raise their little ones. We help each other; that's because we're a family.

Along with the two girls in yellow dresses, a little boy and a baby boy were baptized. I don't have boys, and my girls have long outgrown wearing matching yellow dresses to church, but I still remember the time they were washed.

After the baptism, we sang "Children of the Living God," about "how He loves us with great love."

That's when I thought about my tattoo.

It's not a real tattoo, made by needles and ink, but I'm still marked. That's part of baptism, being marked by God.

Before the baptism last week, we recited catechism about the sacrament. Catechism is just a fancy word for questions and answers about biblical principles.

The pastor asked, "What is baptism?"

We answered that it was a sacrament ordained by Christ, that the "washing with water in the name of the Father and of the Son and of the Holy Ghost" is to be a "sign and seal" that we belong to Jesus, wholly and forever.

Like a tattoo that can't be rubbed off or removed.

Life gets grimy, and it's easy to think that the dirt and sin are winning. But for those whom God has sealed, all they have to do is think about how Jesus washed their grime away the moment they believed in Him. The water of baptism is just a sign, like a tattoo.

The real washing takes place in the heart.

I've heard it said that God has a tattoo. The prophet Isaiah wrote, "I have engraved you on the palms of my hands" (49:16).

I like that. I like baptisms at my church. I like watching brave little boys who wince as the water hits their hair and shy little girls who cling to their moms' skirts. I like adults who kneel to receive the water and men who wipe away their tears because it's so good to be washed clean.

I like thinking about being tattooed by God the moment I was baptized into Christ.

Most of all, I like knowing that God's tattooed too—with my name.

OH, HOW I LOVE ME, ME, ME

*E*XCEPT FOR TIME out for sleeping and eating, I spent almost all weekend in fervent worship. Of course, my worship wasn't for the God who made me, but for one He had made.

It started Saturday afternoon when a photographer friend came to my house to take my "after" picture, after having lost weight.

So on Saturday I carefully did my makeup and put on my size 8 jeans and soft, black cashmerelike sweater, then smiled my big, cheesy smile as Dave snapped away.

We did indoor shots and outdoor shots. With flash, without flash. After 104 snaps of the camera, Dave ran out of space on the camera's data card about the same time I ran out of smile. Once he left, I downloaded all 104 images onto my computer and clicked on my Photoshop program.

That's when the worship service began.

One by one, I examined and critiqued each photo: *In this one my smile looks forced. In this one my nose looks too big.* I actually liked almost half of the photos and loved about a dozen of them. Of those, I played with the features of Photoshop, zooming and cropping. Some I changed from color to black and white, and I even discovered a tool that makes under-eye circles go away, removes scars, and even covers the annoying rash I had on my chin.

I sat at my computer all Saturday afternoon, enthralled with my on-screen image, and even forgot to eat.

At 5 p.m., I rushed off to church, where I wrestled with directing my attention away from my pictures at home and toward God. Then when church ended I rushed back home to continue my idolatry.

Ironically, the pastor had mentioned idolatry in his sermon. He announced that each one of us would commit adultery—and idolatry—before the sun came up the next day. By that, he meant we would all break the first commandment, "You shall have no other gods before Me," by giving our hearts to something else.

For some, he said, that would mean eating, drinking, money, sex, television, work, even bingo or video games. For me, that meant playing with my pictures and trying to choose the one to have framed and displayed. You know, like an idol.

But even though I was up to my highlighted bangs in idolatry, it didn't register that the pastor had been talking to me! So late into Saturday night and all day Sunday, I sat at my computer. Then Sunday evening, I returned to church for a women's event.

It was on my way there that the proverbial lightbulb went on. However, instead of feeling guilty and like bug slime, I started to laugh with delight. That's because by using the photo I liked best of all, God showed me a wonderful picture of His heart.

Although it's not the most flattering of all the photos Dave shot, it's the one I kept returning to all weekend. It's the one I e-mailed to friends.

Taken out on my back porch, the photo shows me against a plain stucco wall, caught in a ray of light. I'm relaxed; my smile is genuine and not forced. I still remember the warmth of being in that ray of sunlight on that cold porch.

I laughed at how many hours I had spent focused solely on my image, but only because I understood deeply that I'm one of God's own and not even my idolatry could remove me from the light of His smile.

That's because it has nothing to do with how well I do or do not perform, or how holy or unholy I am. My acceptance by the One who made me is only because of Jesus.

I am in Him, and that's who the Father sees when He looks at me—He sees Jesus.

What a beautiful picture that is.

THE STATS DON'T COMPUTE

I'VE WRITTEN THESE words many times before: My husband and I met, married, and fell in love—in that order. They're some of my favorite words, because statistically, logically, we shouldn't have lasted longer than the six months someone had predicted.

But here we are, thirty-plus years later, still married, still wanting to be married.

In 2001, when the Navy base where Barry worked in Orlando closed, he transferred to Jacksonville. The original plan was to sell our house and then for me and our youngest daughter to join him. However, once he got there, he learned that his job was not permanent. And because the powers that be in the Department of Defense hadn't given him a job-ending date, he stayed in a sort of limbo.

So my daughter and I stayed where we were, with Barry coming home to visit as often as he could.

At first, when friends found out that I wasn't joining my husband across the state, some voiced concern. Some feared the 130-mile separation would hurt our marriage.

It didn't. If anything it made it stronger, different, healthier. Sadly, some of the very friends who feared for me saw their own marriages break beyond repair.

Statistically, logically, ours should've been the one to break, especially when the darkness hit and my husband was depressed. Now that it has passed, we say it was the worst, best thing that could have happened to us and to our marriage.

At the darkest part, Barry would tell me I should leave him, to find happiness elsewhere. He said he loved me too much to see me hurting because of him. I told him I would never leave. He told me I was nuts.

And then he disappeared for a week. He had gone to a favorite hiding place of his in Georgia, to think and play putt-putt golf. I didn't know where he was until he called me one Sunday. The darkness had left him. He was going to be okay, he said.

I knew it was for real when he called again to make plans to build a condo with me. "Just for us," he said, "for forever, as long as we both shall live." What God had joined together on May 3, 1975, no one or nothing could put asunder.

One of our favorite things is spending time at the beach. For my birthday one year, Barry bought me a machine that makes ocean sounds, and sometimes when we're home and not at the beach, we'll listen to the waves crashing and pretend the ocean is outside our back porch.

Marriage isn't easy. Loving feelings ebb and flow, like ocean waves. After thirty-plus years we've learned to ride them out. I think that's why I like listening to my sound machine. It reminds me of the constancy, that through the dark times and the blah times and the good times, we have remained—only because God remains.

One day Barry came home for seven brief hours, but in many ways they were some of the best hours of our married life. We rode bikes, swam, read the newspaper. Later in the afternoon we went to a wedding. Of course, Barry made the usual wisecracks about "prison" and "ball and chain" and "pain and suffering," but during the wedding he kept me close. Afterward, before he left to go back to Jacksonville—he had an early class in the morning and couldn't stay for the reception—he told me that he hated to leave.

Marriage is difficult, but good. Absence makes the heart grow fonder, but so does the everydayness of being together, riding bikes, swimming, reading the newspaper. Maybe it's what God had in mind when He brought the woman to the man in the Garden of Eden and said, "For this reason a man shall leave his father and mother and hold fast to his wife, and they shall become one flesh" (Genesis 2:24, ESV).

As I've written many times before, my husband and I met, married, and fell in love—in that order. After all these years, I *still* don't know why we're still together. Statistically, logically, we shouldn't be. I just thank God that we are.

RUDENESS *and* GRACE

IN THE WORDS of the great theologian Britney Spears, "Oops...I did it again." Seems I offended someone. Again. Unfortunately, I don't know who, or how. All I know is that I did.

My daughter told me when I stopped by the restaurant where she works. That's why God invented daughters, to point out their mothers' faults. As we sat debating who, of the two of us, is the most shallow and superficial, she stopped midsentence and said, "Mom, some lady thinks you're rude!"

Then she told me that some women at one of her tables were discussing a column I had written, and one of them told the others that I had been rude to her.

"Were you rude?" my daughter asked.

Not knowing who the woman was, I didn't have an answer. "Not on purpose," I told her. "You know how I am."

Sadly, she does.

Just a few weeks ago I wrote about being a "high-level, First-Degree Jerk," and this more or less proves it. I don't mean to be rude; I don't like being rude. I just am. It comes naturally to me.

I remember one time attending a job fair at a community college in California. I had been taking classes, but I wasn't some recently-out-of-high-school student. I was in my thirties, a mother of two, without excuse for what I did.

Spotting a popular local radio personality at a table, I barged over to him and uttered something forgettably clever.

He looked at me with surprised disgust. That's when I noticed the dozen or so people waiting patiently in line to speak to him, including a young woman I recognized from my biology class. She was the one speaking with him before I interrupted.

Pretending that someone was calling my name, I turned and waved to no one and slunk off.

Because God loves and disciplines everyone He considers His child, He wasn't going to let me get away with shrugging it off and avoiding the woman I had been rude to. Dropping biology was out of the question, too.

Sometimes the voice of God's Spirit is called the "hound of heaven" because it hounds you to do the right thing, even in matters some might call trivial. However, where sin is involved, to God it's not trivial, and I knew I needed to apologize for my rudeness.

Saying "I'm sorry" is hard enough with people you know, but with strangers it's often more difficult because you don't know how the other person will respond. *What if she screams at me? What if she calls me vile names and makes me feel like worm spit?*

For a day and a half I agonized, rehearsing my apology. As I waited for her before class, I thought my heart would beat itself out of my ears I was so nervous.

Although I don't remember what I said when she finally arrived, I'll never forget her response to my apology.

She looked at me blankly. "You were rude? I don't remember." With that, she shrugged and went into class.

I remember being stunned. I had prepared myself for a dose of what I had coming to me, but instead received a tiny taste of the mercy of God.

We don't always get what we deserve. The hound of heaven who drives us to face our sin is also the merciful Father who takes pity on our ignorance.

Ever since that episode I've tried to be aware of my rudeness to people. Ideally, I try to catch myself before I do it, but that doesn't always happen.

My point in all this is to say, if you're reading this and if I've ever offended you, I'm truly sorry. Like I said, I don't mean to be rude; I don't like being rude. I just am. And I appreciate having it pointed out to me because I genuinely want to be better. Not so I'll be loved and adored, but so I won't dishonor the name of Jesus.

A LOVE THAT'S REAL

MR. ARTHUR WHITE called one day with a request. Even though he's ninety years old and has outlived two wives, he wants to know what love is and asked if I would explain it.

That's a tall order, and I doubt I could explain it in my remaining seven hundred or so words, even if I fully understood it myself. But because you sincerely want to know, Mr. White, I'm going to attempt it.

When I was in the seventh grade, I loved red-haired Paul Minardi with all my thirteen-year-old heart. We held hands and kissed, and when we broke up after six months, I thought my heart would be damaged beyond repair. But then blond-haired Scott Huseth came along, and I loved him just as I had loved Paul Minardi.

But that wasn't love. That was "I love how I feel when I'm with you." That was love of myself, which isn't reserved just for teenagers. Even adults confuse warm feelings with love. Just look around. Relationships begin and end on a whim. When the feelings go away, we think love has gone, too. But that's only because we don't know what love is to begin with.

In *Fiddler on the Roof,* Tevye asks—implores—his wife, Golde, "Do you love me?" She tells him, "I've cooked for you, washed your clothes, cleaned your house, given you children. Milked your cows! After twenty-five years, why talk about love right now?"

Tevye wants to know about love. Everybody wants to know about love. So, Mr. White, don't think you're alone with your question.

I think love has nothing to do with feelings. I think love is a deliberate choice of one's will to act on behalf of another person's best interest. Sometimes it involves feelings, but sometimes it doesn't. It always involves the highest good of the object of one's love, and sometimes that's not easy.

Sometimes what we think is loving isn't. For example, I used to wake my daughter up every morning. *What a loving mom,* you probably think. However, it would have been more loving of me to let her to use her own alarm clock. Real love would risk having her oversleep and be late for school or work. That's in her best interest.

This brings me to another thought about love: Real love is tough. It stands up for right and against wrong and fights to maintain its purity. Even against popular culture and opinion, real love stands for truth. Real love is selfless and sacrificial. It's stubborn. It doesn't cop out and do the easy thing.

Mr. White, is this making any sense to you?

You mentioned that you're not a religious man, but that you're questioning. You're looking for love, and while I can guarantee that you'll never find it in a set of religious principles, creeds, or doctrines, you will find it in God.

I guess that's my best answer for you. The Bible says, "God is love." I've heard it said that humans can possess and express love, but love is not our basic nature. Love, on the other hand, is something God is. Everything He does is because He is love. He can't be anything else. *God is love.*

Jesus, God the Son, said the greatest demonstration of love is to lay down your life for another. Then He went and did just that. But He didn't die for His friends. He died for His enemies. That's you and me. That's love.

Mr. White, the Bible says that God is love and love comes from God. So if you want to be loved, you need to go to Him. Likewise, if you want to give love, you need to get it from Him as well.

God's love is vast. Awesome. Limitless. Surprising. It fills up all the empty places inside you and gives you enough to pass on to others. The best part: God's love doesn't wait until you've cleaned yourself up. On the contrary, God loves you in your messiest mess. In all your brokenness. In all your sin.

Mr. White, as plainly as I can say this, God loves you. And if you can own that, I promise you that you'll never need to search for the answer to your question anywhere else ever again.

FRUITY *for* JESUS

*B*EING FROM CALIFORNIA, I've heard all the jokes about "the land of fruits and nuts." If that's true (and I'm not saying it is), then I would have to say I'm more nutty than fruity, although becoming fruitier is my goal these days.

I remember visiting my grandmother in Los Angeles and going to Farmers Market, the famous Farmers Market on 3rd and Fairfax, where everything is bigger, better, brighter than anywhere else and where you can buy glossy California navel oranges the size of cantaloupes (and cantaloupes the size of the Goodyear blimp).

Now that's fruit.

I also remember the first time I ever saw a Florida orange. My in-laws had shipped us a box one Christmas, and when I opened the box and discovered the mottled green- and yellow-skinned fruit, I thought it was rotten and threw it all out. After all, California citrus is the color of orange Crayola crayons.

It wasn't until we moved to Florida that I learned Florida oranges are "real" oranges. Even so, when it comes to favorite fruit, I'm still partial to overpriced, chemically enhanced, fake-looking California navels.

When it comes to being fruity, however, I'd much rather be the real thing.

Last week at church, the pastor talked about being fruity for Jesus. Those weren't his words; he talked about "the preeminence of love." He spoke about how you can do great things for God and be so proficient at what you do that God's kingdom is advanced and people are blessed, but if you're not fruity, you're not doing as well as you may think.

By fruity he meant loving. If you don't have love, you're nothing but a noisy gong or clanging cymbal. If you aren't loving, you've somehow missed the point.

Lots of times as I'm sitting in church listening to the sermon, I'm taking notes. *Yeah, yeah. This is good; I can use this in a column. Wait—slow down! You're talking faster than I can write!*

Sometimes I'm thinking, *Boy, do I know somebody who needs to hear this.*

But last week's sermon was directed at me, as if God Himself tapped me on the shoulder and whispered, "Listen up, honey. This one's for you."

"Love is patient, love is kind," the pastor read from his Bible. "It does not envy or boast; it is not proud. It is not rude or self-seeking, is not easily angered, keeps no record of wrongs, doesn't delight in evil, but rejoices with the truth. It always protects, always trusts, always hopes, always perseveres. Love never fails."

That's fruity love.

Even before the pastor said anything, I had already been thinking about how "nutty"—or hard—my love is. Or like a California navel orange that looks good on the outside but is dry and tasteless on the inside.

However, before I had a chance to feel condemned, the pastor admitted that he, too, is nutlike, and so is most everyone else, but that none of us are doomed to be nuts forever.

We can be fruity because Jesus grows the fruit in us. The pastor reminded us that the "love is" passage isn't a list of what to do, but is a description of who Jesus is. He is patient, He is kind....

That's the answer to the fruit/nut problem. As my pastor said, "Before love is a behavior in you, it must be Someone you meet." We can take our nutlike, loving-deficient hearts and meet with Jesus; then His love will transform us and bear fruit.

It works like this: He loves us first, and that prompts us to love others. His patience with us allows us to be more patient with others. Likewise, it's His kindness, His goodness, His gentleness and faithfulness that are produced in us. It's His fruit that makes us fruity. Like an orange—it doesn't grow from a tree by its own efforts, but the tree produces it from within.

So that's my goal these days, to draw closer to Jesus, who is love personified, that His love may be produced in me, that I may be less nutty and more fruity.

A fragrant fruit for Jesus.

BELOVED, HOLY BREAD

*T*HERE'S NO OTHER WAY to say this: I'm in love. My beloved's name is Panera, a local bread bakery and café. It was love at first bite.

What Starbucks is to coffee, Panera is to bread. If you've never tasted red onion and rosemary focaccia fresh from the oven, you haven't lived.

The trouble is, I love bread, but it doesn't love me. Or maybe it does, since it seems to cling tightly to my hips and around my middle, and eating too much of it does unpleasant things to my insides. So even though my true love is less than an hour away, I've had to keep my distance. Heartbreaking, isn't it?

I thought about my beloved last week as I covered a first Holy Communion service at a local Catholic parish for the newspaper. I thought about being hungry and tasting and eating as forty-five second graders anticipated eating the Bread of Life for the first time.

As they filed in, the girls looking like little brides in their white dresses, and as the choir sang, "Come to the table of plenty," I thought about what truly satisfies. Later someone read, "Taste and see the goodness of the Lord."

I felt hungry, "slightly famished" as one of my daughters used to say, and considered driving all the way to Panera for lunch, but I wasn't really hungry for focaccia, or even a cinnamon scone. Instead, I was slightly famished for what the second graders dressed in white were about to taste: Holy Communion with God. Tasting the Bread of Life.

Different churches have different ways of serving Communion. Some churches have real loaves of bread, and Communion receivers tear off a piece and dip it in the cup of wine or grape juice. Some use bits of matzo crackers, unleavened bread. The minister may take a whole matzo and hold it up for the congregation to see its stripes and piercings, reminding the famished, "This is the body of Christ, broken, beaten, and pierced for you."

The minister will do the same with the cup of wine and say to the thirsty, "This is the blood of Christ, which was shed for you."

In some churches, the people get out of their seats and go to the altar to taste God; in other churches, the elements are passed from one hungry person to the next. The Catholic way is to go to the altar to receive a small white host and either dip it in the wine or drink out of the cup. Whichever way it's done, it's still hungry people desiring to be filled: mind, body, and soul with the goodness of the Lord.

Years ago, one of the jokes in our family was that my husband insisted that bread from paper bags tasted differently than the same bread from plastic bags. So I would go to the same bakery every day and ask for a loaf of Italian bread in a paper—not plastic!—bag. I'd bring my girls with me and say to the woman behind the counter, "Give me this day my daily bread."

She would laugh, and my daughters would roll their eyes as only teenage girls can and say, "Mom, you're so lame." But before we would even make it to the car they would moan that they were "slightly famished" and beg for "just a piece."

Sometimes, as I'd break off a hunk and hand it to them, I'd say, "Unlike this, there's another Bread that never goes stale, Who sustains life, and Who satisfies the deepest hunger. This is the Bread you should beg for."

Again, they'd roll their eyes and tell me I'm "such a mom." Maybe so, but I know what it is to be famished and to try to satisfy my hunger with everything other than God. I know they do the same—we all do.

So my prayer for them and for all of us is that next time hunger strikes, we won't settle for red onion and rosemary focaccia, no matter how heavenly it may be, but head straight for the table of plenty.

"He who feeds on this bread," Jesus said, "will live forever." Those who feast on Jesus will never be hungry again.

Prayer *for* Lost Things

HAVE A FEELING I'm in the middle of God answering a prayer. However, it's not one of those answers that makes your mouth drop open and leaves you speechless—like the other day, after tearing my house apart looking for my daughter's heirloom diamond ring that I had misplaced. I asked God if He would pleeeeeeeze help me find it.

Immediately, I discovered it in a box in my closet. It could've been a coincidence rather than an answer to my prayer, but my mouth dropped anyway.

My prayer, which I think God is in the middle of answering,

isn't about finding lost things. I don't remember praying it, but I must have asked God to show me my sin, because that's what He's doing. On the other hand, maybe He's doing this as a freebie, as if to say, "I know you didn't ask, but I think you should know."

Take today, which is Wednesday as I write this: Already He's shown me that I've lied twice—about stupid stuff—and I e-mailed a friend a bunch of gossip. When I balanced my checkbook and discovered an error that netted me a bunch of extra bucks, I thought about putting the money in the offering at church, but I bought purple pillows for my couch instead. Then I harbored bad thoughts about the person who didn't rinse toothpaste spit out of the bathroom sink.

Those are the only the sins I'm willing to tell you about. I don't dare tell you the rest. I'd be too ashamed. I'd have to leave the area. Or shoot you.

Just when I think I'm doing okay in the sin department, I find that I'm not.

Recently I was with a group of women at a conference. I told them, "Real joy is knowing the depth of your sin." I told them about a saying we have at my church: "Cheer up! You're worse than you ever thought possible, yet God's grace is greater than you can imagine."

Just when you think you're doing okay—and maybe you are, compared to the next guy—that's when God steps in to answer your prayer (whether you prayed it or not) and shows you how not okay you really are.

When He does that, it's rarely pleasant. I've yet to have God tap me gently on the shoulder and deliver a handwritten note on lavender-scented stationery listing my sin. It's usually more like when you're fifteen and sneaking back into the house at midnight after taking your parents' car out for a drive and your dad meets you in the living room. He turns on the light, and you know you're toast.

However, with your dad, sometimes you can talk, cry, or sweet-talk your way out of your toasting. Plead insanity. Lie. After all, your dad's a sinner, too. But with God, you can't do any of that. You can't fake it, and you can't fool Him, so it's best not to even try.

"Real joy," I told the women, "is knowing the depth of your sin." That's because only those who know it can fully appreciate God's great forgiveness. It's not only the big, bad stuff I've done that nailed Jesus to the cross, but the stupid stuff, too. It's the good I fail to do.

Whenever I start thinking I'm not so bad, God lovingly steps off His throne in heaven and turns on the light to show me that, yes, as a matter of fact, I am quite bad. The good news is that when God shows me my sin, it's not because He doesn't love me, but because He does. He loves me enough to answer my prayer to be shown my sin, whether I've prayed it or not.

Real joy isn't asking for, and then finding, a lost ring. Real joy is knowing the depth of my sin, and then looking to the Cross to find the greatness of God's forgiveness hanging there.

CHANGE MY FACE, O LORD

O OFFENSE to my Aunt Gladys, but when I look in the mirror lately, I see her face.

Actually, it's a combination of Aunt Gladys, my mother, and Uncle Tommy, chin whiskers, mustache, and all.

It's rather frightening.

It's also disconcerting. In my mind, I don't look like what I really look like. In my mind, my skin is smooth and clear and doesn't sag.

In my mind, I'm not quite as cute as I used to be when I was fifteen, tan and petite, and wore hip-hugger bell-bottoms. I'm not *that* delusional. But in my mind, I'm not ready to accept that I'm looking more like Aunt Gladys every day.

I love Aunt Gladys, but she's in her eighties and I'm not. In my mind, I'm more like twenty-four, which is twenty-plus years younger than I really am.

Sometimes when I look in the mirror, I'll take my fingers and gently push the skin on my face upward toward my ears to make the creases around my mouth disappear.

"Yeah, that's what I look like!" I'll tell myself. But then I eventually have to let go of my face and watch it return to its current (and most likely, permanent) saggy state.

Then I'll push the skin up once again and wonder how much plastic surgeons charge for a face-lift and whether they would throw in a nose job for free. Or maybe a more defined chin.

No offense to Aunt Gladys, but I want a new face.

I was thinking about that this morning as I opened the daily devotional book I keep at my desk, *Grace for the Moment* by Max Lucado. Today's reading was called "God Changes Our Face."

Isn't that so like God to know what we're going to be thinking and then have the answers waiting for us at the perfect moment?

I bet God has a good time being God.

In today's reading, Lucado writes about how God invites us to see His face so that He can change ours and how He uses our regular, imperfect faces to display His glory.

Lucado writes, "He loves to change the faces of His children. By His fingers, wrinkles of worry are rubbed away. Shadows of shame and doubt become portraits of grace and trust.

"He relaxes clenched jaws and smoothes furrowed brows. His touch can remove the bags of exhaustion from beneath the eyes and turn tears of despair into tears of peace."

How does God do that? Lucado says that God changes our faces through worship.

After I read that—after I laughed at God's ironic timing—I

ran to find a mirror. (I confess; I briefly pushed at my saggy face. Force of habit.)

Then I began thanking God, not for my face, but for His.

There's a benediction that goes: "The LORD bless you and keep you; the LORD make his face shine upon you and be gracious to you; the LORD turn His face toward you and give you peace" (Numbers 6:24–26).

Don't you love that? Wouldn't you like that to be true of your life, of your face, to have God shine His upon you? That's another way of saying that God looks down from heaven, singles us out, and smiles on us.

"Oh, yes," He says. "That's one of my kids. I think I'll bless her and be gracious to her and give her peace."

When God does that, when He pours out His grace and we're caught up in the wonder and the beauty of His smile on our lives, it shows on our faces. If it doesn't, then we haven't truly worshiped.

I want a new face. I want one that reflects God's face as He smiles upon me.

So, Lord, may Your face shine upon me. Be gracious to me, Your needy child. Give me Your peace—and change my face, I pray.

FIRST, YOU CRY

*F*IRST, YOU CRY.

That's what former NBC News correspondent Betty Rollin wrote in her autobiographical book about her journey through breast cancer.

I'm not at the "first, you cry," stage; the doctors aren't even 100 percent positive that the "suspicious" spot on my mammogram is cancer. It might be nothing. There might not even be a journey. This may be just a dip in the road.

Then again, it might be something.

Life is like that. There's a time and place for everything under heaven, as the Bible says.

A time to be born and a time to die. A time to weep and a time to laugh.

This past Sunday at church my pastor announced that our dear sister, a wonderful woman named Jane Johnson, had died on Friday. She was only fifty-five. Brain cancer had invaded her life in a massive way.

I remember chatting with her each week at church before worship began. She wore great wigs and brightly colored clothes and would laugh about having "only half a brain."

Actually, that's part of worship, too—God's people laughing together. Tuesday was her memorial service—God's people weeping together.

We sang, "Whatever my lot, Thou has taught me to say, it is well, it is well with my soul."

The pastor called Jane a "pistol." Jane made people laugh.

When the doctors told her she had cancer, they gave her two weeks to live. She lived several years after that.

"Jane is more alive now than ever before," the pastor said on Tuesday. "Dancing with Jesus," as I say.

That may be, but we who are left still grieve the death of our friend.

My husband always says there are only two things you can be certain of in life: that you won't get out alive and that the IRS will suck you dry.

Good people suffer. Bad people prosper. Couples who desperately want children remain infertile while the most unfit to parent seem to be the most prolific. Cancer happens.

Life is like that.

And none of it makes sense unless you know in the core of your being that even the most awful blow you're dealt comes from the hand of a loving God.

Some people say God has nothing to do with the evil that befalls us, but I find that a terrifying thought. If anything—sickness, tragedy, war, even the IRS—could escape God's good hand or hijack His authority, then it would be greater than God himself.

But the God who sets the seasons and hangs the moon in the night sky and causes a baby to coo at her mother also decides who will bear cancer and to what degree. Who will miscarry. Who will be the one to stand at a graveside and who will be the one eulogized.

One of the most amazing things about people who believe in God is their ability to give thanks and proclaim His goodness when it makes no sense to do so.

Unbelievers shake their fists at God and shout, "If You're so good, then why did (fill in the blank) happen?" But only those who trust that everything under heaven comes from the goodness of heaven can sing through their tears, "It is well with my soul," and mean it.

Jesus said that in this world we will have tribulation and trials, distress and frustration—and death. But He also said we are able to be of good cheer. We can take courage, be confident, certain, and undaunted because He has overcome the world. By His death and resurrection He has deprived evil of its ultimate power to harm the souls of those who trust in Him.

I don't know if I have breast cancer. If not now, maybe someday I will. Someday, somehow, some form of tragedy will strike me. That I can be sure of.

But I know God. I know I am known by Him. I know that whatever my lot—even if at first, I cry—it is well, it is well with my soul.

GRACE HATH BROUGHT
ME SAFE THUS FAR

THIS PAST WEEK, I discovered that it's humanly possible to hold your breath for an entire week. From the time my doctor called to say my X-ray looked "suspicious for early signs of breast cancer" until the radiologist said, "benign," I don't think I breathed.

During the week of holding my breath, I learned a few things. I learned that I am loved by friends, who called or sent notes and e-mails or stopped me in the market to say they were praying for me. I'm overwhelmed and amazed. Everyone should be as richly loved as I am.

I also learned that the words I scribble each week, sometimes willy-nilly and without great thought, God uses to affect those who read them. I don't always know why I write what I write. Sometimes I'll have an opening sentence and then just babble on until I get to the end of my allotted space and hope it somehow makes sense and communicates the grace of Jesus to those who desperately need a touch.

Last week's column was one of those. A dear young woman wrote to say that she, too, was waiting to hear from the pathologist, hoping for the word *benign*, yet fearing the word *malignant*. A man wrote to tell me of his possible prostate cancer. They both agreed that, yes, God is in control, but as finite humans, they were scared and holding their breath. Others wrote to say they were scared to see a doctor.

Although I try not to preach when I write, I'm going to now: If you're a woman in your forties or older, get regular mammograms. Be afraid not to! Research from the American Cancer

Society shows that regular mammograms are currently the best defense against breast cancer. They can detect early stages of cancer up to two years before a lump can be felt.

And mammograms don't hurt. When I speak to women's groups I often read a piece called "Preparing for Your First Mammogram." In it the writer suggests practicing by freezing two metal bookends and then asking a stranger to use them to smash each of your breasts as hard as she can for as long as she can.

Everyone laughs at that story because that is what we fear. But what we fear is rarely what is.

The truth is, finding breast cancer early gives women the greatest chance of survival and the best options for treatment. Mastectomy isn't always automatic. Chemotherapy doesn't always make you sick or cause you to lose your hair. One woman I know went through radiation treatment while managing her business and raising her children as a single mom.

Also during the week I held my breath, I learned that the majority of women who are called back for a do-over mammogram or a biopsy hear the word *benign*. I learned that that's one of life's sweetest words.

But the sweetest word of all is *grace*.

During the week I held my breath, I experienced grace beyond measure. As I drove to work each morning and tried not to think about all the "what ifs" that threatened to rob me of my peace, I sensed a Presence beside me, answering my every fear:

If it's cancer, I will be with you. If you lose your hair and get sick to your stomach, I will be with you. If you cannot work, if you lose your breast, even if you lose your life, I will be with you.

Grace rocked me to sleep at night and gave me a song to sing when I awoke. Grace even gave me a sense of adventure to face whatever might lie ahead and to get the Big Story. (For a journalist, it's all about getting the Big Story.)

But I also learned that God has already given me the Big Story to write. The Big Story—the Biggest Story—continues to be grace.

It's as we sing, "'Tis grace hath brought me safe thus far, and grace will lead me home."

It's grace that keeps us safe, even when we're holding our breath.

Tales *of the* Bizarro World

E LIVE IN a Bizarro world. Back in the 1960s there was a Superman comic book series Tales of the Bizarro World.

Bizarro Superman lived on Htrae, a square planet where alarm clocks dictated when people went to sleep, ugly was beautiful, and upside down and backwards were normal. All Bizarros were imperfect duplicates of other living things; they were illiterate and spoke with poor grammar.

Although our planet is round, it's still a Bizarro world where increasingly, encroachingly, evil is good and good is evil. The Bible warns against that happening. The ancient prophet Isaiah pronounced "woe" upon those who declare it and who push it upon others. *Woe* being much more than just experiencing a bad hair day. Woe meaning great sorrow, grief, and misery.

You don't mess around with the stuff of God.

In our Bizarro world, 86 percent of Americans say they believe in God. According to an ABC poll, 89 percent of Americans are in favor of keeping the phrase "one nation under God" in the Pledge of Allegiance. However, the 11 or 14 percent of Americans who don't believe, and who are most vocal about it, appear to be running the Bizarro show.

The other day, someone on the radio said, "Why don't the 14 percent just shut up?"

Fortunately, they have the right to voice their opinions. Unfortunately, they're trying to silence the majority, and they seem to be winning. This is a Bizarro world.

In 2003, Alabama Chief Justice Roy Moore lost his appeal before the U.S. Supreme Court to save a granite monument of the Ten Commandments that he placed in the judicial building. He faced a five-thousand-dollar-a-day fine if he didn't remove it.

According to an Associated Press story, Ayesha Khan, an attorney for Americans United for Separation of Church and State, announced back then, "It's time for Roy's rock to roll!"

Woe to those who call evil good and good evil.

In 1980, the U.S. Supreme Court ruled that the Ten Commandments could not be posted in public school classrooms. So far, it has not ruled on them being displayed in government buildings, but because this is a Bizarro world, that day is fast encroaching.

However, as the Reverend Rob Schenck, founder of the Ten Commandments Project in Washington DC, pointed out, our entire system of law is based on English Common Law, "which had its moral foundation in the Ten Commandments."

Schenck told *USA Today*, "The Commandments are a constant reminder of a higher moral authority than us. We are not the ultimate arbiters of right and wrong...the laws of God are higher than the laws of men."

Because the Ten Commandments refer to God, Supreme Court Justice John Paul Stevens said they can't be displayed publicly. Yet the Declaration of Independence refers to "God." Congress starts its day with a prayer to "God." Even every session of the Supreme Court begins with the announcement: "God save the United States and this honorable court."

How bizarre is Stevens's logic?

In our Bizarro world, even if the 14 percent wins and all evidence of God is removed from the public arena, God's law would still remain preeminent because God remains God. He is Creator; we are only His creation, even for the 14 percent who don't believe that. In a Bizarro world, it's bizarre, not to mention dangerous, to believe otherwise.

In the comic book backwards world of Bizarro, Bizarro Superboy tells Bizarro Superman that he wants to see the dull movie *Slowest Gun in the West*. His father tells him, "Okay, you disobeyed me all day, so you [are] entitled to a reward!" However, even Bizarro Superman recognizes his folly, when in another issue he says, "Me unhappy! Me don't belong in [a] world of living people. Me don't know difference between right and wrong, good and evil!"

Woe to us who do know the difference yet continue in our Bizarro ways. May God have mercy on us all.

Random God-Musings

*S*OME DAYS too many random thoughts vie to be the one I choose to write about, so today I'm jotting down several brief God-musings. Perhaps one of them will be helpful to you.

This is why I believe in God the Father, Son, and Holy Ghost. Actually, there are lots of reasons why, but the one that stands out most is this: I didn't have to do anything to believe. Not only that, but no one else did anything either.

People talk about evangelism strategies and four spiritual laws and witnessing techniques—and all that is good, but God doesn't need it to get a person to believe.

When I believed on May 30, 1978, I was not reading Christian books, listening to Christian radio, watching Christian TV. No one had shared a gospel tract with me; I was not attending church. No altar call, no "Let's sing the first, second, and last verses of 'Just As I Am.'"

Just one day I didn't believe and the next day I did. I had felt like a dog's chew toy being fought over by two slobbering mutts, being pulled and torn between two kingdoms, and then on that Monday morning about 9:45 a.m., I was crying in the bathroom at work and a woman named Rita came in and asked me what was wrong. I told her I wanted Jesus to save me, and that's when He did.

Just like that.

God is not a formula or a set of principles or handwritten slogans on placards. We don't have to hit people over the heads with our Bibles or beat salvation into people with the Cross of Christ.

But God does use people to share His good news. All I'm saying is that He saves whomever whenever He wants, and He can do it in spite of our best efforts to either help or hinder.

When I think of what I am most ashamed of, topping my list is how I really feel about God. I don't fully understand it, but the other day I got a glimpse into how I must hurt Him.

I had cooked my husband sausages, sauerkraut, and mashed potatoes for dinner and had forgotten to buy a loaf of French bread. Plus, we were out of ice cream. So I picked up my keys to head to the store.

He said I didn't have to go, but I wanted to. He seemed genuinely surprised and touched that I would do that for him, and that bothered me. Then when I returned he said several times, "Thanks for going to the store," which *really* bothered me. Why would he think that I wouldn't want to do this for him? Does he think I'm a monster?

Just as I was about to say, "Why are you so surprised?" God said that to me first.

"Why are you so surprised when I do something nice for you?" He asked my heart. He asks that often, and often I am ashamed to admit that I secretly don't think He is good.

Jesus is not a cliché, and Bible verses are not feel-good panaceas, and I repent of every time I've ever told anyone, "All things work together for good" and "Just trust Jesus."

While that's all true, for a deeply wounded person, such statements are like pouring alcohol on a festering wound. It's too easy for people like me, who have not suffered, to toss glib, simplistic answers to people who are inside a pit, clawing to survive. But tossing answers to them doesn't help.

Better to get in the pit with them and hold them until they see that Jesus is in the pit with us both and has been all along and will eventually redeem the whole pit situation and it will be glorious, but maybe not today.

I'm not sure it's possible to love God, at least not the way He should be loved, but I know it's possible to know that He loves me. I am nearly insane with longing to have others know God's smile, and I feel impotent when they refuse His love. I often refuse it, too, and I know better.

We humans are so messed up.

I Wonder, I Worship

*I*F YOU DON'T count people or God, or maybe cake with buttercream icing, I think what I love most in life is wonder. I love the sense of surprise mixed with curiosity, of awe and bewilderment and delight all rolled into one emotion.

One night last week I slept in the moonlight. I had gone to bed at the usual time in the usual way and then was taken by surprise by the moon peeking through the blinds. It was big and round and brighter than I had seen moonlight in some time—and I opened the blinds and crawled back into bed to watch the still and silent nighttime show.

It felt mystical and magical, and as I marveled at the incredible amount of light reflected by this hunk of rock so many millions of miles away I thought, *My Father made that!*

Theologian Ravi Zacharias says that "wonder interprets life through the eyes of eternity while enjoying the moment," always being careful to give recognition to wonder's source.

It thrills a person to her knees.

Of course, lots of things thrill—roller coasters, receiving flowers at work when it's not even your birthday, still fitting into size 8 pants after a month of eating too much cake.

But wonder, although it thrills, goes beyond goose bumps and heebie-jeebies and happy surprises. Wonder goes beyond because it's from beyond. Wonder is that response from the creature when the Creator does something marvelous and immeasurably more.

Consider the color green. Tree after tree after tree—how many different shades and hues of green can there be? And how is it that green is such a soothing color on the eye? Or how is it that the sound of the ocean could lull and calm a restless spirit or the feel of sunshine on one's face could warm the coldest of hearts, a breeze could stir one's very soul?

My Father did that. My Father does that, and only He knows how and why and when and who needs a dose or two of wonder to bring a person to her knees.

Saint Julian of Norwich once said, "Truth sees God; wisdom gazes on God, and these produce…a holy, wondering delight in God."

I don't think you can have wonder without delight, and I don't think you can have delight without worship. Not true wonder and not true delight.

We live in such cynical times, although I suppose every time has its cynics. It makes me sad that lots of people think that believing in God is a neurological disorder, as Bill Maher (*Politically Incorrect*) says, or a result of a lack of education, as Andy Rooney (*60 Minutes*) says.

How sad for them. How sad to think that people refuse to acknowledge that God is and that the things He does inspire wonder and worship. How sad not to be able to sleep in the moonlight and experience the delight of thinking, *My Father did that.*

I have a friend, a new Christian, who uses the word *awesome* regularly and often. Rain and thunder and lightning are no longer weather nuisances, but are "awesome displays of God's power." Dusk, dawn, sunrises, sunsets—all "awesome," all wonder-full. Life is now a curious adventure, a wonderfully awe-full challenge, a gift from Creator to creature, from Father to child. Even the difficulties are wonder-full because God is in them and works His wonders through them.

D. H. Lawrence once said, "When the wonder has gone out of a man he is dead."

On the flip side, you might say that when a man is filled with wonder he is fully alive.

Despite what the cynics say, it truly is a wonderful world.

FACING *the* FEAR FACTOR

I'M AFRAID I have a confession to make: Unlike everyone else in North America, I'm not a fan of reality TV. I'm especially not a fan of *Fear Factor*. Watching people getting shocked while grabbing live eels or eating Madagascar hissing cockroaches ratchets up the heebie-jeebie factor in me.

Just the names of some of the show's stunts make me cringe: "drowning closet," "rat pit," "worm coffin." The show's only redeeming quality is that it allows people to face their fears. When that happens, when you do the thing you're afraid of, fear loses and you win. However, eating hissing cockroaches is just stupid.

When it comes to fear itself, I'm afraid the two of us are well acquainted. I vividly recall my earliest fear factor memory when, during the Cuban Missile Crisis, Sam Lang said that the Russians were about to drop a poison mushroom bomb on us and our eyeballs would pop out. I ran all the way home from school, panicked, and dove under my bed. Fear often sends me hiding. Occasionally, however, it makes me act like a witless moron.

When my husband and I were first married, we went to New York. That was back in the 1970s, when we watched a lot of shows like *Baretta* and *Kojak*, and I pictured New York City as riddled with gangsters and bad guys with itchy trigger fingers, carrying submachine guns and waiting for short, green-eyed girls to use as target practice. Not only was I afraid of gangsters, but I had included psychos and international spies on my list of things to fear in New York.

After our flight had landed, Barry told me to wait with our luggage while he checked on a rental car. I moved to hide behind a post and saw a man in a fur hat. *Obviously a Russian spy*, I thought.

Frozen with fear, I watched him look around and slowly reach into his overcoat, I assumed to pull out his submachine gun to *rat-a-tat-tat* my brains out.

With only seconds to save myself and my husband, who would surely be next on the man's hit list, I screamed across the airport terminal, "Barry! Duck!" Then I hit the floor, covered my head, and waited. When nothing happened, I looked up and noticed that the man had pulled a piece of paper from his coat and walked over to the pay phone.

Barry just laughed!

The fear factor tends to make people crazy. Either you overreact and do something moronic, or you let it paralyze you with worry. Sometimes you can face it and do the thing you fear and make it lose its power over you.

But sometimes you can't.

Life is getting increasingly fearful—war, the threat of more terrorist attacks. My daughter once dreamed of living in New York but doesn't want to anymore, at least not now. She's afraid. Not "watching too much *Kojak*" afraid, but "we have a real and vicious enemy" afraid. And unlike facing a fear of hissing cockroaches by eating one, facing this enemy isn't that simple.

So what do you do with this type of fear? You don't hit the floor and cover your head. You don't scream, "Duck!" Instead, you run. You run to the One who laughs at our enemies, and you hide in Him. "A mighty fortress," as Martin Luther called Him.

For those wrestling with their own fear factor, hear what God says: "Do not be afraid that some plan conceived behind closed doors will be the end of you. Do not fear anything except the LORD Almighty. He alone is the Holy One.... He will keep you safe" (Isaiah 8:12–14, NLT).

If you fear—reverently respect—Him, then you need fear nothing else.

HOLY WIND, HOLY FIRE

AYBE IT'S BECAUSE I hadn't been looking very hard, or maybe it's because God's ways are not my ways and He tends to operate the universe, including answering prayer, without checking with me first. Whatever the reason, last week I finally found my focus Scripture verse for the year, even though the year is half over.

One year my Scripture was Ephesians 3:20, God is able to do "immeasurably more than all we ask or imagine." That one still gives me goose bumps to think of how God has done "immeasurably more" in my life. Another year my Scripture was about how "nothing is impossible with God" (Luke 1:37), which is a pretty good verse for a skeptic like me.

This year, the word I'm sensing God wants me to dwell on is about the wind. In His famous "You must be born again" conversation with religious seeker Nicodemus, Jesus said the Holy Spirit is like the wind. It "blows wherever it pleases," He said. "You hear its sound, but you cannot tell where it comes from or where it is going. So it is with everyone born of the Spirit" (John 3:8).

As I went to church last week, I thought about the wind-words of Jesus. Then when the pastor read that very passage, it was as if God tapped me on the shoulder and said, "Listen up, child. I want you to hear this."

So I listened up as the pastor talked about not being able to control the wind and how futile it is to try. We can't create it, not the real thing anyway, and we can't stop it. We can't rope it, cage it, or tell it which way it should blow and have it obey.

When my mom was little, she thought the trees made the wind blow. That always makes me laugh, but I can see how a kid might think that. At church, the pastor said that sometimes people think they can make the wind blow. Not the wind like a nor'easter or a Chinook or a Santa Ana, but the Holy Spirit's wind. He said a person can't decide when to be born or when to be born again. If we could control our own or someone else's salvation, that would rob the wonder of God doing it all Himself.

That's the awesome part. That from start to finish, God moves in and changes a person's heart while we just stand around watching the trees blow.

Since God knows what's in a person's heart, even if he or she isn't aware, God must've known that I'd been longing for some wind to blow. I hadn't been silly enough to think I could make it happen, but I thought maybe it would never blow, at least not in the direction I wanted it to.

Then, as if to prove a point or make an exclamation, or maybe simply to encourage my heart, as I left church and started walking to my car, a gust of wind caught my breath. *How like God to stoop from heaven to send such a perfectly timed message*, I thought.

Actually, instead of going to my car, I went back into church. Someone was singing "I Will Never Be the Same Again," which is what happens when the wind of the Spirit blows into a person's life. Just like once you're born you can never go back, once you're born again by the Spirit, you're never the same.

The pastor had said you can't control the wind, but you can always see its effects—it messes your hair or blows your toupee off. It blows away the ashes, moves mountains of sand. "If nothing's disturbed, there's no wind," he said.

So I've got a new Scripture verse for the year. I had thought it was late in coming, but then I remembered that God's never late. Not with the wind, not with His marvelous workings in a person's life.

"God's making all things new," the pastor said. That's what happens when the wind blows, and that's what I'm going to be looking for.

Only Sinners Allowed

*E*VERY DAY on my way to and from work I pass my church. Right now it's in the process of being built, with huge cement slab panels forming a "contemporary French Gothic style" sanctuary.

To me, it looks like a cathedral. It's going to be awesome when it's finished.

Earlier this spring, folks from my church would come and sit on bleachers for hours at a time watching the walls go up. We're counting down the days until it's finished.

I love my church. Not the building—after all, we've been meeting in a gymnasium—but the people who make up my church. I love the whole idea of church, of strangers who become family. As I was telling a new member of the family, "We're a strange bunch and pretty messy, but our Dad loves us."

Several weeks ago I took an informal poll around town asking, "Do you regularly attend church, and if not, why not?"

None of the answers surprised me. Some said scandals in the leadership and too much emphasis on money contributed to their loss of faith in organized religion. Others said too many people go to church just out of habit or to be seen; there's too much judging of people based on their appearance, too much gossip.

One person, who used to attend regularly, stopped after the church split because of a dispute about a new building when it became apparent that building the brick and mortar church was more important than building the spiritual church.

Churches do great harm to people sometimes.

Groucho Marx once said he wouldn't belong to any club that would accept him as a member. Likewise, when it comes to church, even a good one, as soon as you or I join, the quality of its membership drops severely.

But that's good news.

Although nonchurchgoers have lots of reasons for not going to church, I think one of the main reasons is that they don't understand what a church is. I don't think many churchgoers understand either.

For some reason, people seem to think God lets only good people into His church. So they think they have to clean up their lives before they go. Then once they're there, they think they have to stay good. Or at least pretend that they're good, because, after all, they're church members now for goodness' sake!

But then they start noticing that some of their fellow "good" church members aren't so good after all—some are even occasionally outright bad—and they're appalled. Disillusioned and disgusted.

But churches aren't for good people, because there aren't any of those. Not even your Great-aunt Ida, who has never missed Sunday school in all her eighty-seven years, is good.

Instead, God lets only sinners into His church.

If everyone knew that from the start, then no one would be surprised when the person in the pew next to them acted like a sinner. The church wouldn't be filled with "hypocrites," another reason people give for not attending church.

In his book *Church: Why Bother?* author Philip Yancey likens an ideal church to an Alcoholics Anonymous meeting, where membership means admitting that you're broken and need fixing and that you need other broken people to walk alongside you and hold you up. Everyone's equal because everyone's a mess.

In a column last year I wrote, "One of the things I like best about my church is how freely everyone shares their messes. ('Oh, your kid's in jail? So's mine!')." That still makes my friend Bob Brashear chuckle. He's part of my church, too.

God is building His church, one sinner at a time. We are weak; we are strange. We're not good, but our Father is, and He loves us dearly. He's also in the process of changing us to be more like His Son, Jesus, one step, one day at a time. We're not there yet, but we are getting better.

My church is scheduled to be finished in October or November, but that's only the building. The real church, the one that God is building using sinners, is still in process.

That church, too, is going to be awesome when it's finished.

I'm so glad to be counted among its members.

BELOVED BEARCAT

*S*OMEONE CALLED the newspaper recently asking about bearcats, as in "Home of the Bearcats," which is written on the side of a local middle school. The caller had never heard of a bearcat.

Although I'm not sure what the middle school knows about them, I'll tell you what I know.

My husband's name is Barry, but his father always called him Bearcat. I call him Bear. He grew up in New York, a sports jock from the time he could throw a baseball. He's strong and pigheaded, tenderhearted and tough.

When we had a renegade armadillo digging up our yard, Barry would grab a shovel and stand poised to kill. He'd growl and snarl around the house and make menacing threats. However, when it came down to actually offing the intruder, my mean husband would be down on his hands and knees in the yard calling, "Here, armie. Here, armie. Go home!"

Anybody who calls an armadillo "armie" and tries to shoo it away isn't a bloodthirsty killer. Actually, as a middle child in a family of three boys, Barry's a peacemaker and a caretaker. He was always the one his dad called on to take care of his aunts. Even now, he's still caring for them.

Barry wanted sons, but God gave him daughters. He still can't figure out women, although he once told a pregnant woman in labor, "I know just how you feel."

I tried to explain to him that, no, you don't know just how she feels, but he insisted that he did. "The pain can't be any worse than living in a house full of females!" he said.

He's cute when he's being a moron.

Barry's an overcomer. A speech impediment and a serious back injury from playing youth football have given him a compassion for underdogs and those in pain. I've always known him to have a heart of mercy.

He knows a lot of stuff, too. He can take a house apart and put it back together. He knows about money and machines and how steam boilers work. He's got a memory like a computer and can probably tell you the 1972 New York Yankees lineup, and who won the Super Bowl in 1968.

He can also tell you about every one of my screwups since we met. His good memory is both a blessing and a curse.

Although we don't share the same commitment of faith, sometimes he surprises me. I'll be worried and fretful over things I have no control over, and he'll say, "Has God ever let you down? Won't He take care of you? You say you believe—so believe."

He calls me the "world's greatest Christian" and thinks I can't lie, cheat, or steal. I think he has a blind spot when it comes to seeing the real me. But then, I have a blind spot when it comes to him, too. I know all his faults, but I love him anyway. For better or for worse, just as I vowed.

We've had a hard time this past year, but we're finally pulling through it. We're stronger for it. I've toughened up. He's softened a bit. At one point we talked about splitting up for good, but that's an oxymoron. Splitting up is rarely good. A long time ago, the two of us became one flesh. God joined us together, and to split would mean being violently torn apart. He's the one God has given me to love, and I can't imagine loving anyone other than him.

I don't know what a bearcat is, but I know I'm in love with one. On our first date, he bought me ice skates. He's a fanatic about keeping the bathroom clean. He thinks drinking coffee should be a sacrament and that "defiling" it with cream and sugar should be a sin.

He loves any movie starring Clint Eastwood, Charles Bronson, or Sean Connery.

He rolls his socks and uses my head as a target as he throws them across the room.

He drives me crazy…and I'm crazy about him.

Thank you, Lord, for this bearcat of a husband.

SAINT (INSERT YOUR NAME HERE)

IN CASE YOU ever wonder what saints eat, the "saints at the house of Brashear" eat just about anything that's not moving. This past Tuesday, the saints—the people in my life group—ate roast pork, sweet potato casserole, and Harriet Eich's green beans that she brings every time the saints get together at "the house of Brashear."

Bless her sainted heart.

Sometimes I write about eating with this group of people I call my family, but I've never written about the family being saints. That's because most people think of saints as being "saintly," with golden halos around their heads, and the saints that eat at the house of Brashear every second and fourth Tuesday of the month don't fit most people's mental image.

After all, I'm one of the saints. Me, a saint. Isn't that a hoot?

When we got together for dinner last week at the house of Brashear—"we" being mostly folks from my church, about twenty total when we're all there—we talked about saints.

One Patron Saint Index on the Internet lists 3,621 saints. There's St. Expeditus, patron saint of procrastinators, and Amand, patron saint of bartenders. If you have an earache, there's Polycarp of Smyrna; or if you have a fear of rats, there's Gertrude of Nivelles. St. Zita is the patron saint of lost keys.

My name, however, is not listed. Neither is Mary Ann Fulkerson's, nor Tim Ott's. None of the Brashears are listed as saints, and not even Harold Eich's name is there, and he's pretty darn saintly, in that golden halo way.

Some of the saints listed on the Index did some saintly stuff, such as being kind to animals (St. Francis of Assisi) and saving storm-tossed sailors and giving gifts to the poor (St. Nicholas). St. Joan of Arc was martyred for her faith, and St. Patrick supposedly chased snakes out of Ireland. But I don't think Rhett Vardaman, one of the Tuesday dinner saints, ever did anything as saintly as any of that. His wife, Tracy, stays home with three small children, which takes the patience of a saint, but I don't think that qualifies her for sainthood.

After dinner at the Brashears' house, the saints meet in the living room. We pray for one another, share good and not so good news. Then we open the Bible together.

This past week we read, "To all in Rome who are loved by God and called to be saints: Grace and peace to you from God our Father and from the Lord Jesus Christ" (Romans 1:7).

All of us who were present are loved by God. We, too, have

been called to be saints, having experienced the grace that comes from the Father and the peace that comes through faith in Jesus.

That's what makes us saints.

Not that we feed birds or take vows of poverty or are beheaded for our faith. What makes us saints, what makes anybody a saint, is knowing that we are by nature far from saintly and have no way of ever achieving sainthood by our own merit. It's *sola fide* (faith alone) and *sola gratia* (grace alone). That's how some of the most rascally among us can ever call ourselves saints.

Take St. Augustine of Hippo. If he lived today, we might call him a player or a gigolo. He's said to have once prayed, "God, give me chastity and [self-restraint], but not just now." But once God called him into faith in Jesus and gave him the title of "saint," his prayer became, "Our hearts were made for you, O Lord, and they are restless until they rest in you."

That's what saint-ness does to a rascal. It changes the wickedest heart to one that's filled with praise to the Almighty.

Who knows? That might even happen to you one day. Then you can be a saint, if not at the house of Brashear with me and the rest of the gang, then one in your own home.

You, a saint. Isn't that a hoot?

GRACE *in the* ORDINARY

*T*HESE ARE ordinary days. That's what a Catholic friend told me. In the Catholic calendar, in between all the fancy days like Advent and Lent, Epiphany, Easter and Pentecost, the days are called ordinary days.

Plain old days. Just ordinary. Nothing fancy. Kind of regular.

I looked it up on the Internet and found that there are a whole lot more ordinary days than nonordinary ones, which pretty much describes life. A whole lot of ordinary with some fancy thrown in here and there.

Some folks think that's a bad thing, but I'm not one of them. I love daily and regular and plain and same.

At Elsie Meloche's 102nd birthday party, she talked about the games she remembered playing as a kid—jacks and tag and hopscotch. She lamented that being a kid is just too complicated these days.

I'm not 102, but I tend to agree. Once, I was telling someone about how my sister and I used to sit on the curb outside our house and play in the gutter water. The person looked at me as if I had said I liked to eat worms on toast. So I said, "Hey, if you've never played in gutter water and made dams with rocks and Popsicle sticks, then you haven't lived."

These are ordinary days.

The sun rises and sets. The rain falls in the late afternoon. Grapes are ninety-eight cents a pound.

The other day I watched lizards play on my front walkway. I pulled a few weeds. I scoured my kitchen sink and told my husband I loved him. I ate a grilled cheese sandwich for dinner and washed my kitchen floor with warm water and a bit of ammonia.

My daughter called to say that my granddaughter had gluesticked paper all over the back window and the hot Georgia sun had baked it on and that it was annoying to scrape all the paper bits off, but amusing all the same.

One summer when we lived in an apartment in California, my kids and all the neighbor kids spent nearly every day in the carport playing a game they called Zoom-a, Zoom-a. They flattened a cardboard box; then as one kid sat on it, another would drag it. By the end of each day they were as dirty as coal miners, but it was good. It was all good.

It was ordinary and so very, very good.

When you think about it, as grand and glorious as God is, He mostly uses the ordinary to speak to people. When the Israelites crossed the Jordan River on their way to the Promised Land, God told them to collect stones from the middle of the river to use as memorials.

Jesus talked about sparrows, about gardens and sheep, about pennies and cups of water given in His name. He used bread and fish to feed thousands, bread and wine to symbolize His sacrificial death.

He healed with mud and spit, made furniture with His hands, was crucified on an old rugged cross. He made the ordinary sacred, and He makes our ordinary lives extraordinarily sacred as well.

Sometimes life is big and grand. You win the lottery, eat filet mignon, go on *Oprah*. But mostly you don't. Mostly you just floss your teeth and wait while your tires are being rotated and balanced. You clean lint out of the dryer trap and shop for canned stewed tomatoes.

You say your prayers and count your blessings; you change the porch light when it goes out; you eat ice cream right out of the carton. And if you're lucky or fortunate or blessed—whatever you choose to call it—God meets you there, right smack in the middle of the ordinary. Father, Son, and Holy Ghost joining in while you fold your socks.

In *The Valley of Vision*, a Puritan prayer says, "Thou hast made summer and winter, day and night; each of these revolutions serves our welfare and is full of Thy care and kindness."

The sun rises and sets. Kids glue-stick paper to windows. Lizards play. Babies cry. God draws near.

These are ordinary days.

THE LOBSTERS THAT
DIED *for* MY SINS

HAT STARTED OUT as a day of celebration and merriment at the Kennedy house last week ended in crustacean death and destruction.

It was the grand Launching of the Water Softener Day. After weeks of planning and piping and repiping and more repiping, after multiple trips to Lowe's and The Home Depot and countless hours of deep concentration and contemplation over chlorine content in the water, one day last week my husband put the final touch on the installation of the Water Boss water softener in our garage, thus and forevermore making our hard water luxuriously soft.

We had planned to celebrate the festive occasion with a lobster dinner. All day we looked forward to our lobsterfest extravaganza and discussed in detail beforehand who would pick them out and what time we would buy them. Timing is everything when buying lobsters.

As the day progressed, things didn't go exactly as anticipated. The water softener leaked and my husband made an emergency trip to the hardware store, leaving the lobster-choosing and transporting to me.

I arrived at the market at the agreed-upon time to ensure optimum freshness, picked out two ugly, yet potentially delicious, crawly things and brought them home.

However, I should have sensed trouble when the usually white-coated meat/seafood department people weren't behind the counter and a non-white-coated guy came from the front of the store to help me. As he fished two squirmy, overgrown crawdads from the tank with a rakelike device and dropped them into plastic bags, something didn't feel right.

Since I couldn't remember how we had transported lobsters from store to home before, I didn't think to question this method of packaging. Besides, we live only two miles from the store. When we lived in Maine, we bought lobsters all the time and once took a dozen of them for a ride to the in-laws' house in upstate New York. They were packed in a box with ice and seaweed, and my feet rested on top of the wiggly box for the entire six-hour ride. Only one lobster died in transit.

Last week's lobsters survived the ride home and were alive when we put them in the bathtub to await their execution while the water boiled on the stove, but they died before we could kill them for our food.

Maybe we could've cooked them anyway, but since it's usually better to be safe than sorry, my husband took the bodies and disposed of them in the woods. Later, we ate eggs and toast while buzzards feasted on thirty-eight-dollar lobsters.

It put a funk on the whole day.

We didn't know whom to blame. My husband said I should've called him from the store so the water could be boiling at the moment I arrived home, thereby bypassing the bathtub. He even hinted that perhaps the tub wasn't cleaned properly.

I thought the fault lay with the guy who just plopped the lobsters into bags without ice or even a sliver of seaweed to frolic with or munch on.

And where was God in all of this? Why didn't He intervene and save our lobsters and our celebratory supper? The day, the week, the whole month was ruined!

Yes, I'm fully aware of how utterly trivial this is—and that's my whole point.

I think most of us do well in significant crises. Human nature is often at its best in catastrophe. But it's the little, petty annoyances that test our character and expose our true selves. Where was God? Holding up a mirror for me to take a look.

I moped about those lobsters all night. I wanted my money

back. I wanted justice and revenge and punitive damages thrown in. And pie!

Most of all, I wanted not to know that something so minute could set me off. I don't like being shown the depth of my shallowness. I much prefer wandering through life with blinders on, unaware of the sin that dwells in me.

On the other hand, the best part about being shown your sin is knowing that God's forgiveness covers it—all of it.

I just wish I had learned that on a night we planned to have soup.

Seeing Grace Clearly

I'M HAVING a terrible time these days. My old glasses decided to stop working. Or maybe it was my old eyes. Whatever the case, I needed new glasses and went to the eye doctor, and now my new reading glasses are about three times stronger than my old ones that quit working.

While my eyes are rejoicing that they can read again, my feet aren't too happy. It seems that I can see to read with my new glasses, but I can't see to walk. As a result, I've been falling a lot lately, or at least bumping into things and people. I even missed the floor when getting off the couch, only to find it—the floor, that is. Good thing I'm well-padded.

I went back to the eye doctor for a different pair of glasses, these with progressive lenses. They're supposed to allow me to read and walk, theoretically at the same time.

As I write this, I've only had them a few days, and I'm feeling quite seasick. I've been called dizzy before, but this time I really am.

The woman who fitted these glasses on me warned that they would require some getting used to. She said to keep my head still and train my eyes to move. I've been trying to do just that, but it's not easy. I'm still walking into walls, and I have to feel around the counters of the newsroom to keep from crashing into coworkers.

When I was younger, I bought a pair of glasses with clear lenses just to wear so I would look studious. But now that I have to wear them to actually see…well, studious or not, wearing glasses has lost its thrill.

I have a vision problem, but not just with my eyes—it's also the way I look at life sometimes. Sometimes I'm so busy looking ahead that I miss what's right in front of me, or I think I see danger and trouble where there isn't any. Or worse—I don't see danger or trouble or temptation and fall right into it.

Years ago I read an article about the need for "godly glasses," or the need to look at everything through the eyes of Scripture. For example, Scripture tells me to fix my eyes not on what I can see, but on what I can't see. What's going to be but isn't yet.

However, sometimes I'm shortsighted and see only what's on top of me. I don't even look at what might be.

When I learned that I was pregnant with my youngest daughter and two weeks later my husband lost his job, with my limited vision I could only see us living on the street and eating birdseed. A friend, however, saw a tremendous opportunity for me to trust the Lord and to look for all the ways He would work miracles in my situation.

At the time I couldn't do anything except trust, and as I did, I saw God perform countless wonders on my family's behalf.

I think that's how God wants us to see our troubles, as opportunities to see Him work. But we need eyes of faith and godly glasses for that.

Scripture also says to "fix our eyes on Jesus." When I start to see myself as not so bad, then one look at Jesus on the cross reminds me that even the so-called good deeds I've done drove those spikes through Him.

On the other hand, when all I can see is my sin and I start thinking I'm too far gone for God to ever forgive me, then a glance at Jesus lets me know that I'm not. No one is.

As I'm getting used to these new glasses, trying to see and walk at the same time, I'm reminded in this life of faith I'm walking to fix my eyes on what I can't see yet and to fix my eyes on Jesus.

Like these glasses, it takes some getting used to. I'm still going to stumble around and sometimes fall, but I'll make it.

Someday I will see clearly.

Someday my faith will be sight.

GOING CRAZY

I MUST HAVE somehow clicked something on my computer recently, because now every morning awaiting me in my e-mail inbox is a daily stress tip. On second thought, maybe it was someone else who did the clicking, someone who decided that my clenched jaw and semipermanent scowl are unbecoming and that I need some de-stressing in my life.

However it happened, I'm glad, and I look forward to my daily reminder.

Mostly the tips are common sense: "Get enough sleep." "Do one thing at a time." "Put things away." "Clear off your desk." Then it gives a brief explanation about how each tip can help a person de-stress. Each one ends with the question: "Why make yourself crazy?"

Good question.

Ironically, every week when I sit down to write my column, Grace Notes, I usually begin by making myself crazy. First, I put enormous pressure on myself: *Better make this a good one. Better not say anything to show my ignorance. Be funny. Be insightful. Be filled with the Spirit. Or at least be able to fake it one more time.*

Next, I add the pressure to write something worthy of my calling as a Christian communicator. Then the doubts creep in: *What if I write something heretical and my pastor reads it and excommunicates me from the church? What if I make the Pentecostals happy but tick the Catholics off? What if I cause the Baptists to never invite me to speak to their women's groups or the Methodists to regret inviting me to their teas?*

Then there's the pressure of my Thursday afternoon deadline. *What if it's 11:57 a.m. Thursday and I still don't have anything to say?*

After I've made myself crazy to the point of wanting to quit my job to sell shoes at the mall, I pray: *Lord, what do You want me to say this week?*

He always answers with one sentence or one thought, one Bible verse, one nugget of grace from the God who loves His people. So here it is for today:

Why make yourself crazy?

At the final Passover meal with His beloved friends, Jesus had just spelled out for them what was ahead. Judas had left to betray Him; He had told Peter, who had declared his undying devotion only moments before, that the disciple would deny even knowing Him.

Then Jesus told them, "Do not let your hearts be troubled. Trust in God; trust also in Me."

In other words, don't make yourself crazy worrying about "what ifs." Don't make yourself crazy thinking about all the "could haves" and "should haves" and "why can't Is?"

Don't make yourself nuts about what other people might, or even will, think. Don't make yourself sick about potentially messing up, because eventually you will mess up. That's why Jesus died.

That's why He gives us grace. That's why we need it desperately.

We all drive ourselves crazy needlessly.

The Reverend Billy Graham once talked about "borrowed" troubles. He said worrying about what might happen makes even the smallest trouble seem huge.

"Worry is an old man with a bent head," he said, "carrying a load of feathers he thinks is lead."

He advised that instead of borrowing trouble by constantly worrying about the future, listen to Jesus' promise: "Peace I leave with you; my peace I give you.... Do not let your hearts be troubled and do not be afraid" (John 14:27).

Why make yourself crazy? Whatever it is that keeps you awake at night or has you clenching your jaw during the day, give it to Jesus to take care of. Then:

Get enough sleep. Do one thing at a time. Put things away. Clear off your desk.

Don't lend out books that you expect to be returned. Don't be so self-conscious. Smile at someone.

Accept that life can be awkward at times. Accept that you will, at times, fail but that doesn't make you a failure.

Trust God. Pray.

OH, MY ROTTING BONES!

*S*OMETIMES, the stuff you learn at church is deadly. This summer we're learning about the "seven deadly sins." Actually, every sin is deadly, but these are the biggies:

Greed. Envy. Gluttony. Lust. Pride. Wrath. Sloth. Every other sin springs from these.

The deadliest part about them is that you rarely know they're killing you.

Last week's sin was envy, as in, "Envy rots the bones." As in, "For where you have envy and selfish ambition, there you find disorder and every evil practice" (James 3:16).

Usually, once I get to church and the service begins, I find that I've inadvertently prepared for the sermon, which is not always a good thing. For example, the week we learned about greed (which I prefer to call "avarice" because it sounds less soul-deadly), I "prepared" by sitting at my computer for an hour before church searching for pillowcases to buy online. I also prepared by spending my offering money the day before on—I can't even remember what.

So, I was *well*-prepared to hear the story of the rich young ruler who was unwilling to sell all his possessions, give to the poor, and follow Jesus, that he might be rich in heaven. I was also well-prepared to be reminded that Jesus, not pillowcases, is my treasure and that when I think I want my life filled with stuff, what my soul really wants is to be filled with God.

"The enjoyment of God is the only happiness with which our souls can be satisfied," the pastor said. He added, "God's not saying, 'Put Me first in your life.' He's saying, 'I am your life.'"

Just as I had prepared for the greed sermon, I also inadvertently prepared for the one on envy. I knew that was the sermon topic, and I smugly felt confident that I didn't have a problem with it. Then I checked my e-mail before I left for church. (Note to myself: Stay away from the computer before church!)

A woman who makes me nuts wrote to say that she was leaving to attend the annual trade show for Christian publishing. When I read that, steam came out of my ears and my eyeballs popped out. As far as I'm concerned, anybody in the northern hemisphere could go to this event and it wouldn't bother me, but not her.

I don't even know why I didn't want her to go, since she's not my competition. I could have gone—I could be there right now, schmoozing and filling my tote bag with free stuff. But I chose not to. Still, knowing she's there makes me nuts. My green eyes got a lot greener last week.

Most preacher-type people would say to pray for the person you envy. But I don't want to. Instead, I want to list all my grievances against her right here, right now. If I thought I could get away with it, I'd do it, too, and it might even get past an editor. However, it wouldn't get past God. He's been known to smite people with boils and plagues of locusts, although He often just lets people stew in their own envy until their bones rot.

Last week at church I noticed my bones starting to rot, especially when the pastor said, "We envy others because we want to be envied." Then he said that the result of envy is a crazed ego ("Everything belongs to me").

How did he know that's what I think?

Once again, I was reminded that God has given me all the honor and position, opportunity, and prestige that He wants me to have. By wanting someone else's, or by not wanting another person to succeed, I end up destroying myself. You can't walk or even stand up straight with rotting bones. You end up crumpled on the floor in a heap with ravens and buzzards pecking at your flesh.

Envy is that deadly. So is greed. So is all sin.

Of the seven deadly sins, so far I'm two for two. I have a feeling that at the end of summer I'll be seven for seven. That's why I can't say it enough: Thank God for His grace.

GOD, *the* HOLY PLUMBER

*M*Y FRIEND MIKE told me God fixed his toilet as a direct answer to prayer.

Ooh-kay.

And he didn't just say, "By the way, I prayed about my toilet and God fixed it," but, "This is so cool! You'll love this! God fixed my toilet! I prayed about it, and He fixed it!"

He said this past year has been extremely difficult for him, and he's been praying some deep, heavy-duty prayers. So when his toilet backed up and refused to unclog after several days of plunging, he took a chance that God would stop His serious work of running the universe and listen to Mike's "trivial" request.

He was shocked with amused amazement and delight when, after he prayed, he tried the toilet handle and it flushed. He said because of the timing he knew without a doubt God had fixed it, as if God was waiting for him to ask, he said. When he did, that's when God fixed it, and not before.

A few days prior to God fixing his toilet, Mike asked me if I ever pray about trivial things. Probably everything to God is trivial in comparison with His greatness, but Mike was talking about the human concept of trivial.

I pray about trivial things all the time, I said, although I couldn't think of anything recent. Once I anointed my daughter Alison's car with cooking oil, laid hands on it, and prayed for a healing, but it still didn't run right, and then the inside ceiling lining fell down and we had to secure it with safety pins and thumbtacks.

In all my years of praying, I haven't tried praying about a toilet. Mike, however, is new at praying and he's game to try anything, trivial or otherwise.

I told him that I think God answers "trivial" prayers for the same reason He answers deep, heavy-duty, "important" prayers—so that when the answer comes our mouths drop open and we say, "Wow! There really is a God!"

That was Mike's reaction, although not mine. I doubted that God fixed his toilet. Another friend speculated that maybe it was all the plunging and the Drano Mike had dumped into the bowl. Maybe it was just a coincidence.

That was my initial thought, too, but then I changed my mind. If God is in control of every molecule of the universe and He times and plans everything to happen at the precise moment and not one nanosecond early or late, then it's more than reasonable to conclude that the timing between Mike's prayer and the (voilà!) toilet flush is no coincidence.

Besides, it served a God-glorifying purpose as Mike told everyone, "God did this thing for me," and pointed people to the work of the Almighty in his life.

Later, Mike and I talked more about how it must be a total hoot for God to do fun stuff for people, like unclogging toilets, and that sometimes religious people take prayer way too seriously, maybe more seriously than God does.

Maybe God wants His kids to pray about clogged toilets and lost keys and broken knobs off dryers. Maybe God wants us to eat more ice cream and throw rocks into ponds and spit off bridges.

Maybe He loves it when we play practical jokes on each other and sing karaoke badly, when we make up silly poems and take pleasure in the absurd. Maybe that's where we find Him.

Life is difficult, and God meets us in our struggle. It's painful, and God comes to us in our sorrow. Mike said the clogged toilet was a metaphor for the way his life has been these past few years and that God fixing it was a tangible reminder that He is also fixing his life.

Forgive me if this is a graphic and unpleasant subject, but life is often unpleasant.

Life is also not trivial but sometimes frivolous. It has moments of levity and bits of fun. So why not include God in all of it? Why not come to Him with everything and anything?

Is there anything that's truly too small for God to be concerned with?

Maybe He really does fix toilets just because we ask. Maybe Mike's the only one who ever thought to ask.

SPURRING EACH OTHER ON

RECENTLY, I joined a new church. Not really, but I did join a gym. And the more I go, the more I'm seeing how churchlike it is.

I joined because I had reached a point in my life where I knew I needed help. I had tried to do things on my own, take care of myself and all, but that wasn't happening. To be honest, I was doing all the wrong things and lying to myself about it.

You know how it is. You buy a bunch of chocolate or doughnuts or whatever it is that's your secret indulgence, telling yourself that it's actually good for you, or at least not so bad. But inwardly you know that what you're doing is destroying you, and you're powerless to do anything about it. You come to a point where you know you need help.

That's the first step to joining a church—to joining Christ. It's admitting, "I need help!"

So, I joined this gym. What I found most attractive is its ordinariness. Everyone who goes there, including the women on staff, is ordinary, just like me. Nobody's buff. Nobody can crack walnuts with her biceps. In other words, nobody's perfect and nobody pretends to be.

Just like church. At least, just like church is supposed to be. I know some churches expect their members to be perfect, or for heaven's sake, pretend that they are. But that's not the way Jesus wants His church to be. He wants His church honest and real. Nobody's perfect; that's why we're there in the first place.

At my gym, all the stations are together in a circle. Everyone faces everyone else; we're all in it together. No one's left out; no one's allowed to go off alone. It's designed as a community.

Just like church.

The way the gym works, each person spends only thirty seconds at each station in the circle, then moves on to the next. You can come at any time and join in the circle wherever there's an open station. You're in with those who have been there a while and those who have just started. But you're all together, moving in the same direction.

Again, that's just like church. Not everyone joins the faith at the same time, and some are further along than others. But it's still one church, moving in the same direction.

My gym is also like church because the members who have been there a while encourage the ones just joining. Newcomers ask, "Will this really work?" and "Will it always be this hard?"

Those who have been there a while say, "It's hard work, but just do what you can at first. It will get easier. I promise."

It's easier because we're all in it together and there's a lot of "You're doing great!" going on between the members. It's amazing what a little encouragement does for a person. It's also amazing how working and sweating together can create bonds among strangers.

The writer of Hebrews instructed believers to consider how they might spur one another on toward love and good deeds and not to give up meeting together, as some were in the habit of doing, but to encourage one another (Hebrews 10:24).

It's like that at my gym and at my church. We tell each other, "Don't give up! Keep going! You'll be so glad you did."

We're all in it together, but we're also in it alone, exercise- and faith-wise. We collect and come together as a membership, but we join as individuals. We each work out our own body, just as we each work out our own faith.

But we do it together.

Some say that they can worship God alone on the golf course or out in a boat fishing. In a sense that's true. But those who avoid corporate worship miss out on some great moments of being the church. We were created for worship, and we were created to be together, spurring one another on.

So don't give up. Come out and join us—and keep going. You'll be so glad you did.

KNOWN *by* LOVE

HEN MY YOUNGEST brother was little, he would run through the house singing, "They'll know we are Christians by our love, by our love; yes, they'll know we are Christians by our love"; then he would slug my other brother, and they would beat each other senseless until Mom or Dad intervened.

That's not unlike the way some church members behave with each other.

Although my brother was too young to appreciate the irony of the situation, church members who sing about love while beating each other up don't have that excuse.

But I digress.

A few weeks ago, I spoke at a local church's women's group. I'd met the pastor before and had also talked with one or two of the women. From my experience, church women's groups are generally nice, but you never know when you might meet up with a group that sings about love but doesn't live it.

A few days before I was to speak, I thought I had my topic all set. I have a standard talk that I often use with groups of this type, and between you and me and God Almighty, I can deliver it in my sleep. Consequently, because God Almighty already knows this and tends to disapprove of presumption, as I gathered my notes together I sensed Him say, "You're not doing that talk."

I've learned that when you go ahead and do what God has told you not to, you often end up falling on your face. Instead of my autopilot talk, I knew that God wanted me to talk about being real, which can be scary. Some groups, especially the kind who sing about love and then beat each other up, don't like speakers who talk about being real.

Real means exposing sin and calling for repentance. Real means toppling sacred idols and unmasking secret strongholds. Groups who like to beat up their members don't like real. They prefer clinging to the illusion that they have it all together, and they prefer their speakers do the same.

But these women weren't like that; I knew that from the moment I got out of my car, when a woman named Dok, who had come to the United States from Korea, grabbed my tote bag to carry inside. On our way into the church, she teased with several other women. You can't tease if you don't love, at least not the way these women were doing it. I sensed realness.

As the rest of the women entered, there was lots of hugging

and kissing. Not phony "air kissing" either. Plus, there was boisterous laughter and some crying going on, too. All evidence of being real.

During prayer time, no one said, "Please pray for my Aunt Beulah's friend Rose's gallbladder." With this group, the prayers were intimate and personal. Because they loved each other, they felt secure, huddling around each other, holding each other's hands as they prayed. I felt the smile of God on their lives, and I wanted to shout, "Way to go!"

I also remember thinking, *I have nothing to say to these women.* They didn't need to be told that's it's okay to be real, that they can be free in Christ even to fail because they've been forgiven and are deeply loved by God. So my words were more reassuring than conscience pricking because they were already doing what pleased the Lord; namely, loving each other.

Afterward, they crowned their "Woman of the Month" with a decorated cardboard crown and a glittered sash and showered her with sincere praise. They talked about filling a laundry basket for a woman who was expecting a baby any minute. Everybody received a package of note cards as a gift; then we all ate cake, standing up in the kitchen. They continued loving each other—I almost didn't want to leave.

That's what happens when you encounter real love. It draws you in and makes you want to stay smack in the middle of it. When you find that kind of love in a church, you know that God is in their midst and that the members genuinely know Him.

Just like my brother's song, that kind of love is worth singing about.

The Good News About Bad News

*F*IRST THE BAD news. Isn't that what people generally want when given a choice?

"I've got good news and bad news. Which do you want first?" someone will ask.

"Give me the bad news," most will reply.

I've been thinking about that lately—bad news first. "We're having liver and okra for dinner, but we're having pie for dessert." "You have three cavities, but you don't need a root canal." "You owe the IRS a thousand dollars in back taxes, but you're going to Disney World."

I've been thinking about bad news first in the context of how people come into a relationship with Christ; it starts with the bad news.

Recently, a friend visited my church. I've been inviting her for a few years and had almost given up because she didn't seem interested, although she doesn't seem to mind me talking about "that gospel stuff," as she calls it.

But even though she doesn't roll her eyes, she hasn't seemed all that jazzed about it. No jumping up and down because God smiles on His own. No high fives because of forgiveness of sin.

When we're in my car and I'm playing Jars of Clay and the Blind Boys of Alabama singing "Nothing but the Blood of Jesus" and I'm slapping the steering wheel to the beat and dancing in my seat because of the song's message, she'll look out the window or search her purse for gum.

A few weeks ago she decided out of the blue to come to church with me. She had attended church sporadically throughout her life, and I was thrilled that she would finally hear the good news of the gospel. My pastor has a way of letting you know that if you belong to Jesus, you are forever safe and secure, much-loved, and cherished by God the Father.

It's all good stuff.

When church was over, I was eager to know what my friend thought. To me, that particular church service was especially full of grace. The pastor had presented God as passionately loving and wildly adoring. The music focused on God's amazing love and "no condemnation now I dread; Jesus, and all in Him, is mine."

I waited for my friend to gush and squeal, or at least crack a smile. But she didn't. Her face was ashen as she said, "Wow. I never knew how bad I am." Then she talked to me for about an hour about how the pastor had pointed out her sin, as if she were the only one in the sanctuary, as if he had a direct view into the inner workings of her heart and mind.

She said she felt ashamed and unholy, un-good, un-everything she should be but isn't and can never be. At the same time, she was practically giddy to have discovered that about herself. She said she wanted to go again to hear more about her sin.

It was as if we had been at two different services. She had walked out feeling the weight of her sin; I walked out feeling freed from mine.

I almost blurted out, "You missed it! You missed the whole point—it's *good* news of forgiveness and grace!" However, I kept quiet as she talked about stuff she had been carrying for a lifetime, stuff that she didn't realize until that moment had separated her from God.

Actually, that had never bothered her before. God was just an interesting idea at best and at most someone or something she would deal with someday. For my friend, that someday was upon her, and she was miserable and feeling wretched about herself.

A pastor friend once said that until we live in the bad news, we can't fully appreciate the good news. We have to feel the crush of our sin and own our part in the enormity of Christ's suffering before we can even begin to grasp the depth of His grace, the scope of His mercy, and the immeasurable cost of His forgiveness.

I well remember living in my own bad news and remember even more clearly the moment when I finally heard the good news. Likewise, I look forward to the moment when my friend hears it, too.

Maybe afterwards we'll have pie.

GRACE *to* SEE ME THROUGH

RECENTLY, I wrote about the gym program I'm involved in and how much like church it is. Since November, I've been going religiously; I'm working hard—I want so badly to see results.

The catch is, to see results you have to first be measured. The gym lady whips out her tape measure and writes down the evidence of your slothful living and reckless eating. Then each month, she does it again and gives you a "report card" showing inches and pounds lost or gained.

My first month showed a weight loss of only one pound, but a decrease in body fat and a total of seven inches lost. I was ecstatic! I felt motivated, pumped. *Thank You, Jesus! Let the burdens of my hips roll away.*

To compare it to church, it's like the early days of my faith, when everything was peace, love, and joy. I would pray; God would answer. *Rah, rah, sis-boom-bah.*

The next month, I increased my time at the gym. I thought if I worked even harder, surely God would reward me even more. But my next report card showed that I had gained weight and had only lost less than an inch.

How could that be? I'd worked so hard. It didn't seem fair, especially as I kept hearing others sharing their success stories of double-digit losses.

Once again, I thought about church and a person's faith journey and how sometimes your best efforts seem to be in vain. How sometimes you pray about a situation for months, years, even decades—and nothing changes. How others' prayers are answered all around you, yet God remains silent to yours, and you feel like He must be playing some cosmic joke on you.

I'm not alone in thinking that either. Every once in a while I get an e-mail from a young girl who asks good, hard questions about life and faith. Her last question involved not feeling God's presence. Her unspoken question was: "If I don't feel God's presence, does that mean I've done something wrong?"

I assured her that sometimes God seems far away, but that's so we will exercise faith and believe He's there even when everything looks otherwise. That we'll keep on going even when we don't see results.

I also told her that other times, when you're not even looking for Him, God will just show up. Flood your soul with His presence, give you a song or a sign, something to remind you that He sees your struggles and knows your discouragement, confusion, and doubts and that He hasn't forgotten you.

My own words came back to me when the woman who measured me saw my disappointment and said, "Don't pay attention to the numbers. You're doing great."

However, I didn't feel great—I felt like crying. Even so, I found my place at one of the exercise stations and started working. I thought about how if I could just lose ten pounds I'd only be twenty-five pounds overweight. I thought about other situations, ones that break my heart if I think about them long enough, and about how tempting it is just to quit the faith and go with the flow, not against it anymore.

Then I remembered something one of Jesus' followers said to Him. Things had been getting tough for the disciples. Following Jesus wasn't as fun as it had been in the beginning, and some were quitting. Jesus asked His closest men, "Do you want to leave, too?"

Peter answered, "Lord, to whom shall we go? You're the only One whose words give eternal life!"

Just then, as if God Himself entered the exercise studio, the background song changed. With apologies to the Monkees, I started singing to myself, "…and then I saw His face. Now I'm a believer. Not a trace of doubt in my mind…I'm a believer, I couldn't leave Him if I tried."

Thank You, Jesus!

Friend, when you can't feel His presence, when you can't see Him working, when your best efforts make you feel like you're moving backward, when you want so badly to see results of your faith and you feel like quitting, there's only one question: To whom else would you go?

And there's only one answer.

Thank You, Jesus.

"Good" Contrition Isn't *an* Act

LTHOUGH TODAY I consider myself Protestant, when I was a little girl I attended a Catholic church. I remember my church as being old and dark, with lots of dark wood and stained glass.

Dark wooden doors lined the inside walls, which I now know were confessionals, but long ago I thought they were either broom closets or where they kept the devil.

When I was seven, I learned that behind those doors sinners confessed their sins to the priest and I was expected to do the same. So, usually on a Saturday morning, I would enter the church, dip my fingers in the holy water, and wait my turn to confess my sins. However, at seven, I didn't think I had any sins to confess, so I made stuff up. "I harbored bad thoughts." "I hit my brother." "I told three white lies."

Real sin, the sin that Jesus died for, was murder or robbing banks, or so I thought.

After I'd go through my sin list, the priest would say, "Now make a good Act of Contrition." I don't know if Catholics still do that, but back then it meant reciting a prayer that began, "O my God, I am heartily sorry for having offended Thee." Only, at age seven, I thought it went: "O my God, I am partly sorry," which is probably closer to the truth.

In the Gospel of Luke, Jesus attended a dinner party at the house of a man named Simon. Right in the middle of everyone eating canapés, a notorious "sinful" woman burst through the door, fell at Jesus' feet, washed them with her tears, and poured expensive perfume all over them.

With raised eyebrows, Simon thought, *If Jesus were really a prophet, He'd know what kind of trash this woman is who's stinking up my house with her tearful display.*

Jesus, knowing Simon's thoughts, told him a story about two men's debts. One owed about $750, and the other owed about $750 million, and neither could repay. Nevertheless, the money-lender canceled both men's debts.

"Now which man loved the moneylender more?" Jesus asked.

"The one who owed more," Simon replied.

Bingo.

Then Jesus told Simon that the "sinful" woman loved much

because she had been forgiven much. "But you didn't even offer me a hot towel to freshen up," Jesus told him.

Some people think that Jesus was teaching that the woman was "forgiven much" because her sins were greater than Simon's, but I don't think that's it. Although murder is more heinous than punching one's brother in the arm, all sin is grievous to God and all sin separates us from Him.

I think Jesus was pointing out that the woman's gratitude was great because she saw her sin as great. Her tears were a "good act of contrition," coming from a genuine, contrite heart. Simon, on the other hand, had little love or gratitude because he didn't recognize his sin as being particularly terrible. If Simon were to step into a confessional, he might make up sins to confess to the priest, too.

The reason prostitutes and "sinners" loved Jesus so much was because they recognized that their sin and their debt was great. But just as great is the sin of Simon and of people like you and me, who consider ourselves not so bad when we're really bad to the bone. I may not be a serial killer, but I often fail to do the good I know I should. I don't rob banks, but I often think of myself more highly than I ought.

As sin, I may think these things are not so bad until I realize that they are the sins that crucified Christ. A spike went through His hand because I yell at my kids.

When I'm confronted with my great sin, I want to fall at the feet of Jesus and cry out, "O my God! I am heartily sorry!"

That's when Jesus, just as He did for another sinful woman at His feet so long ago, reminds me that I am already forgiven, and because I am, I can go in peace.

Blessed are those whose sin is great, for greater is God's forgiveness!

INTO EVERY LIFE *a* LITTLE PDI MUST FALL

*E*VERY ONCE in a while life is PDI—Pretty Darn Idyllic. I had a good week.

For the two people left in the western hemisphere who haven't heard: I'm going to be a grandma! Oldest Daughter came for a visit and presented me with an "I (heart) Grandma" bib. I'm still laughing and crying about the news. It's something I've wanted for a long time. New life in my family! Grandpa-to-be is happy, too.

Life is PDI. God is good.

Also this week, Youngest Daughter graduated from high school without tripping over her shoes. She didn't lose her cap or forget her name. She's outgrown her desire for assorted body piercings and Skittles-colored hair. She loves me. She even likes me—most of the time.

Life is PDI.

I had my entire family home with me this week. Even my "boys"—the son-in-law and the boyfriend. We did the family dinner thing. We all went to church. They sat in the front row with me. The boyfriend straightened out my silverware drawer and washed my dishes. No one cried. No one yelled. No one slammed doors. (Not even me.)

God is good.

The hard situation I'm dealing with these days doesn't seem so hard anymore. A desperate prayer I prayed was answered in an amazing way. God is good. He gives more than sufficient grace.

This past week, I received a handful of letters and heard the news that my first (now out of print) book will be rereleased. The other day I found a bathing suit that isn't too terrible. (Life may be PDI, but I'm still a bit doughy in the middle.)

I'm loved. I'm secure. I have a purpose and a calling—and a great hairdresser. I enjoy my job. I love the people I work with. I adore my boss.

My car's not making any weird noises, and the azalea plant a friend gave me a few weeks ago is still alive on my screened porch. Big Lots has my absolute favorite hairspray—for eighty-eight cents.

My washing machine hasn't eaten even one of my socks all week. My mom and dad called from their home in Mexico to say hello, and I got to tell them that their baby's baby is going to have a baby. Not only that, I just learned that a Baptist preacher and writer friend in Shreveport, Louisiana, prays for me every morning at 9:45. Is that not cool? Is life not PDI?

Yep, God is good.

Sometimes words seem so inadequate. How can I describe the soaring of my spirit? How does one find the words to explain the refreshment of an unexpected cool breeze on an otherwise still, stifling, humid afternoon? Or the music of my children's laughter? Or the complete sense of well-being I felt this week as I awoke to the gentle breathing of my husband, the one I love most on earth?

Sometimes life is struggle and pain. Boredom. Confusion. Discouragement and despair. Most of the time, though, life is just there. It's routine. Same old stuff. A bowl of Cheerios at the kitchen sink every morning and *Jeopardy!* in the recliner every night.

Sometimes life has you yawning. Sometimes you're crying because that's all that's left to do.

But sometimes you laugh because for a brief moment, a day or a week, life is PDI. God is good. Not that He isn't good when you're crying. I've been in church services where the pastor says, "God is good all the time," and the congregation replies, "All the time, God is good."

God is always good. Life, however, isn't. Not always…but sometimes.

Sometimes it's PDI. Pretty darn idyllic. God sends a breeze. He answers a prayer unexpectedly. He shines His light into your darkness and plops hope into your life just when you need it most and expect it least.

Sometimes He sends you a week where everything works. He's that kind of God.

Amen? Amen.

ABBA, GIVE ME *a* WORD

CHRISTIANITY TODAY article, "Dirty Qur'ans, Dusty Bibles," posed the question: If Leviticus or Jude suddenly disappeared from Scripture, would we notice?

The article contrasted the violent reactions to real or unsubstantiated accusations of "Qur'an abuse" to the almost nonreactions to similar "Bible abuses," such as when the "Palestinians holed up in Bethlehem's Church of the Nativity in 2002 had used Bibles as toilet paper."

Ted Olsen, author of the CT article, said that Christians may think the greatest threat to Scripture is an "outright ban" of the Bible, but it's not. The greatest threat is the nonreading of it. The nonthinking of it as more important than food. The noncherishing it as the final authority of how we are to live our lives.

Olsen pointed out the major difference between how Muslims view the Qur'an and how Christians view the Bible. He said that to a Muslim, the Qur'an is "divine—a 'recitation' (that's what Qur'an means) of God's words, unfiltered through human speech," and therefore, "must be ever kept safe from the world's muck and filth."

The Bible, while it is the very word of God, isn't divine in itself, but reveals the divinity of God: Father, Son, and Holy Ghost. It carries divine authority because it comes from Divinity, a pastor friend said.

Jesus once told some religious Bible scholars, "You have your heads in your Bibles constantly because you think you'll find eternal life there. But you miss the forest for the trees. These Scriptures are all about me! And here I am, standing right before you, and you aren't willing to receive from me the life you say you want" (John 5:39–40, *The Message*).

But that's not what's on my mind right now. What caught my attention was the article's scenario of a sudden disappearance of Leviticus or Jude.

Truthfully, if Leviticus disappeared, I would probably be happy. Several years ago, our church had a read-through-the-Bible-in-a-year thing, and I got stuck in Leviticus with all its detailed explanations of how to make sacrifices and regulations about clean and unclean foods and what to do about boils and mildew. I never finished reading it and went directly to Joshua (skipping Deuteronomy and Numbers, too).

So I wouldn't mind if Leviticus disappeared. But what about the tiny book of Jude—just twenty-five verses? After reading the CT article, I went to my Bible to see how I would feel about being suddenly Judeless, and I got stuck again, but not stuck like "Leviticus is so boring my eyeballs are crossing." I got stuck at the first two verses, the greeting no less, because of its richness:

"To those who have been called, who are loved by God the Father, and kept by Jesus Christ: Mercy, peace and love be yours in abundance."

To those who have been called—singled out, invited, divinely selected, set apart, and appointed.

To those who are loved—welcomed, fond of, with deep affection, beloved.

To those who are kept—guarded and protected from being

snatched away, from being lost or spoiled, kept from perishing.

Mercy—kindness toward those who least deserve it.

Peace—the tranquil state of a soul assured of its salvation through Christ, fearing nothing from God, content with one's earthly lot.

Love be yours in abundance—lots and lots and lots.

Wow. All that in twenty-six little words.

Back in the fourth century, young monks would often approach an elder in the monastery and say, "Abba (Father), give me a word." The elder would give the monk a phrase from Scripture and send him off to learn it for himself. The monk was then expected to dissect and chew it, meditate on it, and put it into practice until the word became a part of the monk's being.

So it is with us today. So it is with me and Jude. I am called and loved by God the Father, kept by God the Son, given mercy, which I need, peace, which I crave.

As for the rest of Jude, maybe I'll read on. Right now, I think I'll stay stuck. Abba has given me a word.

Waiting *for the* Wind *to* Blow

BECAUSE I'M WRITING this the day before Christmas, I haven't opened any of the presents underneath the Christmas tree in my living room. But I'm sure I will love them all.

Either that, or I'll fake delight. Moms learn to do that after years of receiving macaroni-glued-on-cans pencil holders and ceramic wise men that look like gnomes.

One of my favorite gifts is the "Jesus plate," which has baby Jesus looking oddly like a manatee. However, of the gifts that are yet to be opened, I doubt any will top the gift God gave me a few years ago.

At first, I didn't know it was from God—I thought it was just the gift picked out by the secret Santa at work who drew my name. But the more I thought about it, the more I realized that the wind chimes came not from a coworker, but directly from God Himself.

A few weeks prior to that, I had decided that my focus Scripture verse for the coming year was to be John 3:8, where Jesus talked about the wind. Shortly after that, nearly every day a breeze would come from nowhere, catching me by surprise and delight, as if my Father was whispering, "I'm working on your behalf. I'm answering your prayers. I'm making all things new—just hold on."

Back then, I needed something to hold on to, so I held on to the wind.

Day after day, my thoughts focused on the wind, the holy wind of God, blowing through my life, changing me, changing those around me.

One particular windy night, it was the first service in my church's new sanctuary, and I watched my then two-year-old granddaughter gaze in awe at the building. "House!" she cried in awe and delight.

Her parents—my daughter and son-in-law—told her, "That's God's house." She ran as fast as she could into God's house, tripping over herself, eager to make herself at home in God's big house.

The wind began blowing in my little one's life.

I find it ironic that, even though I had been watching and waiting and looking for the wind, I didn't recognize God's gift, sitting on my desk. Instead, my first thought upon opening it was, "Wow, I don't hate this!" (I'm notoriously hard to buy gifts for according to my family.)

Made from metal, the chimes softly and delicately tinkled as I held them by the string and let the breeze from the overhead air-conditioning vent create music. Then I put it back in its box and brought it home, where it sat on my dining room table for a few days. It wasn't until the following Monday, as my friend Tara and I prayed for God's holy wind to blow in a certain situation, that I realized the significance of the chimes—that they were, and are, a reminder from the holy Creator to me, His doubting, skeptical child, that He is God on my behalf and always will be and that He doesn't want me to miss witnessing His work in my life.

How awesome is that? It took me a while to find a place to put my gift from God. I wanted it to be where I could hear it, so I would know when the wind was blowing. However, I didn't want it outside where the wind blows naturally. Instead, I hung the chimes from a lamp in my living room. That way, when and if the wind blows and I hear the chimes make their delicate music, I'll know that it's caused by the holy wind of God blowing supernaturally. Besides, it's in my house, in my heart, that I most need to experience God's holy wind.

Knowing my Father as I do, I won't be surprised to one day hear the music and to feel the breeze of the Spirit blowing through my life, changing me and changing those around me.

Blow, Spirit, blow.

WALKING *by* GRACE

*A*S PART OF a local fitness campaign to improve cardiovascular health, I agreed to wear a pedometer for five weeks. Actually, I agreed to walk ten thousand steps a day, every day, for five weeks and be part of a team where I work. The pedometer helps track each step.

Although my job consists of ten-hour days of marathon sitting in front of a computer, with an occasional sixty-six steps to the bathroom or forty-eight to the water fountain, when I agreed to this, I didn't think it would be a big deal. I figured my regular exercise workout several times a week would net at least a million steps, give or take a couple hundred thousand, but I figured wrong.

It seems that despite all the bending and stretching and pushing and pulling and lifting (and sweating and breathing) that I do during an average workout, the actual steps involved are minimal. Maybe fifteen hundred max per workout.

So far, I've only reached ten thousand steps twice, and it's making me nuts trying to find ways to up my totals. I even tried moving my pedometer (also called "that blasted clicker!") from my waist to my shoe. Since my particular clicker doesn't measure stride, just steps, I found that if I wear it on my shoe I can sit at my desk and tap my foot and net a few hundred steps.

But that's cheating. I felt so guilty that I tried walking backwards to reverse the numbers and, therefore, atone for my cheating, but it didn't work. Sometimes you just have to confess your sin and move on.

I've even started wearing the clicker to bed in case I walk in my sleep. It's fifty-two steps from my bed to the kitchen. On a good night, if I can't sleep, I can get in several hundred steps just wandering around my house.

Hey, every step counts.

Last Saturday I got up early to walk the trail near my house. As I did, it gave me time to think. Here are some of my walking thoughts:

* Speed doesn't matter. To my pedometer, a step is a step, whether I run or walk. As long as I keep moving forward, I make progress toward reaching my goal.

* Likewise, the goal doesn't change. In the fitness campaign, the goal is improved cardiovascular health, a better heart. In my spiritual life, the goal is to be made more like Jesus. Again, a better heart. In both areas, however, just being human means I'll never reach 100 percent, but that doesn't mean the goal isn't worth the effort.
* If the goal seems unreachable, break it down. Ten thousand steps a day for five weeks is 350,000 steps, which is overwhelming to think about. Even ten thousand a day seems difficult. But if I make small goals and reach them, then that encourages me to keep going.

   It's the same with walking by faith. It's daily, hourly, moment by moment. *God, please lead me. Help me. Guide me. Just get me through today. Step by step. Day by day. Your grace is sufficient, even if I don't feel it.*
* It matters where you walk. Leaving the path can get you sticker burrs in your socks, and walking foolishly can get you into moral, legal, ethical, and spiritual trouble. It's a whole lot easier just to walk where you know you should in the first place.
* How you walk affects others. Because I'm part of a team, the entire Sunday afternoon I spent reading on the couch affected the team's total. As part of God's family, it matters what I do. Grace sets me free, but freedom doesn't mean I have license to do whatever I want and potentially cause a brother to stumble.

So…walk in a manner worthy of the Lord, fully pleasing to him, bearing fruit in every good work and increasing in the knowledge of God. May you be strengthened with all power, according to his glorious might, for all endurance and patience with joy, giving thanks to the Father. (Colossians 1:10–12, ESV)

Amen!

You Don't Know God

*Y*OU DON'T know God."

That's what my pastor told me a few weeks ago. Of course, I don't think he realized that he was telling it to me personally, but I took it personally.

He was talking about the people we want to see in heaven someday and about the insert card in that week's bulletin. He said that we should write down the names of five people we want to see come to faith in Christ.

He didn't ask us to put their names in the offering plate or post them on the church website or anything like that. Just write them down and tuck the card in our Bible; then pray for each name.

"If you think there's someone too hard for God to reach, then you don't know God," he said. "You don't know what He's able and willing to do in a person's life."

I took out my card and jotted down my five names, just shaking my head as I wrote. And then I couldn't stop at just five. As more names popped into my head, I started filling up every inch of my card. I didn't count, but it's safe to say there are close to twenty names.

The more names I wrote, the more I shook my head. I even laughed as I wrote a few of the names. I know God, but...

That got me thinking about impossibilities. Miracles and such. I have no trouble believing that God made the universe out of nothing or that Jesus turned water into wine. I believe in the Resurrection and that a virgin gave birth to the Son of God. I even believe that a fish swallowed an old-time prophet named Jonah and burped him out on the beach three days later. But I'm not too sure about some of those names written on my card.

"You don't know God," my pastor had said.

That got me thinking about even more impossibilities. Once, Jesus walked into a home where a little girl had just died. He told the mourners, "She's not dead; she's just asleep."

But they knew better. They knew an impossible situation when they saw one. They knew dead. However, they didn't know God. They didn't know that the One standing in front of them was God Himself. God, who simply walked over to the dead girl, took her hand, and raised her back to life—as if there was nothing to it.

That's the point, isn't it?

For God, there is nothing to it, whether it's raising the dead or drawing people to church on a Sunday morning or ultimately to the Cross.

"I am the LORD, the God of all mankind," God told the prophet Jeremiah. "Is anything too hard for me?"

Well, now that You ask, there's that matter of all those names written on my card.

I don't know why I have such a hard time believing that God can change the lives of people I know. For years I've listened to and chronicled the faith stories of hundreds of people who have encountered the living God. I know God! I've seen His hand in people's lives. I've experienced His power in my own life.

But…

Jesus told His disciples, "With God all things are possible."

So I'm back to thinking about impossibilities these days. I'm thinking maybe they're not so impossible. After all, Jesus made a blind man see. He changed water into wine. He changed me.

Who knows, maybe a long time ago someone put my name on a card and shook her head. Maybe she laughed to think that I would ever set foot in a church service, let alone believe.

Maybe her pastor told her, "If you think she's impossible, then you don't know God."

Maybe there's really no such thing as impossible after all.

Goodness Like Apples

THE OTHER DAY I was talking to a couple of older men—one on a tractor lawn mower—and the lawn mower man asked if I was the "lady from the paper who writes about religion." I said I was. Then he said he tries to be a good Christian himself.

I laughed and said the term "good Christian" is an oxymoron, then returned to the newsroom.

Later that afternoon the non–lawn mower man called to ask what I meant by "good Christian" being an oxymoron. He said he had flunked Sunday school so wasn't up on the lessons. I told him that you can't be good and be a Christian because to be a Christian you have to admit that you're bad.

I was just being glib with these two men, but not really. And to make sure I wasn't just blowing smoke, I did a search for the word *good* in the Bible and found that people can "do good," be "rich in good deeds," and "live good lives," but people cannot "be" inherently good. Goodness as a character trait is attributed to God alone.

You may argue that lots of people are good. You may argue—and I would tend to agree—that some Christians are nasty and angry and mean and that many who don't claim to be Christians are kind and giving and selflessly generous.

But are they "good"?

In Buddhism, the ultimate goal is to reach enlightenment, which is said to be achieved through developing a perfect morality—being "good." In the Five Precepts, the moral code of Buddhists, Buddha instructs his followers to abstain from: harming any living being, stealing, sexual misconduct, false speech, and intoxicating drinks and drugs.

On the flip side, Buddhists are to practice kindness and consideration, generosity, sexual fidelity, honesty, and are to develop clarity of mind. These are all good practices, and if one can carry them out consistently, one might appear good.

But does appearing good and doing good equal *being* good?

Can bad people do good things? And why should we do good at all if we can't ever be good as a result? Yikes! I probably should've kept my mouth shut with the lawn mower man, because now I can't stop thinking about this.

Still, I think most people want to be good, and most probably think that they are. My pastor often asks two probing questions: "If you were to die tonight, do you know for certain that you would go to heaven?" and "If God asked you why you think you should be there, what would you say?"

He says lots of people give variations of the same answer: "Because I'm a good person."

But according to what (or whose) goodness scale? Good compared to whom? Without a universal standard or guideline, how does one know what's good enough?

There's no security in that.

But for those who believe they're not good and can't ever be good on their own, there's great security. That's because God only loves sinners, scoundrels, and screwups. He only loves bad people who know they're bad and who despair of any hope of becoming good by their own devices or good intentions.

Because God alone is good and because He loves ungood people, He offers His goodness in exchange for our un-goodness. That's the essence of Christianity.

I like that. I don't have to try to be good, because I can't be. But God can be good in me and produce goodness through me and in spite of me. Goodness is a fruit of God's Spirit in the life of a Christian.

It's like apples.

Apples don't grow because they try to; they grow because the tree produces them. (Yes, I know there's soil and fertilizer and bug spray involved, but that's another subject.) The point is, apples can't grow by themselves and people can't be good on their own and there's no such thing as a good Christian. But there are fruity Christians.

At least that's how I see it.

HAND-RAISING GRACE

MY FRIEND JOAN called to ask if I knew anything about raising my hand.

"Like wanting to be picked as a game show contestant?" I asked.

"No, like raising your hands at church," she said. "I don't do that and I'm not sure I could. But if I'm missing out on something, I'd like to know what it is."

I told her that worship comes in a variety of forms and expressions and that hand-raising isn't "better" than non-hand-raising; hand raisers aren't more spiritual. I also told her that it has a lot to do with culture. If you grew up in a hand-raising church, or say if you're a hand-raising sort of person in your everyday life, it's just what you do when the music starts.

I've seen hand raising at rock concerts. I've also seen regular church hand raisers snarl and snipe at each other out in the church parking lot, yet as soon as they get inside and the first chorus starts, their eyes close and their hands go up in the air as if on autopilot.

So, hands up or down isn't an indication of how spiritually attuned you are or how engaged you are in your worship, I said, which brought the discussion to the real question: What is worship? Is it an attitude? A state of mind? Is it an activity—"praiseandworship"—swaying, singing, eyes closing, feet stomping?

Is it as I remember as a child—sitting straight-backed with hands pressed together and thumbs folded, trying to effect a posture of holiness? Is worship ritual and liturgical grandeur, pomp and ceremony? Or is it something else entirely?

I believe worship is infused in everything we do, ordinary and not, inside the church accompanied by piano and organ as well as at home with our kin. It's what happens when the Word of God is alive and active in and through every cell of our being and we respond with a wholehearted "Yes!" to the God who made us.

That might make our hands go up in the air, but it might not. It might make us weep, or it might make us sit still and think. Whatever worship inspires us to do, it should, however, never be devoid of God. That sounds elementary, but it happens.

Kathleen Norris, author of *Amazing Grace: A Vocabulary of Faith*, writes about attending a worship workshop that was dry as dirt. As the worship facilitators approached the lectern, briefcases in hand, their faces had the same expression Norris recalled seeing on her mother's face "when she had to give one of us kids castor oil."

She describes singing songs of psychobabble gobbledygook and that she craved refuge in the long-ago hymns of the faith, saying they often act as icons for her, "a window pointing toward the holy."

Worship need not always be foot-stompin' lively, but it must be sound theologically.

Last Friday night I attended a worship concert. The band—a bunch of scruffy young guys—played old hymns set to new music, centuries-old words and electric guitars. What made it worship-inspiring was the richness of the words we sang: "What can wash away my sin? Nothing but the blood of Jesus; what can make me whole again? Nothing but the blood of Jesus.

"Oh! Precious is the flow that makes me white as snow; no other fount I know, nothing but the blood of Jesus."

I remember singing and thinking, *Yes! This is it! This is worship; this is what life's all about!*

It wasn't just emotion, although it stirred my emotions. It wasn't the music, but the words of the gospel—"nothing but the blood of Jesus."

It's as Norris starts out in her chapter on worship: "Worship is primary theology." It's basic—God inhabiting human hearts, making them clean and whole and healed. It's gospel, pure and simple.

So, Joan, if you're reading this, here's how you know if you have worshiped: The question is not "Have I raised my hand?" but "Have I humbled my heart?"

If the answer is yes, then you haven't missed out on anything.

Driving *with* Mercy, Grace, *and* Hope

I USED TO LOVE bracelets in a neurotic, obsessive way, but now I don't, although I still like them.

Back when I loved them to distraction, when I had so many that I couldn't fit any more of my "pretties" in the glass jar on my bathroom counter, I made three more and hung them from my rearview mirror—car bracelets.

Using pewter alphabet beads and assorted green glass beads, one bracelet spells *mercy*, one spells *grace*, and the third spells *hope*.

They hang from my mirror, and as I drive anywhere and everywhere, as the bracelets jangle with the bumps in the road, I'm constantly reminded that mercy, grace and hope go with me.

Of the three, I'm not sure which is my favorite or the most important or even if you can have one without the others. They all seem to go together, and as I drive along, they wrap around each other, separate yet intertwined.

Although I probably should pay attention to the traffic, often when I'm out driving I'll think hard about these three bracelets and what each represents.

For example, take mercy. If you've ever been a teenage girl who used to sneak out of the house to meet some guy your parents had forbidden you to see and then got caught, you understand what it is to plead for mercy.

And if you've ever had a kid who scribbled "I love you" on a bedroom door with permanent marker, you understand mercy from God's perspective. The crime deserves a whack on the behind, but mercy prompts you to offer a hug instead.

A few weeks ago my mercy bracelet broke and the beads spilled all over the inside of my car. I found most of them, but not the Y and the E, so I drove around for a few days with just *hope* and *grace*, which was okay, but I missed the *mercy*—and I love mercy.

So I bought another Y and E, restrung them and put *mercy* back in its place. That's when I noticed I had misspelled it as *mecry*, which I decided isn't all that inaccurate. After all, mercy is something that "me" cries for—"Don't give me what I deserve!"

That brings me to grace. If mercy is not getting what we deserve, then grace is getting what we don't deserve.

Sometimes I get mercy and grace mixed up. I think they're similar, but grace, the unearned and undeserved favor of God, is outright crazy. My pastor illustrates it this way:

Someone breaks into your house and brutally murders your only child, and you go down to the jail and bail the murderer out. You take him home and adopt him, give him your child's room, his stuff, his inheritance, even his name—then you take the murderer's place in the electric chair.

"That's grace," he says.

It's good to be reminded that we are all murderers who killed the Father's only Child and that God has made provision by His grace for us to be restored and reconciled to Him, our slates not only wiped clean but Christ's perfection credited to our accounts.

It sounds crazy, but that's what grace is. Actually, it's not so much crazy as it is otherworldly. I think we humans can be gracious, but we cannot *be* grace. We cannot manufacture it. That belongs to God alone.

Last is hope, and I think hope is what helps us to last. Hope helps us to keep going when we want to stop or retreat. Hope prods us to not give up when every cell in our bodies cries out to fling ourselves off the ledge.

Hope gives us courage and strength and endurance. It looks at the bars of the prison we're in, stares at the emaciated or bloated or wrinkled or sallow face in the mirror, stands at the side of the hospital bed or the grave, feels the sting of the salty tears and the weight of the sorrow, and looks beyond to the laughter and the freedom and the everlasting, eternal, neverending peace.

They form a trinity: grace, mercy and hope—and we need all three.

Grace saves us. Mercy brings us near to God. Hope points the way home.

WHAT MOMS WANT

HEN MY daughters were younger and Mother's Day would come around, every year they would ask the same question: "Mom, what do you want?"

And every year I would give the same answer: "I want you to make your beds every day, keep your rooms clean, and be nice to your sister."

Then they would laugh and say, "No, Mom—what do you really want?"

My theory is that mothers never get what they really want for Mother's Day. My mom always asked for a shower cap, and my grandmother always asked for a wallet. They got perfume and bath oil.

Once I polled some friends about what they really wanted for Mother's Day. One stared blankly and said, "An entire day without hearing, 'Buy me, drive me, fix me, get me, or give me.'"

Another said, "To have somebody else put the toilet paper on the roll."

Other women asked that their favorite hairbrush not be used on the dog, their eyeliner pencil not be used for homework, and their good washcloths not be used to wipe out the fish tank.

Mothers never get what they really want.

Maybe it's because we want the impossible. We want a baby *and* we want sleep. We want healthy toddlers *and* couches that aren't smeared with graham cracker slobber. We want active teenagers *and* sanity. We want well-adjusted adult children who move out of the house (and stay out), *and* we want them to be our babies again.

Last Mother's Day was my first as a grandmother. This Mother's Day will be my last with a child at home. By the end of this month, my youngest daughter will be moving to North Carolina to finish school and start life as an adult. She had a practice run for a few months last year when she moved out, but it didn't "take."

This time she'll be five hundred miles away, not fifteen.

It's what I want for her—autonomy, independence, new horizons, new opportunities. But I also want her three years old again, wearing that blue dress with the big white collar and bright pink bow and her dirty high-top sneakers, tugging on my arm and asking for a "jinka juice."

I'd settle for her not leaving her shoes in the kitchen for me to trip over—even just for one day!

Like I said, moms want the impossible.

That's okay, because nothing is impossible with God. So with that thought, here's my Mother's Day want list. It's what I really want, not for myself, but for my daughters:

Alison and Laura, above all, I want you to know that you are loved. Your dad and I love you imperfectly, but you have a Father in heaven who loves you perfectly. We have and will disappoint you, but God never will. I want you to know that deeply and intimately.

I want you to be fulfilled in your life. To find something that gives you purpose and meaning. Something that as you do it you can say, "This is why I was created!"

I want you to sleep well at night—to live with a clear conscience and without guilt. No worries because you know that God has you firmly in His grip.

I want you to laugh heartily. I want you to sing and dance and play.

I want you to live in grace, not obligation. I want you to experience worship, not drag yourself to church because it makes Mom happy. I want you to know that belonging to Jesus is a good thing, not a burden.

And, even though you're far away, what I really, really want…I want you to make your beds every day, keep your rooms clean—and be nice to your sister.

Happy Mother's Day.

PARABLE *of the* FEATHER PILLOW

THE DAY BEGAN like any other. With a billion things to do and not enough time to do any of them, in the middle of it all life happened. Up until then something had been gnawing at me for years, and that day I finally received the answer I had been looking for. As if from heaven itself—actually, from a magazine article—I learned that, yes, you can indeed wash a feather pillow in the washing machine and dry it in the dryer.

I realize that there are things in this world of far greater concern, but I'm a simple woman. A simple woman with a favorite feather pillow that was long overdue for a cleaning.

I can't even begin to tell you how excited I was at the prospect of a clean pillow. I'd been thinking about bed bugs and microscopic icky things playing in my ears at night, and I was starting to be concerned, but not enough to buy a new pillow.

I *loved* that pillow.

Although I didn't have much time to spare that day, I calculated that I had enough time in between errands to get my pillow washed and dried before bedtime.

Because God is merciful, my beloved pillow made it all the

way through the spin cycle without a hitch, or so I thought until I discovered an important truth: A layer of wet, matted fowl feathers plastered on the inside of your washer tub is a good indication that your pillow fabric has a tear in it somewhere.

When that happens, you have a Situation. Most Situations call for someone with a level head and common sense, but since no one with either of those qualifications was nearby, I was left to my own devices. Since I loved that pillow and wasn't ready to trash it, I rescued as many wet feathers as I could, scooping them up with my hands and stuffing them back inside the now large hole in the pillow fabric.

Because I'm not a complete idiot, I knew enough not to use my electric sewing machine to close up the wet hole. My favorite pillow wasn't worth the risk of electrocution, or at least jamming the needle in the wet fabric. So, I stapled the tear shut, tossed the pillow in the dryer, and went into the house to work at my computer.

About the time the dryer started making strange groaning noises, I opened the dryer door to find that my pillow was dry. And clean. And a bit toasty—and that most of it had escaped into all the available openings of the dryer's drum, behind it, in the lint trap, in all the hoses—everywhere.

I spent the rest of that entire afternoon poking at and pulling and plucking feathers out of every crevice of that dryer, determined to get my pillow back. At one point, I tried stuffing the feathers back into the pillow fabric, but dry, fluffy feathers don't behave as well as wet, goopy ones do. In the end, most of the feathers ended up inside my vacuum cleaner (which now needs a new motor, but that's another situation altogether).

The good news is, although I'm out a favorite pillow, the washer and dryer are now feather-free. And my point in all of this you ask? Well, mostly that I've been dying to tell that story ever since it happened.

I guess the point is this: Sometimes life hands us situations that reveal the futility of our own thinking. That when we think we're in control, we're not. Grace allows me to admit that I'm helpless, hapless, hopeless apart from Christ. That I can't do life on my own, and that sometimes trying to hold on to things I think I can't live without only makes my life more difficult. I end up losing them in the end anyway.

It's freeing to be able to own up to my errors. Not just about feathers, but about my sin. Grace lets me know that I can't clean myself up, no matter how hard I try.

Thanks to a laundry room full of teeny fluffs of pillow innards, I'm reminded anew.

GIRLS GONE WILD

RECENTLY, I MET a young girl who's newly in love. She's at the stage where she and her friends dissect every encounter, every look, every phone conversation and syllable uttered by her beloved, searching for every nuance of meaning. She's at the stage where she savors it all. It's agonizingly exquisite. Painfully wonderful. She hasn't discovered his flaws yet. She's still at the stage where he hasn't any. As someone three times her age, I just smile. I know from experience that this stage doesn't last long. The flaws appear soon enough.

Another young woman I know is looking for love. She thought she had found it a few times before, but it wasn't real love. Lately, she's settling for counterfeit love with temporary guys until real love comes along. She knows real love is out there somewhere. There's an emptiness in her being that she knows love can fill and must fill; she's just not sure with whom or how.

This woman and I often discuss love, real and counterfeit. She says girls who are looking for love settle for sex. "Most of them don't have dads," she says. "Or if they do, they don't have the relationship they want."

Columnist Rabbi Shmuley Boteach, a father of five daughters, once wrote about young women in our current culture—girls gone wild. He referenced a *New York Times* front-page story of a fifteen-year-old girl who refused to have sex with her sixteen-year-old boyfriend and the boy cheated on her. When the girl found out, she told her boyfriend that they should both cut class and go have sex. She did so, she told the *Times*, "in order to keep him."

Boteach wrote, "When I read this story, I wondered: Where was this girl's father? Had her father been a strong male presence in her life, she would not have been so desperate for the affection of a scoundrel." He said that when girls grow up secure in their father's love, "they will not be forced at too early an age to worry whether they're pretty enough, smart enough, sexy enough or attractive enough. To their father, they are just perfect. And they will internalize that message in their most vulnerable years."

It's not a stretch to say that this is the essence of the gospel. We're all born looking for a love that we instinctively know exists, but can't grasp. We're looking for that flawless lover but settle for ones who are as flawed as we are. But perhaps more than a lover, we long for a Father, a protector of our virtue and of our most delicate vulnerabilities, an encourager of dreams and a champion of our deepest desires.

In the story of Christ's death and resurrection, God simultaneously whispers and shouts that He has come to be all that we long for. He offers Himself as a perfect man to bear our sin as His own, to gladly "take the bullet" in our place. Every young girl dreams of such a man! Then to prove that it's not just a dream, He raises Himself from death to life and offers that same life to anyone who will receive it.

God as Father provides and protects. God as Jesus presents Himself as a flawless bridegroom. "Your Maker is your husband," wrote the ancient prophet Isaiah. Jesus, the lover of my soul, is totally, madly, deeply, wildly in love with His bride. To be in Christ is to be in love. Safely, securely ensconced in the perfect love of Father, Son, and Holy Spirit.

Although those who are the beloved bride of Christ still chase after counterfeit loves, we do so needlessly. For He is what our hearts long for. So, for my young friend and anyone else who is looking for that agonizingly exquisite real love, I know Someone who is perfect for you. Once you meet Him, I promise you won't need to look any further.

THE GRAVITRON *of* LIFE

*S*ORRY, FORREST GUMP, but life isn't like a box of chocolates ("you never know what you're going to get"). Chocolates are sweet, and even if you get one you don't like, you can always choose another. Or just bite off the chocolate coating and throw out the icky center.

No, life is more like the Gravitron ride at the fair. It spins you around, and then when the floor drops, centrifugal force smashes you up against the side, and you lose your shoes and your wallet— and then when you get off, you stumble and wobble until you finally lose your lunch in the nearest trash can.

Yeah, that's life.

Sometimes Gravitron moments are just mildly annoying and

almost amusing in their absurdity. A friend came in to work Monday and said that he'd paid off the loan balance on his van—seventeen thousand dollars, yet someone at the loan company called to say they were repossessing it.

"But it's paid off," he told the person. "The check's in the mail."

"We're going to repossess your van," the person insisted.

So all week my friend's been hiding his van around town…as the Gravitron spins.

Last week one of my daughters called, in trouble. Nothing dire or life-threatening. Nothing that couldn't be fixed, but trouble nonetheless.

And because I keep trying to reattach her umbilical cord, I stepped onto the Gravitron, pushed the ON button, and sent myself on a wild ride.

By Sunday I had spun myself so furiously with worry that I was throwing my shoes at God, accusing Him of not caring about my daughter or about me, of being cruel, of being a bully, spinning until I was wobbly and feeling sick to my stomach.

Never mind that just the day before my daughter had told me about a stranger paying for her tank of gas, finding twenty-six dollars on the ground, and someone leaving groceries on her doorstep. These were all God's way of telling me that He didn't need me to help Him be God in her life. That calmed me for maybe thirty seconds, until something else set me off and I switched the Gravitron on full-speed and stayed on the ride all day Monday, waiting for the floor to drop.

Even so, in the middle of all the spinning, I still had to do my job, including interviewing a man who works with computers. During our conversation, one side of my brain listened to him while the other side, the side that tends to be fruitcakey, tried to make my daughter's life smooth and problem-free via mental telepathy, which is cosmic insanity, not to mention impossible.

At the end of the interview the man looked at me and said, "When Jesus was in the boat with His disciples and a storm rose and they were afraid, He told the storm to be still—and it was."

That's an odd way to conclude an interview about computers, I thought, but I knew that it was God Himself speaking. Even though my Scripture for this year is "Be still, and know that I am God," I hadn't been doing that. Later I learned that my daughter's current trouble had been taken care of and I had ridden the Gravitron in vain.

I really do hate carnival rides, so you would think I would stop getting on them.

Sometimes the things that spin us out of control are our own doing, like my worrying about my kid. If I scream and spin and wobble and throw my shoes in frustration, it's my own fault. I stepped on the ride. I created the storm.

But sometimes storms rise up and spin us out of control, and it's not our fault, like with hurricanes. It's beyond my comprehension to even try to explain such storms. But—as much as I hate clichés—this I know to be true: Sometimes God stills the storms and sometimes He lets them rage. Either way, He seeks to still His people, which, like chocolate, is indeed sweet.

Maybe Forest Gump wasn't completely wrong after all. Except with God, we do know we'll always get His peace.

I Think I Like Jesus, Too

Earlier this week I attended a seminar for religion writers, "How Religion Shapes Regional and Community Identity."

Prestigious people with prestigious titles came from prestigious institutions and organizations to talk to us about how in the world we should cover this thing called religion.

We discussed the phenomenon of megachurches and how religion affects art.

Someone even mentioned Elvis as a religious icon, with his followers making pilgrimages to religious-sounding Graceland.

We learned about the "supermarket mentality" of people choosing a religious institution that fits their needs and about the new immigrants and the religions they bring with them.

Everyone tossed around words like "religiosity" and "diversity," "ritual," "heritage," and "spiritual."

We learned about demographics and trends.

The program was…interesting, in a statistical, intellectual, antiseptic sort of way—and utterly devoid of Jesus.

However, despite His obvious exclusion from the program, He showed up anyway (even though I don't think the religion experts noticed). He came as I chatted with the man sitting next to me.

"I'm Jewish," the man said. "But I really like Jesus."

Sometimes you encounter people and engage in polite, yet forgettable, chitchat. Other times—"divine appointments" as some say—God shows up in a big way and you're left awestruck.

"Tell me about Jesus," I said. "What do you like about Him?"

The man's eyes lit up. "I like that He got His hands dirty," he said, "and He didn't have an ego. He didn't have a 'Look at me, world!' attitude. It almost makes me cry—His selflessness."

Then he added, "I don't think Jesus would like this meeting."

The man told me that he loves the idea of faith and about how, a few weeks earlier for the first time ever, he prayed to Jesus. "And He answered!" he said. Jesus had touched him in a way he had never been touched before.

Then, because he's a journalist, the man asked me questions. "Do you think Jesus will come back in your lifetime?"

I said that I didn't know.

"When you see Jesus, do you think you'll cry?"

"Yes, I'm sure I will," I said.

Then he asked me what I think heaven will be like. I told him I think we will have really great jobs; maybe we'll be journalists.

"Without egos and jealousies?" he asked.

In between all the religious mumbo jumbo that our newspapers had sent us to listen to, this man and I experienced church. In stark contrast to the careful Jesus-free talk going on in the conference room, this man unashamedly spoke of Jesus. Not "the man upstairs" or a generic "God," but "Jesus."

The name, as one hymn says, that "charms our fears and bids our sorrows cease."

Jesus, the name that's "music in the sinner's ears" and "life and health and peace."

It was by divine appointment that I got to see music on this dear man's face as he spoke the name Jesus. Reverently, passionately, name above all names, Jesus.

It was also by divine appointment that I got to share some good news with him. "I think you're a Christian," I told him. Not in the dry esoteric/ritual and tradition/PowerPoint presentation "Christianity as one of many world religions" way we had been discussing in the seminar, but in the awestruck, "Nothing in my hand I bring, simply to the cross I cling" way. The "Jesus, I have nowhere else to go with my sin but to You" way.

He smiled. "A Christian? You think so?" he asked.

"Yes, I think so," I said.

He smiled some more. I bet he's still smiling.

Jesus does that to you.

Without charts and graphs and statistics, He just quietly shows up on a Monday morning and enters two strangers' conversation, and as religion goes on all around them, He brings life in His name.

Jesus. His name is Jesus.

I think I really like Jesus, too.

THE NEW BEATITUDES

*O*NE OF THE MOST poetic and familiar passages in the Gospels is the Beatitudes, found in Matthew 5 and also Luke 6. Teaching His disciples, Jesus began, "Blessed are the _____," and then He said why they were blessed.

For example, the poor in spirit shall receive God's kingdom; those who mourn will be comforted; the merciful will be shown mercy; and the pure in heart will see God.

Here are a few "blessed ares" that I would like to add to the list:

Blessed are the flexible, for they shall not be broken. That's what my former pastor in California used to say. It makes sense, too. When you're rigid and stiff-necked, unyielding and unbending, you may win the argument or the debate or get your own way or hold the grudge and refuse to forgive, but you end up breaking the relationship.

It's better to be flexible, although that involves stretching and being pulled, using muscles that you might not have used in a while. If you're not used to forgiving or admitting when you're wrong or not only letting others have their say, but also listening to them, it might be uncomfortable until you get used to it.

Blessed are the petty of heart, for God shall whack them upside their heads. This one I know too well. Just recently, my husband decided we should get digital cable. He rarely wants anything, and in the grand scheme of things this is not a hill worth dying on, but I fought it anyway.

It wasn't even over the cost or that I was afraid he would watch reruns of *Law & Order* ten hours at a clip or even mindlessly surf the hundreds of channels. The one and only reason I did not want digital cable to invade my home was because, being already techno/VCR illiterate, I knew that the digital devil would screw up my being able to tape episodes of the *Gilmore Girls*.

That's it. That's the only reason.

I lost my battle—we got digital cable—and I was right; I could not figure out how to program the VCR and became quite snappy. I seethed all night about it and then about toothpaste tubes left out on the bathroom counter and big shoes left where I can trip over them and about how my life was perfect before digital cable interrupted it, blah, blah, blah.

As He always does when one of His children behaves badly, God whacked me upside the head—with grace. My husband installed a device so all I have to do is flip a switch when I want to use the VCR and the cable reverts back to nondigital.

He did it for me, and his kindness brought me to my knees. Likewise, Romans 2:4 says it's God's kindness that leads us to repentance, and repentance makes a soul feel good.

Blessed are the skeptical and doubting of faith, for God shall surprise the dickens out of them. Sometimes you pray and it's as if God is wearing headphones, and you're waving at Him shouting, "Yoohoo! God—it's me!"

You ask Him to change a situation—I know I'm being vague here, but the stuff you want most to happen is generally the most personal—and after years and years of it not changing and just about the time you decide to give up hoping, the thing begins to change. Maybe not completely and not all at once, but enough to let you know that God hears you and has heard you all along, and it so surprises you that you want to yell.

But you don't. Not yet, anyway. You keep it to yourself. Still, your skeptical, doubting heart is blessed.

Blessed are the truly sorry of soul, for God shall make them grin like a fool. Only those who know the depth of their sin and the extent of their unrighteousness can fully appreciate the magnitude of God's forgiveness. And for those who do, there's no greater reason to smile—and the greater the sin, the greater the grin.

Not that I would ever advocate going out and sinning on purpose, but even Martin Luther said if you're going to sin, sin boldly. That way you have something worth repenting over.

So, as we say around my church: Cheer up—you're a lot worse than you think…but God's grace is greater than you can imagine. Blessed are those who know it.

MOTHERHOOD AIN'T *for* SISSIES

I REMEMBER GETTING an e-mail from a friend in Texas a few years ago. She writes books and travels all over the country speaking to women's groups and has a tremendous ministry to imperfect moms, of whom she counts herself as chief.

Her e-mail was one of rejoicing. She told me that her son, the one with a tattoo "the size of a refrigerator" on his back, was finally only smoking pot and would soon marry the mother of his unborn baby.

What kind of mother would be happy about that?

Only the kind who has been on her face before God, crying about a son's cocaine use and begging the Almighty for mercy. *Hallelujah, it's only pot!*

Motherhood ain't for sissies.

When my oldest daughter was ten, she decided to stop eating. For the next year, I watched her waste away. Her skin turned gray; her eyes grew dim. At first she wouldn't eat; then she couldn't eat.

I would bring her to the market and offer to buy her anything there if only she would eat. "Just one bite," I'd plead.

When she wasn't around and I could bear my grief and fear no longer, I would sprawl on my face before God, begging for mercy. "Save my daughter!" I would cry.

It ain't for sissies, this motherhood thing.

I remember when I was about seventeen or eighteen telling my mother, "Why bother telling me no when you know I'm going to do it anyway?"

Although I don't remember what "it" was, decades later my words still haunt me.

I also remember about thirty years ago being in the market with Mom when, right in front of the frozen food section, I looked at her and blurted out, "Mom, I'm so sorry! For everything."

Not the "sorry I got caught" or the "sorry because I'm reaping consequences that aren't pleasant" of my youth, but truly, deeply sorry. For everything.

At first she looked at me as if I had two heads, but then she understood. I cried, she cried, we hugged. She had forgiven me years earlier, for everything. That's what moms do. Maybe not all moms, but my mom did.

Motherhood ain't for sissies.

My oldest daughter is finding that out. My granddaughter spits up on her and stains her clothes. She doesn't sleep when my daughter desperately needs a nap. She fights against the "snot plunger" and screams.

"I'm doing this to help you, silly," she tells her baby. "You want to breathe, don't you?" My daughter said she hates being the "mean mom." After only three months, she's learning that motherhood ain't for sissies.

As a mom, you pour your life out for your children. You laugh when they laugh, cry when they cry. You lie awake at night, waiting for them to come home. You worry. You make decisions you know are right, but are nevertheless agony to carry through.

You make mistakes. Sometimes you get it right.

You risk life and limb for your little ones, even when they're bigger than you, because even when they're gone from your life, they're still your little ones and are never gone from your heart.

Motherhood ain't for sissies. It requires courage and wisdom, stamina, patience, sacrifice, and faith. Even after thirty years, I still don't have what it takes. Not in myself anyway.

Motherhood ain't for sissies, but that's what we are. Only by the sufficient grace of God can we be anything more.

GOD LOVES SLUGS LIKE ME

'M A FRONT-PEW sitter. My pastor thinks I sit up front because I want to hang on his every word, but it's mainly because I'm only five feet one inch tall and have trouble seeing over people sitting in front of me (but don't tell my pastor).

The problem with sitting in the front row is that it's difficult to slink down in your seat and try to hide from God when you're smack in the pastor's line of vision. As everyone knows, pastors have a direct hotline to God. Whenever someone in the congregation is straying, God whispers that person's name in the pastor's ear so he can tailor his sermon to make the strayer squirm.

That's what happened to me just last week.

"How many of you are satisfied with your level of spiritual maturity?" my pastor asked. "In light of that, how do you think God feels about you? Delighted? Disappointed? Mixed feelings?"

I knew the correct answer was "delighted," but I didn't feel delight worthy. First, I had missed church altogether the week before—for no good reason. Wasn't sick. It wasn't even raining. I just didn't go.

On top of that, I hadn't opened my Bible once all week. I picked it up a few times to set it out of the way and eventually covered it up with papers so I wouldn't be reminded that I was neglecting God's Word. I watched a lot of TV last week, too—and not even news or educational TV, but the junky stuff that rots your brain and your soul.

If that's not bad enough, I spent a lot of my food money for the week on clothes I don't even need—I was almost late for church because I was in the middle of dyeing a shirt to go with a pair of pants I bought with my food money.

Although I don't want my pastor to know this, during the first part of his sermon my mind kept wandering back to the shirt in the dye bath at home. Then I thought about how many outfits I could make out of the clothes I bought and what I'd fix for dinner this week on the money I had left.

Then I thought about shoes to go with my new clothes.

Then I thought about my column this week and what I should write about. Since I'd been such a slug all week, I wondered if maybe God had decided to remove His hand from my life.

I sat in the pew looking as holy and sanctified on the outside as I could, but inside I was panicking, trying to drum up inspiration and God's favor. I had left my Bible at home, still hidden under papers; otherwise, I would have opened it and pretended to follow along with the sermon (while trying to come up with a column idea).

"In light of that, how do you think God feels about you?" my pastor had asked earlier.

I figured God was probably disgusted. Just the day before, He had sent a plague upon me: an itchy rash on my face after trying a new "peach tree and coconut" facial scrub. *Locusts and gnats can't be far behind*, I thought.

Then I thought about the words from a hymn we sometimes sing: "Prone to wander, Lord, I feel it; prone to leave the God I love."

I felt it. Oh, boy, did I feel it as I scratched my face and slunk down in my seat and waited for the locusts.

But they didn't come. Instead, I remembered another song we sing: "God has smiled on me; He has set me free. God has smiled on me; He's been good to me."

Hmmm.

How does God feel about me, a wandering, frivolous-clothes-buying, junky-TV-watching, Bible-neglecting spiritual slug?

He delights in me! Not my sin, of course, but me, His wayward kid. He smiles on *me*.

He smiles on you, too. How about that?

CONFESSIONS *of a* CYNIC

*I*T HAPPENED BACK when I was a new Christian, back when I had wide-eyed faith and wasn't as jaded and cynical as I am now.

Back then, I worked with middle school girls at church on Tuesday nights, and one night we had planned a banquet for the girls' parents. Each girl was to bring a dish of food to share.

As inexperienced as I was with this age group, I assumed they would remember. But middle school girls don't remember things like bringing food. Some did, but most of them didn't, and I had a fellowship hall full of girls and parents who were all expecting a meal.

So I did what I do best. I ran and hid in the church kitchen with the other group leader, Cathy. She didn't know much about middle school girls either.

I remember eyeing the back door and thinking about bolting. Not just the banquet, but the whole Christian thing. I had been feeling squeezed in some areas of my life. Things were getting difficult, and it wasn't so fun right then.

Sometimes God puts us in situations that we would rather not be in. Sometimes we're tempted to bolt. Then, just as our hand is on the door, He does something marvelous.

Being the grown-ups in charge, Cathy and I knew that we couldn't stay hidden in the kitchen all night. We needed a plan, or at least a platter of fried chicken. We had neither.

That's when I remembered something Jesus had done when four thousand people hadn't eaten for three days and wanted lunch (Mark 8:1–9). The only food available was a few loaves of bread and a couple of fish. Jesus took it, gave thanks, broke the bread, and gave it to His disciples to distribute to the hungry crowd.

After everyone had eaten until they were full, the disciples picked up the leftovers—seven baskets full.

I decided that if God could do that way back then, He could do it for our hungry crowd in the next room. And in case He didn't, I kept the back door escape as an option.

Even though God doesn't always do as we ask, He always does as we need. At that moment, for many reasons, I needed to see His marvelous hand at work.

When I had gone into the kitchen to hide, there were only a few dishes of food on the table. No one else had come in. No one had whipped up a batch of anything or pulled anything from the oven. But when Cathy and I walked back into the fellowship hall to welcome our guests, the dishes had multiplied.

I still don't know if there were more dishes or if the food inside the dishes had increased. All I remember is that we had more than enough to feed everyone. We might have even had leftovers; that part I don't remember.

I mostly remember being amazed.

Sometimes I wonder if any of those middle school girls even knew they had been recipients of a miracle. Probably not. Same with the crowd that Jesus fed. To them it was probably just another lunch. But the disciples knew. They knew they had nothing. Just a few loaves of bread and a couple of fish.

As I see it, this story has two messages. The most common application is to say, "Give your little bit to Jesus, and He will multiply it to benefit many." That's a good message. Maybe you have a little bit you want God to bless. If you do, I hope He does that for you.

But the other message is that God steps in when we are feeling squeezed and tempted to quit. When we're scratching our heads or crying our eyes out or reaching for the doorknob. That's when God does something so marvelous, so awesome and spectacular, that any thought of bolting vanishes. We're just amazed.

I said I was jaded and cynical, but I'm really not. I can't be—not as long as I keep remembering loaves and fishes and middle school girls and how God met my need for more than just food one night.

FAMILY SECRETS

EVERY FAMILY has secrets, and mine is no exception. I remember when my daughter Alison was four and asked, "Mom, what's a family secret?"

Not known for my common sense, I bypassed the simple definition ("something you don't want anyone outside the family to know") and instead launched into an outrageous example to make a point that she would remember.

"Well, if Daddy wore Mommy's underwear, that would be a family secret," I told her.

Although I quickly forgot our conversation, she didn't, and later on in the week, she informed my mother, "Grandma, want to know a family secret? Daddy wears Mommy's underwear."

Fortunately, my mother already knows I'm an idiot and figured things out. (Or else she determined that some things are better left a secret.)

It could've been worse. Alison could've shared her family secret at church! Then again, what better place to share your family secrets than with your brothers and sisters in the Lord?

At my church, we don't call each other "Brother So-and-So" or "Sister Whomever," but that might not be a bad idea. It might reinforce the fact that we are brothers and sisters, that we are family. That's what my pastor always emphasizes. He says the church isn't *like* a family. Rather it *is* a family.

"God doesn't save individuals and then set them on a mantel as trophies," he told us recently. "He places us together as a family."

My pastor talks a lot about family and not going through life alone. He reminds us often that we go together, interdependently. We go as family, our lives woven together. Eating together, laughing together, weeping together. Holding each other up and carrying our weakest siblings. Together.

We share our secrets with one another. We can do that because we're family, and it's safe because our Father binds us together in His love.

Just this past weekend, my church family honored me with a book signing after church to help promote my latest book. While selling books and signing autographs continue to be a boost to my already inflated ego, that wasn't what thrilled me most about the event. It was hearing my pastor say from the pulpit, "Why would we do this for Nancy Kennedy? We wouldn't do this for any other author. But we're doing this for her because she's family."

What an awesome family I have, too: Gwen Mason, who always remembers my birthday and calls me "daughter." Ted and Betty Santana, who pray for me. Bonnie Hurm, the kindest person I know. Dianne Lakeman, who listens to my "confessions" as she cuts my hair. Mary Ann Fulkerson, who knows my darkest secrets and loves me anyway.

The list goes on.

Yet when I think about this dear family of mine, my thoughts are bittersweet, because some of the people I love most on this earth don't share this family with me.

It's one of the great ironies of life. Although God "sets the lonely in families," as the psalmist wrote, often when that happens, when God places a person into *His* family, earthly families are torn apart. I don't know why that is, only that it hurts like heck when it happens.

Here's a secret for you: For many, many years I went to church alone, and sometimes as I sat there, I couldn't stop the tears. However, I assure you they weren't (usually) "Oh, poor me, I'm here alone" tears. They were more often than not "Oh, poor them" tears.

Poor them, because they didn't and don't know what they're missing, they are, indeed, poorer for it. Poorer, because as they search for family, for love and acceptance, for belonging and meaning, they're not finding it where they're looking. That's because it can only be found in relationship to the Father, the Father who places His children in His family.

That, my friend, is the real family secret, which isn't really a secret at all.

TO LOVE—*or* LEAVE?

*R*ECENTLY I got an e-mail from a woman asking for advice. She said she had married the wrong person and wanted to leave him. The thought of being a single parent and having to work full-time scared her, yet she didn't think that was a good enough reason to stay married.

She said her husband loved her, which made her feel even worse—she actually hated his attention and his efforts to love her.

"I need your advice real bad," she wrote. "I think my marriage is a mistake."

It took a few days to answer her; I didn't want to say anything glib or harmful. It's sobering to have someone turn to you for advice.

Here's some of what I told her:

"Marriage isn't easy—that's a fact. And I'm not sure it's a matter of who we marry as much as it is *who we are* in the marriage. I can understand wanting to leave if a spouse is abusive or an addict or a cheat, but it sounds as if yours is basically a good guy.

"It's rare to find any married person who hasn't thought at least once about leaving. As for me, I'm glad I didn't when I wanted to, for it rarely had anything to do with my husband. Instead, it was more of an inner conflict; my battle was with God.

"Once I understood how deeply loved I am by God, loving my husband followed. And after more than thirty years, I can't imagine being with anyone else. I don't want anyone other than him.

"I hope you find the peace you're looking for. I can understand the fear of being a single parent and having to work full-time if you leave. And you're right. Maybe that's not the best reason to stay married, but maybe it will give you time to work things out internally.

"The grass really isn't greener anywhere. Every relationship has its challenges, and every marriage has its dry times. I've lived through enough of them to know that feelings ebb and flow."

However, I don't want to talk about marriage—at least not in the earthly, man-woman way, but in the God way, as in God loving His people and them not loving Him back. The Bible often depicts God as a husband and His people as His bride.

There's a story in the Bible about a man named Hosea whom God told to marry a whore named Gomer. The more Hosea loved her, the more she chased after other lovers.

God wanted Hosea, a prophet, to experience what He felt when the people He loved chased after other gods. Hosea kept loving Gomer, and God kept loving the Israelites.

Today He loves the church as well. Today He loves me.

As I read the e-mail from the woman asking for advice, I thought about how hard and fast I run from God and how it's His constant kindness in the face of my wanting to stay distant that repeatedly brings me to my knees in repentance.

Sometimes I'd almost rather He be cruel than kind. With cruelty, if you want to leave or reject the other person it's understandable. If you're married to an abuser or someone who cheats on you, leaving is justified. It makes sense.

But leaving or rebuffing someone whose only "crime" is loving you? (And why would someone keep offering love to someone who doesn't seem to want it?) That's *nuts*.

No, that's grace.

It's my opinion that, deep down, people hate grace. We both yearn for and hate being loved and cherished; we hate unselfish devotion.

Take acts of charity for example. Most people would much rather give charity than receive it. We hate receiving because it makes us aware of our neediness.

We hate grace for the same reason. It makes us face the things we hate most about ourselves; that's why we run.

Deep down we know we're unworthy. We are damaged. We are not good. We're undeserving.

Despite that, God loves us.

And as desperately as we might long for another or a different love, as fiercely as we might fight or as fast and far as we might run, the truth is we'll never find one that's better.

FOR STORM-WEARY ELAINES *and* ROGERS

*O*NE OF MY favorite Internet stories is about Roger and Elaine. As they're out driving, Elaine mentions that they've been dating for exactly six months.

Roger becomes quiet, mentally calculating: *Six months…that means my car's way overdue for an oil change.* He's thinking about how his transmission shifts like a garbage truck and how the mechanic better not stick him with another bill for six hundred dollars.

Meanwhile, Elaine interprets his silence as a sign that what she just said is pressuring him into a commitment, and she starts worrying about whether or not her schoolgirl expectations of a knight in shining armor (albeit unspoken) are making him feel inadequate.

She attempts to ease what she perceives to be his fear of her rejecting him, which to him makes no sense whatsoever, since he's thinking about his car. Then there's a lull in the conversation and

Roger realizes he needs to say something, but whatever he says will most likely be wrong.

Get the picture? It's a long story, so I won't finish it except to say that it's a perfect illustration of the vast differences between men and women, how differently we approach situations and process information, how differently we react to crises. It's a wonder men and women get together at all—and a miracle that we stay together, given the way we communicate.

Take these past few weeks of hurricane chaos and stress.

First, let's say Elaine and Roger did get married and now they have two kids, a dog, and a house that they can barely afford. They love each other most of the time, but life gets in the way. It's not like it was in the beginning when their thoughts were only for each other. They each feel that something's not quite right between them, and they're pretty sure it's the other one's fault.

At the first hint that a monster storm's heading their way, Elaine gets on the phone and calls Roger at work. "I want you to come home right now," she says, her voice shrill and shaking. "I don't want to stay here anymore. Why can't we move to Nebraska?"

Roger sighs. "I can't talk right now," he says. "We'll discuss it when I get home." Elaine gets angry and hangs up on him.

She thinks he doesn't care. She had called wanting to hear him say, "I know you're scared, but everything will be okay. I love you, and I promise I'll take care of you—we'll take care of each other." She mostly wants to know that he would move mountains for her if he could.

Roger wants to move mountains; he might even want to run right home to Elaine, but he can't just drop everything. He still has to work—preparing for hurricanes costs a fortune. Besides, it's still too early to do anything anyway (like escape to Nebraska). Roger needs time to think through what he's going to do, how he's going to protect his family—and now Elaine's ticked. *Again.*

She calls back. "I've got it all planned," she says. "We'll leave in the morning—you, me, the kids, the dog (all crammed into our tiny car with two hundred thousand miles on it) and go to my mom's in Iowa, where they don't have hurricanes."

Roger feels emasculated. Elaine feels that Roger's lack of immediate leadership drove her to take matters into her own hands. *Again.*

Both feel misunderstood, but instead of moving toward each other, they move apart, storm after storm after storm. They feel like they're just one gale away from their home being toppled.

I have no wise words for storm-weary Rogers and Elaines, other than to say that men and women were created to complete one another. To build each other up, not tear each other down. I also know that nothing is too difficult, no relationship so torn apart that God cannot repair it. Not just patch up, but make new—even if only one person is willing to change.

As men and women, we might not ever understand each other completely, but through the grace of God, we can weather life's storms together. It starts with one. It starts with you.

Toddler-Shaped Grace

THIS PAST WEEKEND, we were the "Goo-gas." At one point, we were the "Gummas," and I think even "Gooms."

For those who don't speak toddlerese, that's "Grandma" or "Grandpa." My husband and I just returned from visiting our granddaughter, Caroline, in Maryland.

I learned much in the short time we were with her. For

instance, when you're introduced to a child you haven't seen since she was a baby, a bag of M&M's works as a toddler magnet.

I learned how petty I can be if I think the kid likes Grandpa better than me.

I learned how fun it is to go to Toys "R" Us and pile a shopping cart full of stuff I don't have to put together or trip over and how fun it is to buy "doll clothes" for a real, live wiggly doll.

I learned what a good mother my daughter is and that she takes seriously her calling as a teacher and trainer of another human being. I also learned that I have subzero patience for little, strong-willed people and that it's probably a good thing I don't volunteer in the church nursery.

As I watched this child want up, then down, lights on, then off, jacket on, jacket off, I kept thinking, *Kid, if you'd just cooperate, listen to your mom, and do what she says, your life would be a whole lot easier.*

But then I realized she was behaving a lot like her grandmother, who also wants everything her own way *now*, so I kept my mouth shut.

I loved watching Caroline with her daddy, my son-in-law, Craig. When he walks into a room, her face lights up. They play a game where they run toward each other, and then he swerves and misses her.

She always has her eye on him, and she laughs when he picks her up.

But she uses him, too. Since he's tall, he makes a handy ladder. She'll ask him to pick her up, as if she only wants to be held and loved. But then she'll motion for what she really wants: to turn on/off/on/off the light switch or reach a snack in the cupboard.

Not even two years old, and she knows how to manipulate.

People who think children are born innocent haven't observed toddlers. Toddlers bite their dads and kick their moms. They throw tantrums at the mall and grab straws out of strangers' sodas at Wendy's and toys away from other kids.

Toddlers need Jesus.

When Caroline's mother (my daughter Alison) was just barely three, she stood in her crib wearing her fuzzy red Winnie the Pooh blanket sleeper and said, "I need Jesus in my heart."

Night after night, during our bedtime prayers, she kept saying it. At the time, I thought she was too young to understand salvation—"by grace are ye saved, through faith." But when I asked her why she needed Jesus in her heart, she looked at me and said, "Because I sin."

As they say on *Family Feud*, "Good answer! Good answer!"

The Bible says God has put eternity in our hearts, that we're born with a knowledge of Him. Our hearts know that something's missing, that we were created for more than just eating and drinking and going to work five days a week. More than "Life is hard and then you die."

Blaise Pascal said we all have a "God-shaped vacuum" that isn't satisfied until God moves in. If it's God-shaped, then logically, only God can fill it. We need a Father. We need a Savior.

Preachers often say, "God doesn't have grandchildren." That's not a quote from the Bible, although the concept is true. We all stand before God as individuals, with our own individual faith. As winsome as she is, Caroline can't get into heaven by claiming my faith or her parents' faith, only her own. She needs Jesus in her heart because she sins. She needs a Father. She needs a Savior.

So my prayer for my precious granddaughter is that her parents will expose her to the same gospel of grace that once captured their hearts—and that one day, when God whispers her name and bids her to join His family by faith, she'll run into His welcoming arms.

SOMETIMES WE DON'T KNOW SQUAT

FEW WEEKS ago I mentioned I was a front-row sitter at church. Nothing's changed—I'm still short and can't see over other people's heads. I still prefer the front row.

However, it seems a certain family has also taken a liking to sitting in the front row—in *my* front row. In *my* seat.

Because externally I'm extremely polite, I act like it doesn't bother me…too much (although I've let this family of pew squatters know that this particular row is mine, in a friendly, winsome way, of course).

Of course. But they don't seem to get the message.

I casually mentioned it to my pastor one day. He sits in my row, too, two seats over from me. He told me the name of the family. Told me that they usually attend a different service than I do. However, since we only have two services instead of three during the summer, they started attending *my* service, sitting in *my* row, in *my* seat.

For the past few weeks, I've even left my house extra early just to get to church in plenty of time to get *my* seat. But it seems I haven't been early enough. Each week, there they are: front and center. *My* row. *My* seat.

Obviously they don't know—someone needs to tell them—that even before the building was completed, I staked out my spot. I called dibs! Last week, I even came to church a half hour early. Thinking I had enough time, I hung out in the bookstore for a while.

Shouldn't have done that—the pew-squatting family beat me to the front row by ten seconds!

"You snooze, you lose." They didn't actually say that, but…but

I would have. At least, I would have thought it, if I had gotten there first.

I realize this shouldn't be such a big deal. The church is plenty big enough for all of us. There are even other front rows, at least four. But that's not the point. The point is...

The point is...

The point is, it's these seemingly insignificant irritations that God uses to show me my true heart. I don't know about anyone else, but most of the time I think of myself as pretty darned okay. I'm nice to cats and occasionally to people. I've never been in a fist-fight. I refrain from telling people with twelve items in the ten-items-or-less line at the market that they are in violation.

I go to church almost every week, read my Bible, and try to keep at least two or three out of the ten commandments every day. Sometimes I even do something that's not completely self-serving so I can feel holy and proud because of it.

I'm doing okay, I think smugly. *Not as good as some, but definitely better than most. God must be pleased*, I think. And then some rotten pew squatters step in and ruin my feelings of okay-ness. Suddenly, I'm not as okay as I think.

I'm petty and trivial. Ungenerous. Unloving. Ungracious. All the "un" labels I tend to assign to other people.

I don't like it when pew squatters sit in my seat. But even more, I don't like to be shown my true heart—it ain't pretty.

Now I have to decide what I'm going to do about it. I could sit somewhere else, but I might be tempted to feel self-righteous. *After all, I took the high road and you didn't*, I might think.

Or I could get to church an hour early and set my purse down on *my* seat to mark my territory, but that would show everyone around me just how petty I really am. I've even thought that maybe the pew squatters will read this and feel so bad that they'll stop their squatting. But that makes me feel even less okay.

Most likely, when summer's over this family will return to their usual service, and the front row will be empty once again. But it won't ever be the same. I've seen my true heart, and it ain't pretty.

Once again, I need God's grace.

Oh, how I need God's grace.

MOTLEY CREW *and* SALAD *with* CRUNCH

*H*AD DINNER WITH the family this past Tuesday. We're not blood related, although we all have the same Father.

What we are is a motley group of all ages, mostly from my church, but a few from other churches. We've got some babies and some teenagers and some folks in their forties and fifties. Some older ones, too.

We meet for dinner about twice a month. I usually bring drinks or napkins. (I'm not known for my cooking.)

This past Tuesday, however, I brought a salad—probably the best salad anyone has ever eaten. It had dried fruit bits and sliced, toasted honey-glazed almonds, cut up navel oranges, lettuce, and fat-free poppy seed dressing.

As good as the salad was, that's not what made dinner with the family great. It was being together and talking at the dinner table about garden mulch for azaleas and books we're reading and trying to figure out who brought the blueberry dessert.

After dinner, as is our custom, we gathered together in the living room. During dinner, because there are so many of us, we're separated into four or five eating areas. But after dinner, we gather together. That's when the conversation goes from garden mulch to what's really going on in our lives.

This past Tuesday we talked about what we heard from our pastor's sermon the week before. The pastor had spoken about roller coasters and how sometimes you're way up high and all is well, and then you drop. Sometimes you're jerked all over the place; sometimes you're on your way up, and sometimes you're wobbly-legged and green on the ground, puking your guts out.

It's all a part of the ride.

Because we're family, we freely talked about where we are on the ride. These past few weeks, I've been on top. A colleague at work said I'm "sparkly." My life sparkles right now. I'm riding high. Even so, I know it's only temporary. I also know that I'm not up here because of my own merit. That was also one of the pastor's points: "When you're on top, don't forget that it's God who put you there."

On Tuesday, we spent much of our time in the living room listening to and comforting a hurting family member. We've all been low before; many of us have experienced similar hurts. We said so, but not in a one-up or a suck-it-up-and-drive-on way. We shared our stories to let our loved one know that a member of our family is never alone. When one of us hurts, we all hurt.

Because we're family, we cried, because the one we all love cried. We laughed, too, because our Father never lets the roller coaster drop without giving us hope on the way down. Hope makes us laugh, even when we're crying.

"We're called to suffer sometimes, to be refined as if by fire," said our oldest and wisest family member. "But the fire only burns away the dross; it never destroys us."

I love my family. I love the dinners we share together. Sometimes, like when we have ham, I think about not going. (I don't like ham that much.) But then I remember that the food's not important. What's important is being with my family and sharing my life with the ones who know me best and love me anyway.

We have one more dinner together before we break for the summer. I think I'll bring my salad again. (I hope we won't have ham.) Our "last" dinners are usually noisy and hectic. Even though we may see each other during the week, at church, or around town, it's not the same as when we all get together for dinner. That's when we know for sure that we're family. Not "like a family," but a real family, as my pastor often says.

At my church, we call these small family groups "life groups." That's not a fancy label, but it's accurate. We're a group where life happens: the ups and downs and in between. It's eating together and crying together, it's laughing and praying together. It's loving each other enough to tell the truth and holding each other when words fall short.

It's riding the roller coaster together.

That's what families are for. That's what life is all about.

WHAT, ME WORRY?

OF ALL THE THINGS my daughter Alison does well, worrying tops the list. And of all the things God does well, proving her wrong about her worries is one of my favorites.

Several years ago, Alison, husband Craig, and baby Caroline came to Florida to visit, and as families do when they get together, we started telling family stories.

Alison told us that when she was about ten, she thought if she spoke more than three hundred words a day she would lose her voice forever. Every day she carefully tallied her words, and when she reached three hundred, she stopped speaking for the day. (To this day, my daughter is an excellent counter.)

Although she has outgrown that particular worry, because nature abhors a vacuum, she has replaced it with others.

Ever since New Year's Eve 1989, when tainted ranch dressing gave her food poisoning, she has worried about throwing up and is wary of most everything she eats, especially food that I say is "fine." Back in '89, I was the one who had said the ranch dressing was "fine."

When Alison announced she was pregnant, I knew she would worry about morning sickness, so I worried, too. Even though I told her that I never threw up when I was pregnant and "like mother, like daughter," she worried anyway, and I worried about her worrying.

Likewise, when she and her family flew from Tucson to Tampa, I knew she would worry about taking the baby on the plane, that the baby would fret and cry the whole time and people would give her mean looks and say under their breath, "Can't you shut that kid up? I didn't pay to listen to crying!"

Her worrying made me worry. I wasn't worried about her baby fretting as much as I worried about my baby fretting.

Prior to their trip I reassured Alison that everything would be fine. I told her to look for God once she got on the plane because He would be there to help her. I believed it, but I fretted and worried anyway because I wasn't sure she believed it. I also worried because sometimes God allows babies to cry on airplanes even when you pray that they won't. I worried so much about her worrying that I solicited prayer from my friends.

Alison and Craig had taken a midnight flight—with only fifteen passengers on the whole plane. The ride was smooth and dark and quiet, and the baby slept most of the way.

I wasn't surprised, but I was surprised, if you know what I

mean. I had wasted a good fret on nothing. God had come through and answered my prayers; Alison had nothing to worry about after all.

But then she worried about the return trip. God might not be as merciful two times in a row. To add to her worries, the day they left, the baby had a cloggy nose, and Alison worried that Caroline's ears would hurt on the plane. I told Alison that God knew about it 100 billion years ago and it's all a part of His plan, which made her worry even more because sometimes God's plans include babies with earaches on airplanes.

Before she left, I hugged and kissed her and put on my faith-filled face. "Don't worry," I told her.

She slapped her forehead and said, "Why didn't I think of that!"

We laughed, but we knew she would worry, just like I knew I would, too. It's easy to say, "Don't worry," but hard to do, especially when it's something you do best.

Jesus once posed a question to the worriers of His day: "Can worry add a single day to your life?"

The answer, of course, is "No." Worry never changes the outcome of anything. The only thing it accomplishes is sleepless nights and acid indigestion.

Worry chokes faith—but faith also chokes worry.

If your faith is in your circumstances, you'll worry when things don't go as you plan. However, if your faith is in the One who holds all circumstances and their outcomes in His hands, then worry loses its grip.

P.S. The return flight was even smoother than the first.

TESTIMONIES *in* PROCESS

IN MY JOB at the newspaper as the religion writer, I've written hundreds of testimonies of how people have found faith in Jesus. Although some are similar, no two are the same.

Some testimonies are like those of my daughters: They grew up going to church and came to faith as preschoolers. Some, like mine, tell the story of finding faith when everything in life seems ideal, yet an inner emptiness drives them to the Cross.

Most testimonies, however, are stories of wounding and despair, of addictions, abandonment, and abuse, of broken relationships, and bankruptcy.

"When things couldn't get any worse," they say. "When I had nowhere else to turn, when even my parents cast me out and I wanted to die, that's when Jesus came."

However, before Jesus comes, a testimony usually includes a time of questioning God's kindness. "If You're so loving, if You're so kind, how could You let this happen?" is a common question people ask Him.

As people, we ask it because we think kindness means not letting bad things happen. But God's not a person, like us. His brand of kindness often looks opposite. His kindness allows the bills to pile up and the cancer to spread. It allows the cars to break down and the one we think we can't live without to run off with someone else.

The Bible says God's kindness leads to repentance, which is a necessary ingredient for a testimony to be genuine. Repentance is a sincere regret and sorrow for all the ways we try to find life apart from Jesus, coupled with a desire to change. Without both elements, Jesus doesn't come.

As long as there's an inkling of "Maybe if I just make a few changes, try to keep a few commandments, lose weight, stop smoking, go to church, maybe put a few extra bucks in the offering," as long as there's no grief about sin and until there's an acknowledgment of complete helplessness, then a testimony is still "in process."

I have some friends whose lives are testimonies in process. They've expressed an interest in Jesus, but they're not at the repentance stage yet. They still need more of God's kindness in order to come to the place where they know they can't find life anywhere else but in Jesus. Right now they're still at the "bad things piling up" and questioning God's kindness toward them stage.

As their friend, my stomach is often in knots watching them, and I want to jump in and help, make everything better and easier for them. I want to save them from "big, bad God."

I could offer a temporary help, but they need a permanent, eternal one, which only God can provide. My help would only be equivalent to putting a Band-Aid on cancer. My help would only interrupt God's plan for a better help—a *best* help.

When people tell their testimonies and recount all the difficulties that led to their repentance, they often say, "It was the best thing that could've happened."

That's another common ingredient of a genuine testimony. That's how you know Jesus has really come to you. Because His coming is so grand and glorious, because His grace and mercy so fills your soul that your life turns upside down, you can't help but consider the bad things as "best."

When you eventually turn your heart toward the One who loves you most—and you repent and He lifts you out of your despair—that's when you realize that all the time you spent licking dust really was God's kindness after all. That's when you realize you have a testimony, a story of how God's help came to you at the time you needed it most.

So because I love my friends, the kindest, most loving thing I can do to help them right now is to stay out of God's way as, in the words a friend, He "fixes a fix to fix them" and pray for the day that their testimonies will no longer be "in process," but complete and everlasting.

SECRETS *of the* SOIL

HAT I KNOW about growing plants could fill a thimble. So it's no surprise to me that the cute little yellow flowering things I plopped in the dirt under my tree out front aren't doing well. Even the tree, half-leafy and half-not, looks like it needs something, but I don't know what. Our neighbors, however, all have lovely gardenesque areas under their trees and elsewhere. I'm thinking they know a secret.

I hadn't even wanted to plant anything, but because I'm mostly motivated by what people think, I decided that it was time to be like the neighbors and grow something other than lizards and weeds in the under-tree area.

The nice, helpful nursery salesperson asked what I was looking for.

"Plants," I said.

"Can you narrow that down?" he asked.

"Plants that I don't have to care for."

He showed me some junipers and some yellow and reddish-orange flowery succulent things that he said thrive in the hot sun and that the daily afternoon Florida rain is water enough.

How perfect is that?

I plunked down my money and later plopped them into the holes I dug under the tree, poured out a couple bags of mulch to make it look like I knew what I was doing and figured that was that.

The flowery things immediately deflowered, but then came back within a day or two. This repeated itself for a few months, which suited me just fine. But they've been looking a bit sickly lately and not rebounding like they were. I'm considering planting fake flowers. The maintenance involved in growing stuff is not my thing. Maybe I have bad dirt. I don't know.

Last week's sermon at church was one of Jesus' famous parables about dirt and sowing seeds and how some dirt allows plants to grow and other dirt doesn't. The dirt represents our hearts, and the seed is the gospel message. The point is: If we want good plants (a fruitful life) we need good dirt.

The pastor said most people read the parable and think, *I better go home and fix my dirt.* They think that having good dirt is a matter of morality, doing religious things, and trying hard to be holy, and that good dirt looks good on the outside.

But the pastor said that's not it. He said good dirt is that which is broken and tilled, and as hearts go, a "good" heart is one that knows its need for God.

He said that only God can change the condition of our hearts; we can't make our own dirt good by trying, but we can go to Him and ask Him to make our dirt good for the sowing of the gospel message. I'd never heard that parable told that way before.

But even before hearing that sermon, and even before my flowering yellow things started looking scraggly, I had already been thinking about dirt. Actually, I had been thinking about some deep stuff in my life that I can never write about, not because I don't want to, but because it involves other people's feelings. You just can't blab everything.

Ironically, the things that you can't blab are usually the very things that are at the core of your being, the stuff that keeps you awake at night and on your knees in the daytime. But when it involves other people…you just can't blab it, and as a writer it's frustrating to be so confined.

So I tell a lot of my core stuff to the one I call my uncle-dad. He says that the stuff that can't be made public is the good dirt that God uses to grow beautiful flowers. That doesn't help much when it comes to the pitiful looking flowery yellow things under my tree, but it helps with the other stuff. It helps with understanding and even appreciating the dirt a little better—that God Himself has broken it up and tilled it with great care.

Besides, when people look at a garden, they look at whatever's growing, not the dirt. But the dirt…how vital and precious is that broken dirt!

Maybe that's the secret after all.

FROM LIMO *to* LIGHTNING

*A*LTHOUGH TOPS on his list of dream vehicles is a brand-new Ford F-150 Lightning pickup truck, my husband's eyes still mist whenever anyone mentions "the limo."

Back when we lived in California, Barry decided we needed a second car. At the time, we shared a 1981 silver Ford Fairmont, which was perfect for driving people around. However, Barry decided we needed something we could use for hauling water heaters to the dump. Not that we had ever needed to haul water heaters to the dump, but, to quote one of my husband's favorite phrases, "you never know."

So he brought home a 1968 Ford Falcon station wagon, or as I like to describe it, a twenty-two-year-old rumbling, clattering, smoking bucket of tin and rust, the color reminiscent of Cream of Wheat mixed with mashed lima beans and putty. And that's being generous.

Until then, I had had no reason to doubt my husband's judgment. However, when he reached through the back window (which was permanently stuck in the down position), grabbed a clean rag, and began to shine one of the car's few rust-free spots, as he beamed like a proud father with his newborn child, I started to question his mental faculties.

That's when our youngest daughter, who was about six at the time, announced, "Dad, you got a limo."

Obviously, she had meant to say "lemon," which was a whole lot closer to the truth. Still, the name stuck.

Barry had fallen in love with his "limo" from the start. He washed it faithfully with scouring powder and bleach. He installed a radio antenna and connected it to a portable radio with alligator clips and aluminum foil. He superglued a digital clock onto the dashboard and rigged up a push-button horn.

He didn't even seem to mind the protruding spring that kept ripping the backs of his shirts or having to straddle the sagging front seat to see over the steering wheel. He drove the limo everywhere, cheerfully, proudly. Obliviously.

Our daughters hid their faces in embarrassment. I just shook my head in amazed and amused horror, thinking, *"Why would an otherwise reasonably sane man show so much devotion and spend so much time caring for a hunk of junk?*

When Barry bought it for two hundred dollars, it had nearly two hundred thousand miles on it. He drove it for about three years, which included two dozen hundred-mile trips to San Francisco and back—and several trips to the dump hauling water heaters.

During that time, our newer car went through several starters, a radiator, and a set of tires; meanwhile, the limo needed only an occasional air filter. The radio gave out before the limo did! Eventually, Barry sold it for four hundred dollars—twice what he had paid for it.

It was a sad day at the Kennedy house as we watched the new owners drive away. Even the girls and I felt a twinge of sorrow. Barry had loved that ugly car.

I'm not sure why I'm telling you all this except that it's a favorite story in our family. Also, thinking about the limo reminds me of how sometimes people think of themselves as beaten up, ugly, and junky. Not much more than a pile of rust held together by bolts and duct tape.

But God doesn't see those who belong to Him that way.

I take that back. Actually, He does see us that way, just as we are. The Bible says God remembers that we are "but dust." However, if Christ has redeemed us, if we are His, that makes all the difference. Because we're His, He doesn't leave us as we are, all beaten up and junky. However, He doesn't merely patch us together and add a few makeshift improvements using alligator clips and aluminum foil. That's because He's not about "making do," or even making us better. Instead, God is out to make us new.

In a way, it's like taking a "limo" and turning it into a Lightning.

Have Your Cake *and* Eat It, Too—Kinda

I'D BEEN DOING WELL with Weight Watchers, losing weight slowly but steadily. I believe this program works because it's based on freedom. Although not all foods are nutritionally beneficial, no food is forbidden or illegal.

And then the folks at Weight Watchers went and introduced even more freedom and grace to the program: FlexPoints. Briefly, every food has a point value. Broccoli has zero points, a Big Mac with a large order of fries has twenty-six. My daily allotted total is only twenty points, but FlexPoints allows thirty-five "extra" points weekly to use or lose.

The first week that FlexPoints were introduced, one woman at the weekly meeting I attend excitedly counted on her fingers and then cried, "You mean I can have seven extra martinis?"

The leader assured her that she could drink all seven at one sitting if she wanted to, but added, "Although that's probably not a good idea."

As for me, I'm not tempted by martinis, but I am by cake. With Weight Watchers, I'm free to eat cake.

The problem with freedom is that what we think will make us free generally doesn't. Just because I can do something doesn't mean I should.

During the first week of FlexPoints, I made a trip to our new Wal-Mart; I had heard they had a killer bakery department. Although I told myself not to even go, I wound up there anyway, smack in front of the cake display. That's when I noticed a small twelve-ounce cake, which I calculated to be only twenty-eight points for the entire thing. I reasoned that I could take it home, cut it in half, freeze half, and nibble on the remainder throughout the whole week, thus only using fourteen points. (Even though I had thirty-five points to use freely, that much freedom is scary.)

Still, I felt guilty. Cake is generally considered a "bad" food, and I didn't want anyone to see me buying bad food—they might think I'm bad too.

So I looked around to see if anyone I knew was nearby, picked up the cake, then said loudly to no one, "This'll be perfect for Bob's birthday!" Next I rushed to the produce section, piled a bag of lettuce on top of the cake in my basket, and used the self-checkout lane to buy it.

Once home, I cut the cake, put half in the freezer as planned, and then grabbed a fork. An hour later, both halves were safely inside my digestive tract. And even though I had eaten an entire cake in one afternoon, I didn't go over my total weekly points and registered a weight loss that week. However, after the last forkful of cake, I felt sick as a dog the rest of the day, which cured me of my cake cravings, at least for a while.

Some people think that being a Christian means there's a bunch of stuff you can't do, but that's not true. There's more stuff you can do than can't do. Even so, as the apostle Paul warned the church in Corinth (whose motto was: "Anything goes"), all things are permissible, but not all things are good for you. Not everything is constructive to character or edifying to your spirit. Or, as I used to tell my kids, "Just because you can doesn't mean you should."

Paul reminded another church that there are "some acts of so-called freedom that destroy freedom. Offer yourselves to sin, for instance, and it's your last free act. But offer yourselves to the ways of God and the freedom never quits" (Romans 6:16, *The Message*).

I don't think Paul was referring to eating cake, but for some people that might apply. Anything can become a trap: money, power, sex, trying to achieve the most-envied lawn in the neighborhood. But thanks be to God, because of His great love, He has provided a way out of any trap, any pit we find ourselves in, any prison we create for ourselves.

That way out is Jesus. As the psalmist wrote: "You still the hunger of those you cherish" (Psalm 17:14).

Everything may be permissible, but not everything is good for me. But by letting myself be loved by Jesus, by letting Him still my hunger, I can say no to that which would harm me, and still be free to eat cake.

Just not the whole thing.

STIFF-NECKED GRACE

THE GOOD NEWS: I won the free lunch box. The less-than-good news: I've been paying for it ever since.

A few months ago, we had a "most reps" contest at the gym. Common sense warned me not to get involved, but because I've always considered common sense as...well, "common," I tend to avoid it. So on the machine that works the arm and chest muscles, as onlookers counted, I completed twenty-seven instead of my usual twelve or fifteen reps in the allotted thirty seconds.

As I said, I've been paying for my "free" lunch box ever since.

At first it started as a knot near my left shoulder blade, which I thought would go away on its own. But it didn't. Instead, it turned into a major pain in my neck, which led to creaking and cracking and all kinds of scary neck noises.

Finally, I went to my doctor, who did a head turning move that made me wonder if he had once worked as a bare-handed assassin for the mob. He told me to apply moist heat and massage—and to avoid getting into "most reps" contests with people half my age and twice my fitness level.

I did all that, but for the longest time, my neck didn't get any better. It continued creaking and cracking, and it hurt like heck. That's the point I was at prior to going to church last week. As the service ended, out of the corner of my eye I saw my friend Charlie, the raving optimist who prays about everything. That's when I got the idea to pray.

Okay, God, I said, *I know if I ask You to fix my neck, You can, although I don't know why You would. Even so, would You?*

Almost immediately my neck started to feel better. Later, I sent Charlie an e-mail and told him that I think maybe I might believe that God answers my prayers, too, not just his.

He wrote back: "Now, Nancy, are you sure that you think God really answers prayer—deep-in-your-heart-and-soul think it? Without a shadow of a doubt? Praying, knowing full well that God is going to answer? That He hears and is answering even before you pray and that He has known since before the beginning of time that you would pray this prayer at this exact moment and that He has already healed your neck?"

I wrote him back: "Well, since you put it that way—no. I believe it in my head, but my heart can't shake the concept of God as One who 'dangles carrots' and pulls rugs out from under people. My neck is better than it was, however. Now it's mostly stiff. I am rather stiff-necked, now that I think about it."

In God's eyes, stiff-necked is not a good thing to be. When the Lord graciously and miraculously rescued the Israelites from slavery in Egypt and they turned from worshiping Him to bowing before a statue of a golden calf that they had made themselves, He called them a "stiff-necked people" (Exodus 32:9).

They were stubborn and obstinate in their refusal to trust that He knew best how to care for them, muttering about how much better things were back in Egypt. They may have been beaten-down slaves, but at least in Egypt they had leeks and garlic to eat!

I'm stiff-necked when it comes to trusting God with all areas of my life, stiff-necked when it comes to believing that He is who He says He is: kind and benevolent, gracious and gentle. Thankfully, there's help for the stiff-necked like me. In His mercy and grace, God hears the cries of His children and looks past their stubbornness to their fear. It's the fear that His love might not be enough to meet my needs that causes my neck to stiffen, or that He might only taunt me with it and yank it away just as I begin to grab hold of it.

That's when He places a prayer in my heart, *Fix me!* and then He does just that. Sometimes not all at once, but just enough to help me believe that He is able and willing to do more, if I'll only keep trusting and believing.

My neck's not 100 percent healed, but it's better, and so is my heart, for the prize I won isn't the lunch box after all, but yet another glimpse at my desperate need for grace and God's willingness to give it.

AUDIENCE *of* ONE

'M NOT MUCH of a movie buff, but last week I watched *Save the Last Dance*—twice. It's about aspiring ballerina Sara, who dreams of getting into the prestigious Juilliard school of dance.

On the day of her audition, her mother dies in a car accident. Sara goes to live with her estranged jazz musician father in a rough inner-city Chicago neighborhood. Once there, she places her toe shoes, along with her dreams of ballet, in a closet and shuts the door.

A fair-skinned blonde, Sara attends a predominantly black high school, where she strikes up a friendship with Derek, who dreams of being a doctor. He teaches Sara hip-hop dancing, convinces her to pursue her dream of ballet, helps her practice for her audition, and somewhere in between all that, they fall in love.

Other stuff happens, too, but that's the main stuff.

Because every good story needs conflict, there's a jealous ex-girlfriend, a "homeboy" who puts pressure on Derek to dump the white girl and go with him on a revenge drive-by shooting. To further the conflict, Derek's sister tells Sara that good black men like her brother are rare and they should be with black women. Sara's emotions are in turmoil, and she breaks up with Derek.

This spurs him to go back to his homeboy, and Sara gets ready to go to her second audition for Juilliard. As the day approaches, she misses her mother. She tells her father, "I just want someone there [at the audition] who loves me."

He says he loves her and he'll go with her, which is nice and all, but she really wants Derek there. Next, the movie flips back and forth: Sara arriving at her audition, Derek meeting up with his friends. But he doesn't go with them after all. Instead, he turns, runs, and hops the train to Sara's audition, which is a good thing because the homeboys get shot.

Flip to the audition: Sara's name is called. She dances her classical ballet piece. She's good, albeit uninspired.

Flip to the shooting, and then flip to Derek running down the street. Flip back to the audition: It's time for Sara's contemporary dance, a ballet number with a hip-hop element.

She hesitates. She starts. She goofs up. The judges shake their heads.

She asks to start over, but her heart's not in it. Then, just as her dream of Juilliard starts to die a final death, Derek runs into the auditorium—breathless—and runs up on stage.

"I can't do this; the judge hates me," Sara tells him.

Here's my favorite part: Derek tells her, "You were born to do this. Forget about the judge. Ain't nobody watching you but me."

So she dances, with skill and flair and joy. She dances for "someone who loves her."

When she finishes, the "judge who hates her" says, "I can't say this on the record yet, but welcome to Juilliard."

As movies go, this one is predictable, but I loved watching it nonetheless. I watched it twice, just to hear Derek say, "You were born to do this," and then to watch Sara dance.

I suppose you know where I'm going with this: If we're secure in someone's love, it doesn't matter who else is watching or judging. Being loved sets a person free to do whatever it is he or she was born to do.

Even though the application may be as predictable as the movie, if you're anything like me, you need to be reminded often that for those who belong to Jesus, the Father's love sets them free to be and do that for which they were created.

A song we sing at church asks, "Lord, if You mark our transgressions, who could stand?" The answer is no one. But for those whom God smiles upon, not only can they stand, but they can take their dreams they've hidden away, lace up their toe shoes, take to the stage, and dance with joy for the One who applauds from the wings.

Besides, ain't nobody watching but Him.

WELCOME *to* POMOVILLE

*T*HE REVEREND Richard Pratt has called them "pomo sapiens," although the academic term is *postmodern*. We are living in the postmodern era, he said, which presupposes a modern era.

Pratt said modern thinking is now considered old-fashioned, such notions as absolute truth, men not wearing earrings, women not getting tattoos. In modernity, science and rational thinking governed society. Moderns believe that unless it can be re-created or proven in a science lab, it can't be.

Postmodernity arose after the collapse of Marxism, which Pratt said was theoretically the most rational model for a utopian society ever designed. However, the designers didn't factor in man's propensity toward sin, and "All are created equal" eventually became "All are created equal, but some are more equal than others."

And if Marxism failed, then what good is being rational? That's when people's thinking began to shift from rational to feeling/intuitive, or irrational: *If it feels good, do it—even if it will destroy me, even if it contradicts reason, even if it only makes sense to me (and if it doesn't, who cares?).* Today that's the predominant thinking behind what we watch on TV, read in magazines, listen to on our iPods.

As a generation, full-fledged postmoderns are those twenty-five or younger, with their highest value being personal autonomy: No one has the right to impose on another's personal choice. To true postmoderns, or pomos, everything is equal. Christianity is the same as vegetarianism is the same as reincarnation is the same as homosexuality is the same as anarchy. Pick and choose from whatever you like. It's all, you know, whatever.

To a pomo, the only important thing is what's happening now, Pratt said. Take the young man who decided to take a stand against "evil corporate America" and burned down a McDonald's. He thought that what he was doing was a good thing and was actually surprised that he got arrested. Pomos don't think of consequences.

A young pomo friend often tells me about her love life. As she looks for the right man, she's "seeing whoever" in the meantime. Currently she's seeing three guys—I'm afraid to ask how she defines "seeing." From what she tells me, she lives the old Stephen Stills song, "If you can't be with the one you love, love the one you're with."

Pomos believe that sex with a stranger is preferable to sex with a friend because pomos highly value friendship, and sex tends to ruin friendships. However, they also believe in "friends with benefits" (*benefits* meaning sex), and that could be friends of either gender.

They may live as strict vegetarians and fitness fanatics, yet do drugs. They may oppose abortion personally, but be pro-choice. They may say they are "half-Christian, half-Buddhist." It doesn't make sense, but it doesn't have to.

Engaging a pomo in a conversation about the Bible is easy. They will listen intently as you explain all the archeological and historical data about the death, burial, and resurrection of Jesus—and then say, "Cool. Want to go to Starbucks?"

However, if you suggest that they consider following Jesus for themselves, you'll get an altogether different response. Gene Edward Veith Jr. says in *Postmodern Times* that postmoderns' beliefs are function of the will, with no foundation other than their preferences and personality. Because they interpret any criticism of their beliefs as a personal attack, they will become defensive and sometimes angry if you try to change their opinions.

This is our culture. We live smack in the middle of pomo thinking, and past methods of sharing the gospel won't work. Time to put away the "Four Spiritual Laws" tracts. This is not your grandma's evangelism anymore.

So how do we speak to the pomos around us? We begin by listening and building relationships, loving sacrificially and extravagantly, which is exactly what Jesus did when He walked on earth. Then, when we've built trust, we "speak to their damaged places," Pratt said, because their lifestyle choices and often their upbringing are quite damaging.

It's difficult for a pomo to trust Jesus, but not impossible. God continues to build His kingdom one person at a time, and not even the gates of hell—or postmodernism—can prevail against it.

SOMETIMES LITTLE GIRLS CRY

MY GRANDDAUGHTER cried. Not that she hasn't cried before. She's infamous for her "mall meltdowns." Like every two-year-old, she cries when she's tired, when she hurts her toe, or when she doesn't get her own way.

But this crying was different. This time she cried out of sadness. That made my daughter cry, which made me cry, too.

Her daddy, my son-in-law, left Monday to attend Army warrant officer school in Alabama. He'll be gone for six weeks.

For the past few weeks, Alison and Craig had been preparing Caroline, telling her that Daddy's going away to Alabama. She would nod her head, but at two, how much does she comprehend?

Alison said she found Caroline upstairs one day, holding a framed photo of herself with her daddy, and she was talking to it saying, "airplane" and "Alabama," and she was crying—softly, sadly crying.

Alison said she felt helpless. She said it was the first time she realized that she cannot take away her child's sadness, that we all deal with our sadness as individuals and that it's necessary that we learn to process it ourselves. Ideally, to bring it to God.

I don't know how it is with fathers, not being one myself, but I know what it is to be a mother and to feel impotent when your child is sad. You think that if only you can say enough cheerful words (How many is enough?), if you can send the right things in a care package, if you can somehow direct their relationships through mental telepathy and pray hard enough, then your children will be happy. Then they won't be sad. Ever.

But no matter how intense your desire and how tireless your effort, you cannot halt or take away your child's sadness—and that makes you sad, because that's your baby! That's your flesh, and when your flesh cries, you cry, too.

The other day, as I tried feverishly to telepathically control the universe, or at least one daughter's section of it, I came to a dead end. My daughter's two best friends had moved away and she was sad and I couldn't change anything. I couldn't make her friends not move away; I couldn't make new friends materialize. I couldn't make her sadness go away.

I couldn't. I. Could. Not.

King Solomon said there is a time to be born and a time to die, a time to plant and harvest, to weep and mourn, laugh and dance. My daughters and my granddaughter and you and I will have times of sadness. Sometimes for long periods of time, sometimes briefly. That's just how it is. And though we may not like it, such times are necessary. How would we know gladness if we'd never felt sadness? How would we know God's comfort unless we needed it?

I told my daughter, the one who's sad, that I wished I could make her unsad, but I can't. She said, "No, you can't, but I appreciate that you want to."

Maybe that's the only thing, the best thing, I can do for my children. To acknowledge their pain, yet respect and love them enough not to rush in to fix things for them. Taking away their pain—if I could—would be taking away their opportunity to see God step in and do whatever it is that He does that would inspire their faith and make His name known.

I struggle with this daily, hourly. I've talked to other mothers, even those whose "babies" are older than me, and I'm not alone. When their babies cry, they feel it, too.

Maybe that's part of the penalty for sin, the curse God pronounced after Adam and Eve ate the forbidden fruit in the Garden of Eden. He pronounced a life of hardship, of pain in childbearing. Maybe that carries over into child-rearing as well.

But God has also pronounced hope, for He is a God of hope. So, even though this life is filled with sadness, one day God will wipe away every tear from the eyes of His people. There will be no more death or mourning or crying or pain.

But for now, sometimes little girls cry.

Storms *and* Showers

I

T'S NOT THAT difficult. A few spritzes of cleaner, a few swipes with a scrubby sponge. I mean, how hard is it to clean my shower? But for some reason, it has me paralyzed.

I blame it on the recent hurricane. I blame it on 9/11 and the war on terror. Traffic accidents and suicides. Babies dying. Poverty, hunger, disease.

I blame it on the magnitude of needs "out there" and feeling impotent to meet them and wishing everything would just go away. Can't we just all get along?

I'm not even sure if any of this makes sense, but right now I don't even care. Isn't that terrible? I don't care.

Actually, I do care. I care that people in south Florida and Orlando and Wachula and Arcadia are devastated, without water and electricity, without walls to keep them feeling safe. Some lost not only their homes, but also their livelihoods. What will happen to the moms and pops who lost their pizza parlors and hardware stores? What about the waitress who counts on tips to pay her rent and feed her kids—what if the restaurant she worked at was flattened by the recent hurricane?

I need to clean my shower.

At noon Friday, Hurricane Charley was headed straight for my town. We in the newsroom had been in adrenaline mode for a few days prior, getting stories out, preparing for "what if?" It was fun, exciting. As someone on our staff said, "This is why we do what we do."

But "our" storm, as a coworker called it, the storm with our name on it, became somebody else's storm. Somebody else's disaster. Somebody else's devastation.

I can't quite wrap my thoughts around it. Why were we spared?

I do know this: I wouldn't have been prepared. I only have one flashlight, only five jugs of bottled water. Most of my food is frozen/microwavable. I might have some batteries somewhere.

I had packed a bag "just in case"—with my blow-dryer, my bathing suit, and flip-flops. What was I thinking? A category 4 hurricane is the same as a vacation at the beach? (*I need to clean that shower.*)

On Friday my husband had called to say that he was on his way from Jacksonville, bringing his aunt with him. Her mobile home park had been evacuated. My immediate thought: *I don't want her smoking in my house.* What kind of a person thinks about tobacco odor instead of the well-being of a frightened old woman?

My shower...

On Friday afternoon and into Friday evening I waited for "weather." I wanted to see trees bow down and feel rain whip my face. Of course, I wanted my TV and air conditioning to keep working. I wanted to experience "hurricane lite." But the storm had made a right turn, and I barely got wet.

On Saturday, the news team gathered. We had been prepared to go out and find after-hurricane stories of heroics and human interest, but there weren't any. No storm—no stories.

Except.

The stories, which should've been our stories, now belong to somebody else. And I don't know why. Why were we spared? If God is the One who directs storms, why did this one turn like it did?

There's a deeper "why" that's bothering me, however. With all the pain and chaos and need in the world and all the people with hearts that long to help ease suffering in any way they can...why is my heart not like theirs? Why do I not clamber to be on the front lines, in the fray, fighting the good fight? Why is my first thought not to help but to hide? To pack a blow-dryer, to worry about smoke getting in my carpet?

Maybe cleaning my shower is not why I'm so upset after all. Maybe looking at who I really am is beyond what I'm willing to explore. It's so much easier to focus on soap-scummy tile than on my lack of mercy for others.

I don't like this. But I need it. And now I need to do something about it.

JUMBLED THOUGHTS LEAD *to* GRACE

*T*HIS WEEK I've had so many jumbled thoughts. Next week I'm planning a trip to California to attend my nephew's wedding, although that seems impossible considering he's only eight or nine. At least that's how old he is in my mind.

My dad's supposed to wear a tuxedo, which will probably make me laugh or cry.

With all of her mother-of-the-groom duties, I probably won't get to talk to my favorite sister much—I only have one sister, so she's my favorite by default. We've already planned to meet somewhere this spring, maybe in Dallas. There's a great outlet mall in Grapevine, Texas, not too far from the airport.

Since I live in Florida, I miss my sister, but we know that we'll have eternity together. We're hoping heaven will have a beach like the one we went to as kids. We could lie out in the sun and hang with Jesus.

Like I said, my thoughts are jumbled this week, so please forgive me if I switch gears.

The other night I spoke at a women's dinner at Springs Presbyterian Church in Citrus Springs, not too far from my house. If you ever go there, don't get Internet directions or you'll end up way out in the wilderness. Instead, call me and I'll tell you how to get there.

Springs is my church's first plant, which is like a spin-off. I've written about the pastor, Keeth Staton, in probably three or four of my books.

I knew a lot of the women there, and my friend Tara was there, too. I spoke about being perfect, meaning having Christ's perfection by faith so we don't have to knock ourselves out being religious and fake-holy trying to get God to like us. If we're in Christ, He already likes us and won't ever stop.

Anyway, before I got there I had spent a half hour changing my clothes. I had a closet full of nothing to wear and wasn't thrilled with what I ended up with, but what can you do? The point is, I should've spent that half hour praying or at least going over my notes.

Then, when I got up to speak, I realized that I wasn't sure which notes I had brought—I have several versions of the same talk—so I just started talking anyway about what my life would be like if I were perfect. That's when I had another realization: I hadn't prayed, which is how I like to start a talk, not that it's a good luck charm or anything, but it makes you appear holier than you really are. Plus, it's always wise to ask God's blessing.

So I interrupted myself and started praying.

Oh. My. Goodness.

I don't know if anyone else noticed, but the moment I said "Father," God entered that room and unloaded a huge sackful of mercy on me. I felt His smile and I knew that everything I had come to say—about repenting of not only our sin but of our attempts at being good and trying to appear holy to others and to ourselves and to God—I was experiencing fresh.

I knew, knew, knew I had no business being up there on that stage except for grace, which was the whole point.

I'm not sure if I uttered a single coherent thought after that—I remember now that I was so focused on talking about Christ's sacrificial death for us that I forgot to mention His resurrection. So if you meet any of the Springs women, tell them that Jesus didn't stay dead; to prove that He was God, He only stayed dead from Friday to Sunday.

But besides that, or maybe because of that, I don't know, God smiled on me, which was so cool. After thinking mostly about what to wear and how many books I'd sell and what we were going to eat, God smiled, and that felt good.

The one I call my uncle-dad told me that he's preached some of his best sermons when he's been in the deepest sin. God loves sinners who love Jesus, which is a pretty good thought and not jumbled at all, so I think I'll end with that.

THE JOY *of* SOCKS

WHEN HURRICANE Charley hit Florida, I became overwhelmed by my inability to solve everyone's problems and by my deeper unwillingness to at least try. I thought, *If I can't do it all, then what difference would anything I do make?*

Then I got a call from Joan, the youngest seventy-two-year-old I know, asking me to go with her to do the laundry for the health department team that was helping the people hit by the hurricane.

I immediately said no. It would mean taking a day off from work, disrupting my life, making me step out of myself. It would mean being uncomfortable, maybe getting hot and sweaty.

So I hung up the phone, then called Joan right back. I told her I'd have to check with my editor, but unless I called again, to expect me at her house in the morning.

Then I called my friend Tara, who had already gone down south with her chainsaw and crowbar and helped clear debris in a poor, devastated neighborhood. That's what Tara does when needs arise, while I go home and hide.

Tara said that I needed to do this. Even though it sounded like such a tiny thing, she let me in on a secret. The people with chainsaws greatly need and appreciate the people with laundry soap and quarters and willingness to wash their socks. We all need each other.

I began to envision a huge jigsaw puzzle, with my tiny puzzle piece being a piece of the sky with a teeny section of the edge of a roof on a house that was part of a town. Without this one tiny piece the puzzle wouldn't be complete.

Tara was right. I needed to go. I needed to see the significance of my insignificance. It's not important (or even possible) that I do it all. We're not asked to do it all. Just to be willing to be one tiny piece of the larger puzzle.

One of my favorite themes in the Bible is that of a body "joined and held together by every supporting ligament" (Ephesians 4:16). We are cells and mitochondria and cartilage. We're capillaries and cuticles and the thing that hangs down in the middle of the throat.

Some of us remove soggy drywall from houses hit by storms, and some of us wash dirty socks. It's a puzzle, but not puzzling. It's a picture of how things should be and could be and sometimes are. It's life at its best, even amid its worst circumstances.

So we went to do laundry. At the Laundromat, we met Judy, the owner, who had worked her regular job at IHOP all night and spent all that day washing five hundred pounds of clothes for Project Energy workers who had been working all week to restore power and electricity.

We visited a makeshift animal shelter and saw teenagers walking dogs that had been rescued from the storm. One woman stood at a table and groomed dogs all day. Another had the job of consoling a duck whose feathers were quite ruffled.

Whose job was most important? No one's.

Whose was most insignificant? Again, no one's.

I had been fixated on my powerlessness, but now I see where I went wrong. The Bible talks about the good works that God has prepared in advance for His people to "walk in." He's given us a puzzle to construct, and He's distributed the pieces. I had been wrong to set my puzzle piece aside, thinking that if I can't have all the pieces, then my one doesn't count. Together we make a whole—together we are whole.

Not only that, I had fun. Who knew that doing someone else's laundry could bring so much pleasure?

God knew.

GRACE...LIKE A BEAR

THIS PAST WEEK, I've been embroiled in a mystery here in the newsroom. Embroiled, as in deeply befuddled, mixed up, muddled, confused.

Actually, it's been a whole lot of fun, if not a bit distracting.

The mystery involves three small marsupials in blue overalls and triangle "newspaper" hats and three female staff reporters (myself included).

I found my marsupial, a stuffed koala, on my chair when I came to work Monday morning. No note, just the bear.

I thought it might have come from a reader, delivered to the newspaper's office on Friday, which is the day I work at home. However, upon investigation, I discovered that no one had left it at the front desk for me.

Then I discovered that two other female reporters on staff had koalas on their chairs, too. No note. No clue.

Not only that, no one else in the entire building had them, only the three of us.

Curiosity piqued, I ran down the list of possible suspects, but each person I thought could be the one wasn't. Possible motive, but no opportunity.

After even further investigation, we three koala recipients deduced that the deed was committed between 8 p.m. Saturday and 10 a.m. Sunday. It had to have been someone who has access to the building on the weekend and who knows where each of us sits (which would be scary if the bear wasn't so cute.)

I have my theories as to who's responsible, but they're just not panning out. The most likely suspects wouldn't single out only three of us.

That leaves the most unlikely suspects, but even they have plausible alibis.

The only other solution is that the real culprit is an awfully good liar.

I've been working this case all week, and it's still a mystery. However, the more I think about it, the more I think that I don't want to know the identity of the phantom gift-giver. He or she has a reason for remaining anonymous. Besides, it's fun knowing that I've been singled out for a special blessing.

Still …it's a mystery.

What, you may ask, do fuzzy marsupials in blue overalls have to do with grace or faith or anything spiritual? Probably nothing, although the whole being on the receiving end of an unexpected gift reminds me of God's gift of grace.

That, too, is a mystery. A holy God looks down upon an unholy people. He says (and rightly so), "Your actions deserve death!"

So He plans the death—and then dies so the unholy people can live.

Why would He do that? That's the mystery.

The bigger mystery is why would He do that for *me*?

Any theories that I may have about that mystery don't pan out either. If God requires perfect holiness, which He does, then I've blown it. I've done nothing to deserve it, just like I've done nothing to deserve being surprised by a stuffed koala mysteriously appearing on my chair.

That's grace.

It's disruptive. You're going about your day, and then grace appears, often when you least expect it; always when you least deserve it. One day you discover that you've been singled out by the Grace-giver for reasons you may never know. One thing you do know—it's not because of your merit, because you have none, but it's just because it pleased the Giver to do so.

When that happens, you don't try to figure it out, because you can't. Instead, all you can do is give thanks.

Thanks for bears and thanks for grace.

THE BEST BIBLE

I DON'T LIKE new Bibles. I just bought one, a *Spirit of the Reformation Study Bible*, and although I'm eager to read the articles and study notes, I don't like the book's newness. It feels like a textbook. Heavy, stiff. It's not the kind of Bible you can curl up with.

A friend recently bought a Bible. He'd never had one before, and I think he bought this one at a used bookstore. Used Bibles are the best kind.

My friend said that he's going to read it from cover to cover, Genesis to Revelation. I warned him that Leviticus gets boring and suggested that he read a little bit of Old Testament and also a bit of New. (I was afraid he might quit halfway through Leviticus.)

Too late—he said that he had already read it.

My favorite Bible, the one I keep in my car, is almost thirty years old. I bought it for about fifty cents brand new at the American Bible Society office in Portland, Maine. It's maroon paperback and the cover is getting brittle. A corner looks bitten off, and I think the book of James is about to fall out.

My daughter Alison also had a Bible from which the book of James fell out. (I wonder if that means anything.) Too bad it's not Leviticus that's falling out.

Before I loved Bibles, all I really knew of them was that somewhere in the middle it talked about earthquakes and famines, wars and rumors of wars. Since that sounded scary, I never wanted to even touch a Bible, let alone read one.

I've since changed my mind, but I still don't like new Bibles. New Bibles don't have words underlined and circled or whole passages highlighted or notes to yourself written in the margins. Many years ago, in Isaiah 40:11 of my falling-apart Bible, next to "he gently leads those that have young," I wrote: "(the mommies!)."

In Jonah 1:17, where it says, "But the LORD provided a great fish to swallow Jonah," I wrote: "a rescue—a good thing."

My most marked-up pages are in Ephesians, where I've highlighted, underlined, and circled words like "hope," "God's good pleasure," "love," "unsearchable riches," and "immeasurably more."

It's in Ephesians that I found my calling to "preach to the Gentiles the unsearchable riches of Christ" and to explain the gospel of grace in plain and simple terms.

One of the reasons my Bible might be falling apart is because of all that's stuffed inside it, like the decades-old hand-drawn Mother's Day card from my daughter Alison that says, "Moms are specal (sic), moms are nice. Moms take care fo (sic) you, and I like moms."

Another note is from my daughter Laura, which she wrote as a four- or five-year-old. It says: "I am sre Mom Fo Boen you I dtri to Ow Ka." Translation: "I am sorry, Mom, for bothering you. I didn't try to. Okay?"

I have notes from my pastor (he sends e-mail these days) and even notes from myself to God. One says, "There's a song playing in my head that goes, 'Surrender my will to the One who's calling my name.' Please call my name, Lord! Don't let me go!"

I love my Bible. I love the One who wrote it. I hope my friend will love his Bible, too. I hope he reads it to the end and doesn't give up. (Ezekiel gets a bit dry, but Jonah's a fun read.)

Maybe his Bible will become well-worn and comfortable, a catchall for his thoughts and hopes, his dreams and fears. Maybe he'll discover that the answers to any questions are found in its pages, which all point to Jesus, the One who called Himself the Word of God and was and is God Himself.

Maybe one day my friend's Bible will fall apart from use, and he'll lament having to buy a new one. Maybe he'll keep precious notes from his own child tucked away in its pages until the spine breaks and the book of James falls out.

But even if that happens, even if "the grass withers and the flower falls," as the ancient prophet Isaiah wrote, "the word of our God stands forever."

JUST GET JESUS RIGHT

*H*ERE'S A GREAT idea: Let's stop fighting.

All of us who believe in Jesus, let's all stop nitpicking the peripherals and incidentals of our faith. After all, we are all one, right?

I got this great idea even before visiting with the Reverend Doug Shepherd at his auto parts business. His dad was in the auto business and a Pentecostal preacher, too.

As we sat and talked, Doug's eyes danced. He loves his faith; he loves God and loves being filled with the Holy Ghost and all the manifestations that brings: speaking in tongues, being slain in the Spirit, believing in and witnessing miracle healings.

At age nine he attended a tent meeting in Knoxville, Tennessee. He still remembers the sawdust on the floor and lying on the ground, tears streaming down his face, sorry for the wrong he had done, and then receiving the Spirit of God.

"My daddy picked me up and took me home," he said. "I was still speaking in tongues when my mama put my pajamas on me and put me to bed."

He also said that Pentecostalism has been around a long time—that it didn't begin in 1906 on Azusa Street in Los Angeles, but in 33 AD, on the day of Pentecost, when the Holy Spirit blew into the room where the disciples were gathered. It sounded like a violent wind, and tongues of fire fell, and the disciples were filled with the Spirit.

When the power of God came, Doug said, they began speaking in strange tongues. Pentecostals believe that still happens today.

I asked him why Presbyterians like me don't speak in tongues (although some might I suppose). He said they could if they wanted to.

"The promise is for everyone who asks for it," he said.

I didn't tell him that I've asked for it before but never gotten it.

Years ago, a Pentecostal neighbor decided that I needed to speak in tongues and tried teaching me. But as hard as she tried and I tried, it didn't work. Maybe it's like algebra—I could never get that either.

Eventually I told my neighbor that I was content to not speak in tongues and that I hoped she could be content with not trying anymore to make me do it. After that I think she felt sorry for me, the poor, untongued, heathen shlub. She seemed to think Pentecostalism was the only ticket in town. She probably doubted my salvation.

Although I have nothing against Pentecostalism, some people do. Some argue vehemently that speaking in tongues ceased when the Bible was completed and that being slain in the Spirit (falling on the ground in a rapturous state) is from the devil not the Lord.

Not all, but some Pentecostals think that non-Pentecostals are not real believers or maybe we're not as complete. So we've got the "haves" and the "have-nots" pitted against each other, each thinking the other guy's wrong. That's not even throwing the way different groups baptize into the mix. When sprinklers and dunkers get going at each other, you've got all-out combat.

I guess all I'm trying to say is that not all believers in Jesus worship in the same manner, but we all worship the same Jesus. "There is one body and one Spirit," wrote the apostle Paul to the Ephesians, "just as [we] were called to one hope…one Lord, one faith, one baptism; one God and Father of all, who is over all and through all and in all" (Ephesians 4:4–6).

One day God will gather all of His people around Him—Pentecostals and Baptists, charismatics and Calvinists, too. I think He'll tell us all to sit still, and then He'll say that we all got a whole lot of things wrong and that we fought over things not worth fighting about, but if we got Jesus right that's all that counts.

Maybe we'll all shout and dance and the Baptists and Presbyterians will speak in tongues while the Pentecostals sit on their hands and nod, or maybe we'll all have ice cream. Either way, because we got Jesus right we will have stopped our fighting and our Father will be pleased.

But why wait?

WHAT WONDROUS LOVE!

*B*UT HE WAS wounded for our transgressions, He was bruised for our iniquities; the chastisement for our peace was upon Him, and by His stripes we are healed" (Isaiah 53:5, NKJV).

How does one put into words that which is nearly impossible to express? When theater lights came back on, after 126 minutes of witnessing the brutality of Christ's passion as depicted in the movie *The Passion of the Christ*, as men and women wept openly and unashamedly, I had no words.

I'm still not sure what I think, because in many ways this movie goes beyond a mere movie. It's deeply spiritual, and as I often say, "God shows up." When that happens, a person doesn't walk away unaffected or unchanged. I'm still being affected and (I hope and pray) changed.

But knowing that I wanted this column to be about the passion of Jesus in all its meanings, I took notes in the darkened theater. I noted the disturbing, eerie, and evil beauty of the Satan character and the poetic reference to God's curse upon the serpent in the book of Genesis as Jesus crushes the head of a snake in the Garden of Gethsemane.

I noted Mary, the mother of Jesus, being startled by fear, her intuition sensing impending trouble, as she asks, "Why is this night different from any other night?"—a reference to the Jewish Passover and the prophesied sacrifice of God's holy Lamb.

The movie was dirty and grimy, dark yet beautiful. Even the relentless horror of the beatings Jesus bore was disturbingly beautiful. One woman outside the theater afterward described it as a "holy violence," a purposeful violence. Every lash mark, every stripe on His back, He bore with resolve and purpose.

A *Newsweek* cover asked: "Who Killed Jesus?" The movie answered it: You did. I did. But even more than that, it's clear that Jesus gave up His own life freely, willingly, purposefully. It was His passion to be the Good Shepherd who lays down His life for His sheep.

At one point in the movie Jesus tells His followers, "No one takes [my life] from me, but I lay it down of my own accord." It was His plan from before the beginning to bear our sin in our stead.

One of my favorite parts of the movie shows Jesus carrying His cross on the way to Golgotha, the place where He would die. Someone mockingly asks, "Why do you embrace your cross, fool?"

That was His passion. He embraced His cross because of His great love for those He was about to redeem.

Another favorite part is when a man in the crowd, Simon of Cyrene, is ordered to help Jesus carry the cross. As bloodied and beaten as Christ is, as Simon helps Him, He helps Simon to help Him. As beaten and broken as Jesus was as a man, as God, He was in absolute control. That's why He didn't die from his flesh-tearing beatings. That's why He didn't die from shock or from His heart giving out.

It was His plan all along to lay Himself upon that cross and endure His greatest suffering—having the Father turn His face away as He bore the full wrath of God. Then when the entire transaction was complete, His death for your sin and mine, He announced, "It is accomplished." Then He died, His mission complete.

To sum up my thoughts about the movie and what occurred in my own heart, I would say I was struck by the unfathomable, incomprehensible love of God. I left the theater thinking of a line from an old hymn:

What wondrous love is this, O my soul!
What wondrous love is this that caused the Lord of bliss
To bear the dreadful curse for my soul, for my soul.

I don't understand such a love, but that's the passion of the Christ. He was wounded for my transgressions, He was bruised for my iniquities; the chastisement for my peace was upon Him, and by His stripes I am healed.

What wondrous love indeed.

STORIES WRITTEN *by* GRACE

ONE OF THE BEST parts of my job is telling stories. Not the made-up stuff of fiction, but the real life stuff that makes us who we are.

I love to sit with someone and ask questions, and I've learned a few techniques to draw people out and get them to recall the details that add color and texture to their stories. Of course, I also do this when I'm not on the job, which embarrasses my kids horribly. They're forever accusing me of interviewing ("interrogating") everybody—at church, at the market. They're especially embarrassed when I start interviewing their friends.

I don't mean to do this; I just do it. I'm interested in people's stories. Besides, most people like to talk about themselves and appreciate a listening ear. Frankly, I'm amazed by some of the things people tell me.

Sometimes, people's stories contain elements that most would rather keep secret. During an interview, it's not uncommon for me to stop and ask, "Are you sure you want to tell me this? Are you sure you want this printed in the newspaper?"

As a religion writer, part of my job as I listen to a person's story is also to listen for God's story. Before I even take out my tape recorder and notebook, I know that God has a story He wants to tell through the life of the person I'm about to interview. So I listen and take notes and wait for the part of the story where the one telling it says, "And then Jesus came."

That's always been God's story. "The earth was without form, and void; and darkness was upon the face of the deep," it says in the book of Genesis (KJV).

God said, "Let there be light." He set the sun in the sky. He sent the Son to the earth. Jesus came. He intervened. He came to rewrite people's stories, change the endings, turn the pages and chapters of mourning into singing and dancing.

I witnessed this once again this past weekend when I was with a group of women who told me some of their stories, horrific stories of abuse and abandonment and things too awful to print in the pages of a family newspaper.

Their stories had left scars on their psyches, and some were still suffering raw pain. But despite their pain, because Jesus had come, they knew the ending to their stories.

That's another thing I've learned. Every story needs an ending; every story ends. When Jesus comes and rewrites a person's story, the ending has God wiping away every tear of sorrow and erasing every memory of pain. The great ending reveals celebrating and feasting, laughter and joy.

During an interview, as people tell me their stories, I always listen for the ending that I will use when I go back to the newsroom to write. I listen for that one quote or thought that either sums everything up or leaves a strong impact on the reader.

A man who had been married seventy-one years recently told me concerning his wife, "Seems like I've loved her all my life." One need say no more. That's how I ended his story.

Once I know the ending to a story, I keep it in front of me as I write to remind me of where I'm headed, especially if the middle starts to get me bogged down. Middles do that, both in stories and in life. That's why I always keep the ending in sight.

I love telling stories; I love telling God's story. I especially love the part "when Jesus came."

Perhaps God's greatest story is Easter, when He took all our pain and heartache and the sin from all our combined stories and nailed them to a cross. Then He nailed Himself along with them and declared, "It is finished!"

That would be a great ending in itself, but hallelujah, the story doesn't end there. Three days later, He rose from death, proving once and for all that He alone holds the power to rewrite our stories, to change their endings, and to give us hope.

Amen.

COME *to the* QUIET

SHHH. Hush.

Stop all the fighting and sniping. Cease the quibbling and the squabbling over whether "Merry Christmas" is politically correct or not.

Shhh. Quiet. It's okay.

Put away your credit cards. Your kids don't need another computer-digital-anything. You and I don't need any more debt. Our debt is crushing us as it is.

We need a debt canceler.

Be still, if only for a moment. It's Christmas—our Debt Canceler has come.

Off in the distance dawns the light for the nations. The darkness is pierced, and the light will never, can never, be extinguished.

Stop your striving. Take a breath. Breathe deeply the life you've only dared to dream of. The life where you lie down and sleep in peace and awake with joy.

Put down the bottle. Put away your grudge.

Lower your fist. Kiss your kid. Forgive your dad. Love your wife.

The One who has borne our sin is born.

Our King forever, our Prince of peace, our Mighty God, has come to us, to live with us, identify with us, bear our sorrows, give us rest.

So rest. Stop.

Hush.

At my church on Christmas Eve it's our tradition to sing of peace and silence. "Peace, peace, peace on earth and goodwill to all." "Silent night, holy night." "Now let us all sing together of peace."

Shhh. All is calm. Christ has come.

He hasn't come to wage war on retailers. He hasn't come to battle Santa Claus or debate whether or not the fir tree is a pagan symbol. He hasn't come to argue with local governments over crèches and menorahs in the public square.

The government, after all, is on His shoulders. He is Ruler. He is Lord, and He has come to set His people free. To rescue and redeem. To find the lost, bind the wounds of the broken, heal the hearts of the sad and grieving, the lonely and afraid.

He has come to give rest to the weary, direction to the wandering, purpose to those who think life has no meaning. He has come to still the restless hearts of men and women, to give hope to those who cannot even fathom hope, sight to the spiritually blind.

His law is love and His gospel is peace. His yoke easy, His burden light.

He is salve for tired eyes, a hand for the lonely to hold, a lap for the child at any age to climb upon, a shoulder broad and strong on which to lean and to cry.

So rest. Take your shoes off. Turn down the noise. Switch off the TV.

Pray.

Even if you've never prayed before, it's okay.

Do you hear that? Can you feel it? That soft smile? That's your God, the One who came as a baby, a lamb, a lion, a Messiah.

He smiles!

Shhh. Enjoy the silence. Cry if you need to. Laugh if you want to. Stretch out your hands. Touch the splintered cross He was nailed to. Accept the gift.

Embrace the salvation offered by the world's only Savior.

Forget about the sweater that doesn't fit, the broken gadget that needs to be returned. Exchange your broken life for one that's new, your sin for Christ's sinlessness, your unpeace for His peace, your sorrow and pain for His joy.

All your disappointments, all your unfulfilled dreams, all your confusion and brain noise and heart achings, set them down.

Be still now. So very, very still.

"The effect of righteousness will be peace, and the result of righteousness, quietness and trust forever," wrote the prophet Isaiah. "My people will abide in a peaceful habitation, in secure dwellings, and in quiet resting places" (32:17–18, ESV).

It's Christmas and Christ has come to bring us into His quiet, to hush our fury, to still our rage and fear.

Christ is our gift. Jesus is our peace.

So, shhh. It's Christmas.

LEARNING GOD'S WORD, ONE VERSE *at a* TIME

*H*ER NAME WAS Sarah and she was old, but not too old to eavesdrop on the three men talking with her husband. He was old, too.

The men had just popped in for a visit—these particular men generally don't call ahead; they just show up unannounced with messages that tend to knock the socks off people.

As they shot the breeze with Sarah's old man, one of the men said that he would come back about the same time the following year to see the baby. The only snafu—there wasn't a baby, and being up there in age and all, the prospects of one were slim to none. Not that they hadn't tried....

Sarah just laughed at the absurdity of the idea.

Then the man who had been doing all of the talking—who, it turned out, happened to be God—asked, "Why did Sarah laugh?"

Then God added, "Is anything too hard for the LORD?" (Genesis 18:14).

He also said the same thing hundreds of years later to a young Hebrew prophet named Jeremiah.

"I am the LORD, the God of all mankind. Is anything too hard for me?" (Jeremiah 32:27).

I'm telling you this because it's that time of year when God directs my attention to one Scripture verse for me to focus on for the following year.

Last year my focus was "Be still, and know that I am God" (Psalm 46:10), which, frankly, I've failed at miserably. I was and am still anything but still. But even if I haven't been still, I saw God being God innumerable times in the situations in which I was and continue to be the most unstill.

192

In the weeks leading up to learning what this year's verse would be, I was a bit anxious thinking that, because I had flunked stillness, I would be subjected to a do-over or a remedial Scripture year. If I were God, I'd put me in some sort of spiritual time-out until I was Marines-at-attention still, no matter how long it took.

Then I thought about some situations that trouble me, and as I began being as unstill as a person can get—think of a five-year-old the day after Halloween on a Snickers, Baby Ruth, and Pop Rocks sugar high—and as I began to fear God chasing after me with a giant flyswatter or butterfly net, I remembered the story of Sarah, and especially the words of her holy Visitor: "Is anything too hard for the LORD?"

I know that the answer is no, but I started to count on my fingers all the things I thought (and still think) might be too hard.

I'm not going to tell you what they are, but just think of the things that keep you awake at night and insert them here. Chances are your stuff is similar to mine. There really is nothing new under the sun.

Then God directed my attention to something Jesus once told His dearest friends just as He was getting ready to die. He said, "Let not your heart be troubled, neither let it be afraid" (John 14:27, NKJV).

Last year, my verse turned out to be a sort of "buy one, get one free" deal with the gospel words of Jesus, "Come to me all you who are weary and burdened, and I will give you rest," added on to the command "Be still."

Likewise, it looks like I might get another double deal this year: "Is anything too hard for the Lord?" and "Let not your heart be troubled," which makes sense. If there's nothing that's too hard for God then I don't need to let my heart be troubled.

It sounds simple enough. At least I have a whole year to put it into practice. Also, I've noticed that with each passing year, the Scriptures that I've concentrated on seem to build on each other:

"God is able to do immeasurably more...the wind of the

Spirit moves…with God nothing is impossible…He is God…He gives rest…be still…nothing's too hard for Him."

So let not your heart be troubled.

P.S. Sarah had a baby boy.

ANGELS *on* ASSIGNMENT

I'M NOT SAYING it was an angel, but I'm not saying it wasn't. However, the more I think about it, the more inclined I am to think it was.

It happened to my daughter when she was in New York one summer going to summer school. She had only been there a day or so when she and a friend got off the wrong subway stop late at night and ended up in a neighborhood they knew they had no business being in.

Later she told me, "There I was, some stupid kid from Podunk, Florida, and I prayed, 'Lord, please get us out of here!'" She said that immediately an unmarked cab—I didn't know there was such a thing—drove up, and the driver told them to get in.

The whole way back to their school in Brooklyn, the driver didn't say anything else, but the inside of the cab was filled with "Jesus stuff."

I'm not saying it was an angel, but…

Recently, I met a woman who believes in angels, even angels in New York City.

She told me that once, as she walked through Times Square trying to find a certain church, darkness overwhelmed her and she couldn't see a thing. Anyone who has ever been to Times Square knows that the lights make it seem like daytime, even at midnight. But she meant spiritual darkness.

She said she prayed and God sent two angels—big men wearing blue jeans and flannel shirts—who walked in front of her through the crowd. When they came to the church, they turned and disappeared.

She said that another time, when her son was younger and doing stuff he shouldn't have been doing, she prayed and asked God to "send an angel to go get him."

So He did.

The day she told me about that, my daughter had gone to a concert. I had a funny feeling about this concert, so I prayed and asked God to send an angel to go get my daughter.

I'm not saying it was an angel, but...

The next day, she told me about the concert. First, she said that her eyes were opened to evil, that it was at the same time beautiful and grotesque, compelling and repulsive. She told me she seriously thought the lead singer had sold his soul to the devil and that people at the concert were worshiping, "just like at church."

Then she told me about a guy who was standing near her. Just standing, not saying a word, wearing a bright yellow shirt with "JESUS" on the front. She said, "Mom, who wears a bright yellow Jesus shirt to a concert?"

I'm not saying it was an angel, but...

"The angel of the LORD encamps around those who fear him," wrote the psalmist. When one of God's children needs help, the Father sends it. I'm not saying it's always an angel, but sometimes it is.

The thing with angels is that they don't announce themselves; they just show up. Most of the time, they don't look like what you would expect, no "gender-nonspecific" beings with silky hair and feathery wings. They're mostly just people, looking like cabbies and guys in yellow Jesus shirts. They do what God sends them to do; then they're gone.

A long time ago, when I lived in Portland, Maine, a hobo-looking old man was lying across my car. That day my husband was planning to take a trip to Boston for the weekend. I remember being uneasy about him going and praying that God would help me not worry. When I saw the man on my car, I went outside to see if he needed help. But before I could say anything, he told me I had nothing to worry about. Then he began praying a blessing over my then toddler Alison, my husband, and me. Then he was gone.

It was the oddest thing.

I'm not saying it was an angel, but I'm not saying it wasn't. It just makes me look at people differently and look at God with more awe.

He sends angels. How 'bout that?

CARE CASTING

HEN WE moved to Florida from California, we did so with only the things we could fit into two vehicles. That meant selling or giving away fifteen years worth of possessions, which was both sad and exciting.

I hated parting with my big pine bed we had brought to California from Maine, not to mention the coffee table my husband had accidentally autographed. He tends to write hard, and he had been signing checks. After that, if you looked down at the table at a certain angle, you could see a half dozen "Barry Kennedy" indentations. But since we were moving into my late in-laws' fully furnished house, we didn't need to bring any of our things.

So, we moved in—and then I took a mental inventory. How shall I say this tactfully? The house was filled with *tchotchkes*. Let's just say my mother-in-law's taste was not my taste.

At first my husband said we shouldn't change anything. However, because he was and still is outnumbered in our family three females to one male, in matters of home decor, he loses almost every time.

Once the girls and I convinced him that "less is more," we started taking things off the walls and putting them in boxes in the garage. Next came the hotly debated subject of what to do with it all.

Removing stuff and packing it away was one thing; throwing it out was another. It only took a few months of tripping over boxes until my husband realized that it was time to toss it.

Thankfully, one of his favorite activities in life is going to the dump. Each Saturday we'd load up his truck with junk and head for the local landfill to toss our tchotchkes into a huge pit and watch the seagulls scatter.

Some of our youngest daughter's fondest childhood memories involve flinging doodads and whatnots at the dump with her dad. And once Barry realized that clutter contributed to much of our chaos at home, he started looking around for even more things to throw out.

The other night on TV there was a story about a man who hoarded junk. Like an alcoholic who couldn't pass up a drink, he couldn't pass up a thrift store, he said. He owned about two thousand golf clubs, although he never played, and paid two hundred dollars a month for a storage unit just to house his stuff. His children were embarrassed by him, and his wife nearly left him.

Eventually, he was able to throw much of his stuff out, but it wasn't easy for him. The cameras filmed his struggle and then finally the point when he was able to throw away just one thing. Then another. Then another. He was exhilarated—set free!

"I don't know why I didn't do this sooner," he said.

In Billy Graham's devotional book *Hope for Each Day*, the March 17 entry urges, "Unload your distress," which Graham says is the French translation of the Bible's admonition to "Cast all your anxiety upon [God], for he cares for you" (1 Peter 5:7).

It's like a dump truck emptying its load. The truck is of no use if it carries its load forever. Likewise, "we were never meant to be crushed under the weight of care," Graham writes.

Still, we carry stuff around that clutters the mind and weighs the soul down with worry. It's like hoarding junk or living with tchotchkes. It makes us agitated, fretful, fearful, yet we're often unwilling to let go.

For those burdened by their cares, Graham posed the question: If God loved you enough to bear your sin upon His own shoulders, can't those same shoulders be trusted to bear the burden of lesser things?

The answer is, of course they can be trusted because He can be trusted. I've discovered that when I do trust Him and cast my cares, my "soul tchotchkes," upon Him, He takes it all.

He bears it for me. He flings it like junk into a pit at the dump, and I'm left exhilarated, unfettered, free…and wondering why I didn't do it sooner.

My Welcome Home

EXCEPT FOR one shoe that disappeared in transit, everything arrived intact at our new house this past weekend. Met the neighbors, Marge and Al. They moved into their condo the day before we moved into ours. We commiserated about having more stuff than places to put it; Al helped me figure out how the garage door unlocks. My husband is still away at work, so I am on my own.

Ellen lives across the street. Our daughters went to school together.

Herb lives nearby. I took advantage of his thirty-seven years worth of phone company experience as he solved my second phone line problem.

Peggy and Skeet live down the street, but I haven't taken advantage of them yet.

This is our eighth move in twenty-seven years of marriage, and our first brand-new house. I'm still discovering surprising features—like wall switches that apparently don't turn on anything in particular.

I love the cathedral ceilings, although I'm going to need regular visits from the fire department with their hook and ladder truck to change my lightbulbs and dust the ceiling fans. My daughter and I both agree that the bathroom mirrors are extremely flattering, and we are willing to prostrate ourselves and kiss the feet of their makers.

As much as I love our new house, the actual moving wasn't (still isn't) fun. My back hurts from lifting, and my mind hurts from having to remember to call all the utility companies. Plus, we were without a washer, dryer, refrigerator, *and* microwave for several days. Oh, the agony of being spoiled and having to do without!

But now we're in, and it's time to begin the process of building our home once again. The house is complete, but the home still needs construction, each room needing to be filled with the purposes of God.

On Sunday afternoon, a few of my dearest friends came over. I hadn't completely moved in, but I needed a party. They brought dinner, and we sat in the living room on the floor and talked about how I should hang mirrors way up high and where I should place my daughter's photography.

We talked about my old house and how the year I lived there while my husband was working out of town was dark and difficult. It was the year my home crashed down around me, but now it's being rebuilt.

I had invited my friends over to pray and to ask God to fill every corner, even the ones way up high, with His Spirit. We prayed that every activity, every conversation that takes place in this new home, would bring glory to God.

Earlier, I had wanted to choose a Scripture for my new home, but I wasn't sure which one. Then my friend Karen opened my Bible. "This is what God says," she said, reading from Psalm 127: "'Unless the LORD builds the house, its builders labor in vain.'"

Somebody else had put up the drywall and installed the plumbing and put switches on the wall that don't seem to turn on anything in particular. However, it's the Lord who actually built my new house, and He is continuing to build my home, from the foundation up.

The other morning I woke up and looked out my bedroom window at the morning stars. (Note to myself: Put up curtains or blinds ASAP!) From my pile of pillows, I looked around at all the glorious space in the bedroom. Room to breathe! Room to be.

"Why am I here, Lord?" I whispered to the Father. "Why have You given me all this?"

I still don't know the answer, and I might not ever know. It's enough to know that God is building my home and He has placed me in this neighborhood next to Marge and Al, across from Ellen, and down the street from Herb, Peggy, and Skeet, for His purposes, whatever they may be.

Hear, O Lord, my prayer: May this new house be filled with laughter, mercy, and grace. May love abound. May prayer flow freely, and may Your Spirit not be quenched.

Thank You, Lord, for building me a house. Praise You, Lord, for rebuilding me a home.

ONE LITTLE ENORMOUS WORD

HEN I WAS nine, Sam Lang's basset hound bit my lower lip, ripping a hole in my face. At the time I didn't really know what had happened. I had bent down and said, "Hi, doggy," or something like that, and the dog—I don't even remember its name—didn't growl or bark; it just jumped up and tore my lip.

We were in Sam Lang's backyard, and I remember Sam's mother saying, "In my car!" I didn't know where we were going in her car, but I got in the backseat with my mom, and with a washcloth pressed to my jaw, we rode to the hospital. I got forty stitches and still have a scar that runs from the right side of my lower lip to my chin.

Sam Lang's parents came to see me a few days later and brought me a doll, and the two ladies who lived next door brought me lime Jell-O mixed with applesauce and garnished with sour cream. At school my teacher made me sit with her in the teachers' lunchroom every day until my stitches came out.

Ever since then, I've been afraid of dogs when I first meet them, although once I get used to a friendly one I'm okay.

However, as afraid as I am of dogs in people's yards, it's the dogs in my dreams that terrify me. At least they did until I asked God to explain them.

These recurring dog dreams are most disturbing. I'm talking growling, snarling, Cujo-type monster dogs right out of the Stephen King novel. These dogs eat people and fling the carcasses like rag dolls and laugh with un-doglike voices, and they change forms and haunt me. These dogs are pure evil.

In my dreams, the dogs are out to attack me, although I always wake up before they reach me. Still, after one of these dreams, I'm teary and shaky the rest of the day, feeling in need of Holy

Communion or a prayer meeting or something healing and cleansing.

Several Bible passages talk about dogs in the same snarly, evil way. "Deliver my life from the sword, my precious life from the power of the dogs!" wrote one of the psalmists. Quite often, dogs in the Bible are vicious, wild, disturbing, and not at all petlike.

Those are the dogs of my dreams.

Once I asked God if, in my next dog dream, I could finish it before waking up. Here's how it went: The dogs, rabid-looking and in a murderous frenzy, broke out of their fenced area and raced toward me. I froze, panicked. Then, just before they lunged to begin tearing me apart, I faced them. With perfect calm, I looked them in the eye and whispered just one word.

"Jesus."

That's all it took, just the name Jesus, and they stopped mid-lunge, hung their tails between their legs, and whimpered. That's when I noticed that they were scrawny and mangy and riddled with fleas and what was most amazing—they had no teeth!

So I told them to get lost and leave me alone, and they did. They crawled back to where they came from, powerless, defeated.

These dreams, I now know, are profoundly spiritual and not something I often talk about. We Presbyterians don't talk much about the invisible battles that take place "in the heavenlies," battles against spiritual forces of evil, as the Bible says. But these battles are as real as God is.

In 1529, Martin Luther wrote the hymn "A Mighty Fortress Is Our God." In it he says, "And though this world, with devils filled, should threaten to undo us, we will not fear, for God hath willed His truth to triumph through us: The Prince of Darkness grim, we tremble not for him; his rage we can endure, for lo, his doom is sure, one little word shall fell him."

I still have dog dreams, but they don't scare me anymore. That's because I know the one little word that fells the snarliest of evil: "Jesus."

The Word is Jesus.

QUESTION WANTED: ANSWERS PROVIDED

*T*HE OTHER DAY, a friend posed one of the most asked questions regarding Jesus: "What about all the other religions? Why would God create people who would believe in them if it means they're going to hell?"

I stumbled and stammered and ended up not answering except to ask, "Do you really want an answer? If so, it might take a while to explain it all."

She said she was hoping for just a *Reader's Digest* two-sentence version.

I thought so.

Still, I've been thinking about her question all week. Actually, her question is a bunch of questions all rolled into one: How do you know that the Bible is true? Why, or how, is it different from the Koran or the Book of Mormon? Is there really a hell, and how could a loving God send people there?

She wants to know how Jesus could say He is the only way— aren't there many ways? Many truths?

I did tell her that there can only be one truth because the nature of truth is that it's true. And if truth is true, then anything that contradicts it must be false. That's about as *Reader's Digest* as I could be.

All week I've been thinking about how to answer her, assuming she really wants to know. Hoping she'll ask again. I thought about pointing out archeological proof of historic events chronicled in the Bible, like finding the site of Sodom and Gomorrah and never finding the corpse of the risen-from-the-dead Christ.

However, I don't think she was asking about history.

I thought about saying simply, "It's true because the Bible says so," but in this day, that doesn't always carry the weight it once did. You can't assume that people believe the Bible even has authority, let alone is the ultimate authority. Times have changed.

I probably should have told her that God has created each of us with an inner knowledge of Him. Then I could have said that even though we instinctively know of Him, because we're born sinners at odds with Him, we instinctively fight against that knowledge.

That's where her real question comes from anyway.

God is God, and we are not. Sounds simple enough, but we naturally don't accept that. Without saying so out loud, we each secretly want to be God. We want to be the ones to say what truth is and decide which truth to follow.

But because we're not God, the real God, the true God, gets to say what constitutes truth. And if His truth is that we are all doomed from the start, and that He has provided only one eternal escape—Jesus—that's His prerogative.

If we were God, we could choose another way, but like I said, we're not. So we either do it His way or we're fried toast.

There's so much else I could tell my friend, but I've learned that, unless the Spirit of God is actively working in a person's life, our words, even our most eloquent preaching, fall on deaf ears and may even cause the person to harden his or her heart further. Sometimes less is more.

But I'm not giving up. Instead, I've determined to pray that God will bring her to a point where she's hungry for the truth. The true truth. The "Jesus is the only way" gospel truth.

The good news is, I know God can do that, because He does it all the time. He did it in me when I wasn't even looking for truth. I wasn't looking for answers; I wasn't even asking questions.

Maybe that's the truest truth of all: that we don't seek it, we don't seek Him, but He seeks us.

He seeks us, finds us, and as Truth incarnate, sets us free.

WHO LOVES YA, BABY?

I HAVE TWO provocative statements, which will probably raise your eyebrows.

Statement No. 1: I'm wild about three women I know, but not in the way you might think.

Statement No. 2: The kingdom of God is like the commercial for Viagra.

First, the women. They're friends of mine, although we hardly ever go out together. Truthfully, we've never "done lunch," haven't gone shopping. That's usually what women friends do. But with these friends it's more of a "run into each other at Wal-Mart and stand in the aisle for forty-five minutes and talk about life" friendship.

Even though I spill my guts in 750 words or less in the newspaper each week, I'm not an easy person to get to know. I'm quite closed and self-absorbed. That's why I'm wild about these women—they are, too.

That's what we talk about. We talk about how much we love ourselves, but that deep down we really love God and want to love Him and others more than we love ourselves, but that it's not in us to do it on our own. We talk about wanting God to change us and about being terrified of that, because we know that if God changes us, we'll have to change, and change is uncomfortable.

One of the women I'm wild about is a preacher, although she's really just a mom and a wife. But when she starts talking about how awesome God is, I could listen to her for hours. I want to yell and clap and shout, "Yeah, God!" But since I'm Presbyterian, I yell and clap and shout on the inside.

One of the women I'm just getting to know, which is scary for both of us. People think the two of us are both people persons, but we know that we're not. Ironically, that's what connects us to each other. We're two non–people persons struggling together to be more people-ish.

I can be honest with this woman. Christians often tell each other "I love you" and sometimes even mean it, but even though I'm wild about my friend, I told her that I wouldn't say "I love you" to her because right now I mostly only love myself. She said she feels the same way, so it's cool.

The third woman says she doesn't love God, but I have my doubts about that. She says she knows that God's wild about her and is pursuing her, which frankly irritates the daylights out of her.

"Wherever I go, I keep running into Jesus!" she says. Then she makes a shuddering sound, like it's the worst thing that could happen to her. I tell her it's a good thing to keep running into Jesus. Deep inside, I think she knows that. I'm just glad she's my friend and lets me say things like that.

That brings me to my second provocative statement. I was trying to come up with an analogy to explain to my third friend about how the kingdom of God isn't boring and that belonging to Jesus isn't about keeping rules and yawning in church. She's had a lifetime of that. Instead, these days she's looking for life and liveliness and purpose, beyond rules and principles and commandments.

So, I told her, "The kingdom of God is like the commercial for Viagra," the one in which everyone notices there's something different about this one guy. Something's changed, but they can't figure out just what. All they know is that he's got a spring in his step that wasn't there before.

She looked at me as if I had three heads.

Not that belonging to Jesus puts you in la-la land all the time, I told her. Sometimes the faith life is downright difficult. But even during those times, there's an underlying joy.

Belonging to Jesus puts a spring in your step, and when it happens to you, people notice. It makes you whistle and want to clap.

It makes even the most self-centered person you know wild about others. That's because Jesus is wild about us first.

That's pretty provocative, don't you think?

I NEED GOD

I NEED GOD. That's been the theme of my week, my one prayer.

I *need* God.

Last week I bought a bunch of new clothes. Seems I wasn't done. Even after the pastor's ironically timed sermon on materialism (God's against it), this week I bought more.

I thought I needed two identical pairs of black capri pants…but I really need God.

I bought a new set of sheets for my bed and a gold-fringed chenille throw blanket to hang on the headboard. I love the way it picks up the gold in the bedspread, but…

I really, really need God.

This week, I got a letter from a "fan" and a few nice phone calls from readers telling me how they appreciate my newspaper stories. My sister called and mentioned that "Dave from Jazzercise" loves what I write and that he sends my column to his mother, who sends it to someone else.

Stuff like that tends to make my head swell. It tends to make me think, *How did these people ever survive before I came along?*

I went fishing the other day—fishing for approval and applause. I know exactly where the best fishing spots are to reel in the biggest compliments. Hearing about "Dave from Jazzercise" wasn't enough. I wanted to hear more.

Oh, how I need God.

It's easy to admit that you need God when your life cracks. When you don't get the job. When bad news jars you awake at night and keeps you awake until morning. When you kneel by the bedside of a feverish child or the graveside of one you love.

That's when you seek hard after Him.

That's when you know you need God.

But when life is everyday, when you wake up smiling and wear your favorite clothes to go off to a job that fulfills you…when you know that you're good at what you do and you're well-liked and admired…

I need God.

These days, this week, today—

I need God!

Good things keep falling into my lap. I can hardly answer the phone without it being some new opportunity. Possibilities beyond my wildest imaginations are right there, on my horizon. My daughter saw one of my books in a bookstore last week—in London. *In England!*

More than ever, I need God.

I need God. I need His wisdom; I need His grace. In the good times, in the blessings.

Sounds funny, doesn't it? To need God in the blessings.

But that's the truth—I know me too well.

It's in the times of biggest blessing that I'm most tempted to wander. That's when I'm most apt to fall. That's when I think I can do life just fine on my own.

That's when I find myself buying black capri pants and gold blankets, fishing for applause, and sliding into sin.

I need God.

I *need* God.

Oh, how I need God.

SUNDAY'S COMIN'

*E*VERY ONCE in a while I'll sit down to write a column with the intention of writing about one thing, but then I end up writing about something else. It's funny how it happens. I usually keep a bunch of notes scribbled on pieces of paper—collections of phrases, thoughts, and ideas that come to mind throughout the week. However, when I go to put the scribbles into a column, I won't be able to find the papers or I might not even remember what I've scribbled.

Yesterday my notes said: *I met two women in the past couple of weeks I won't forget for a long time*; however, I couldn't remember who the women were! So much for unforgettable.

Today is Thursday as I write this. Thursday is my deadline at the newspaper, and everything that I thought I would write about I can't think of at the moment. Instead, I'm thinking about Saturday. I've been thinking about Saturday all week, although I'm not in a Saturday mood.

But maybe you are.

Maybe God put Saturday on my mind so that I can write about it. Maybe it's because you need to read it.

Let me tell you about Saturday.

In the Gospel accounts of the death and resurrection of Jesus, Saturday was a day of despair for the disciples. The day before, they had witnessed the brutal, humiliating public execution of their friend. They were grief-stricken, confused, terrified, and despondent.

Their hope had died along with the One they thought would change the world. Then they buried Him.

That was Friday.

Then came Saturday. That's the day reality set in.

Friday is when the crisis hits. On Friday you get the bad news

209

and you're numb. Saturday is when the numbness wears off and everything looks bleak.

Dark.

You can't imagine things ever being different. On Saturday your faith is cold. God is silent. You forget what hope feels like. All you can do is cry—you can't even pray.

That's Saturday.

I'm not in a Saturday mood today, but I've been there. That's why I know that after every Saturday, there's always a Sunday.

On Saturday, Jesus was in the grave. The disciples had scattered. Some huddled together in fear. Some went fishing and tried to forget. But when it's Saturday, you don't forget. You can't forget.

That's because you don't know that there's a Sunday coming.

I remember years ago listening to a radio preacher. I don't remember his name, but I'll never forget his message. He said, when all hope is gone, when everything looks black, when Jesus is cold and rotting in the grave…get ready because Sunday's coming.

Only he said it like this: "Sundaaaaaaaaaay's ah-comminnn'!"

Jesus died on Friday. He stayed dead on Saturday. But on Sunday…

On Sunday, the unthinkable happened. On Sunday, the dead rose to resurrected life. Hope was reborn and restored. Sorrow turned to unspeakable joy.

That's Sunday.

And for God's people, Sunday always comes.

But when it's Saturday, when you're in a Saturday mood, you forget. Saturdays do that to you. If it's Saturday for you, I'm sorry. I know what Saturdays can be like.

But Sunday's comin'. Sunday's comin'.

Saturdays can look awfully dark, but Sunday's comin'.

How do I know? Because in a garden somewhere in Jerusalem, there's an empty tomb where a body lay dead one Saturday.

Then Sunday came.

And Sunday will come again.

LOVING GOD BEST

I DON'T LOVE beads anymore. Maybe you didn't know that I did, but I did.

I loved them so much that for several months they took up three-quarters of my waking thoughts, maybe more.

Even now there are three plastic boxes under my bed, filled with beads, all compartmentalized by color. Also under my bed are beading tools and necklace wire and clasps, and thin, stretchy elastic for making bracelets. There's a jar on my bathroom counter filled with finished bead bracelets ("my pretties") and a metal tree with bead necklaces hanging from its branches.

I loved beads and would spend countless hours stringing them together, unstringing them, restringing them.

But I don't love beads anymore. One day I did, and the next day I didn't—just like that.

A few years ago, I wrote a book about idolatry. That sounds like pagans dancing around carved wooden poles, but it really is more like loving beads three-quarters of your waking hours. In my book (*Move Over, Victoria—I Know the Real Secret*) I pose the questions: What holds you? What is your greatest passion? What motivates you, captures your attention, grabs your heart? What's the first thing you think about in the morning and the last thing you think of at night?

When I speak at women's retreats, that's usually my opening question. Then I say, "The correct answer is ___," and pause to let the women call out, "Jesus!" Then I say, "But the real answer, the honest answer, is often 'not Jesus.'"

Once I met a woman who sings for Jesus. Her face was glowy and shiny, and she had framed embroidered Scriptures all around her house and had the local Christian radio station playing somewhere in a back room. She said she never turned it off.

As we drank coffee from mugs with Jesusy sayings on them she said, "I love Jesus best! I want to do only what He wants me to do, go only where He wants me to go, and sing only for His glory."

I mumbled something liar-ish like, "Me, too," but I doubt if I was glowy and shiny-faced like she was. I doubt if the Holy Spirit shines through liar-faced Christians. Maybe He does, but I don't know that for a fact.

I do know, however, that I have moments when Jesus is my first and highest thought. Sometimes I'll listen to a song or read something that captures me and transports me above and beyond myself. Sometimes, ironically, when I'm eyeball-deep in not-Jesus thoughts, God will invade my thinking and remind me that whatever it is I think I can't live without at the moment—beads, olive green cargo pants, or trying to one-up someone I envy—that even if I could saturate myself with it, it still wouldn't satisfy my soul.

One time I actually said that out loud as I played with my jarful of pretties. I had dumped them out on my bed, and as I tried each one on and thought about the colors I didn't have and, therefore, needed for my compartmentalized plastic boxes, I said out loud, "This does not satisfy my soul!"

I'm not big on saying "God said" things because I think sometimes the things we think He says are just our own thoughts and that He is probably up in heaven going, "I didn't say that!"

But this time, when I said, "This does not satisfy my soul," I know I heard God speak.

He said, "Duh."

He says that a lot, I think.

And it didn't make me sad or anything. Actually, it made me glad because I knew that I was His and that I could always go to Him, or He would come to me, no matter how deep into not-Jesus I find myself.

The truth is, if we are His, God loves us whether we are glowing and shining or whether we are stringing beads. That's because

His love for us isn't dependent on what we do or do not do, but solely on what Jesus has done.

Loving beads isn't bad. It's just that being loved by Jesus is better, and believing that is the first step to loving Him best.

MAUNDY GRACE

*N*EWSWEEK MAGAZINE once surveyed several thousand people, asking, "What is the one thing you would like somebody to say to you?"

Of the top three answers, the first was "I love you." The second was "I forgive you," and the third was "Come and eat!"

Don't you love that?

I love you. I forgive you. Come and eat!

At my church, we meet every Maundy Thursday for a Communion service. It's generally quite solemn and sober (yet joyous) as we meditate on the final words and actions of Jesus the night before His death.

Years ago, the seniors of our congregation met before the service began for a potluck dinner, and one year I convinced my friend that it was an all-congregation dinner and that we should go. We were both short on cash, and I was hungry and knew there would be more than enough food for us.

Besides, I also knew that (a) we were loved and (b) even if it turned out that we were committing a heinous sin by not bringing a bowl of potato salad or a pecan pie, we were forgiven. Not that we would be forgiven, but that we already were.

As it turned out, even though we were obviously not seniors, we were welcomed, loved, and forgiven. And well fed.

Although I only did that once—crashing a party to get a free dinner—I think about that night every year as Holy Week approaches. I think about coming to the table, loved and forgiven. That's what Maundy Thursday is about.

The Gospels record Jesus hosting a Passover meal for His dearest friends, the last Passover meal they would share together on earth. The following day Jesus would die, after having been betrayed by one of His friends.

In the middle of the meal, Christ, the King, gets down on His knees and, one by one, washes His friends' dirty, dusty, stinky feet. He lets them know that He loves them, knowing that they will all, one way or another, abandon Him.

After He's done, He tells them that they are to wash one another's feet, to love each other sacrificially and uncomfortably, with no thought to status or even lovableness.

Then Jesus holds up a piece of unleavened bread, breaks it, and says, "This is my body, broken for you." He lifts up a cup of wine and tells them, "This is my blood, shed for you." He urges them to eat, drink, and as often as they do, to remember Him.

Next they sing hymns and go to a garden to pray. That's where the festivities end and the nightmare that is Christ's passion—His arrest, trial, and crucifixion—begins.

Sometimes in our Easter preparations, between Palm Sunday and the ham and the jelly beans and the marshmallow Peeps and the shouting of "He is risen!" on Resurrection morning, sometimes Maundy Thursday gets lost. Sometimes churches skip over it.

For many years I skipped over it, but I don't want to do that anymore. It's part of the story, the whole Easter experience. The repenting as well as the rejoicing, the remembering as well as the glad hallelujahs. The blessed Last Supper was also the first Holy Communion. It's our visual, sensory reminder that He was and is and is to come again and that, in the meantime, we're to love, forgive, and feed one another. It was His "mandatum," his "maundy," or command.

This year at my church we're trying something new for Maundy Thursday. Similar to walking the Stations of the Cross as they do in liturgical churches, we're going to journey in our worship as pilgrims at various stations around the church. To pray, to sing, to listen to the Scriptures being read and explained, to meditate, to confess.

We're going to end up at the Lord's Table, to eat and drink and remember that He was broken and that He bled for those He calls His own. When we're through, we will have heard the top three things people most want to hear: "I love you," "I forgive you," "Come and eat!"

Party crashers who have tasted forgiveness are most welcome.

THE GOSPEL *of* CHARLIE

A FEW WEEKS AGO, I visited with my friend Joan, the one who convinced me to go with her to do laundry for hurricane relief workers after Hurricane Charley destroyed central Florida.

I had gone just that one time, but Joan went back repeatedly. Joan has one of those kind hearts that I only dream of having. I'm hoping that if I spend more time with her, some of her kindheartedness will rub off on me.

Joan has never met an ugly dog. There's no such thing as a stray as long as she has four walls and a roof. She likes people, too; she adopts them as well.

During one of her posthurricane laundry trips, Joan wandered over to the makeshift animal shelter and put her name on about a dozen or so dogs to take home in case their owners didn't claim them. She ended up with Charlie, named after the hurricane that left him homeless.

Charlie is a brown and white cocker spaniel, although when Joan first saw him, he was mostly a ball of matted fur and fleabites.

If you could choose any dog in the world, Charlie would probably not be your first choice. He might not even be your last choice. You might've said, "Put that dog out of its misery."

But Joan doesn't think any dog is too far gone to love. For the past four years she's cared for a severely disabled dog with no skull that was only expected to live for a few weeks when she got him from the vet. The dog looks odd, but it wags its tail when it walks.

Charlie does, too. After being adopted by Joan, after having his matted coat shaved bare, after being dewormed and de-everythinged, after being loved and fed and loved some more, Charlie has turned into a brand-new dog. He was recently certified as a service dog, a dog with a purpose.

I was thinking about Charlie and about another brand-new (human) friend while watching a video clip at church last week, a scene from *The Passion of the Christ*. Carrying His cross to Golgotha, Jesus tells His mother that He is making "all things new."

Although the Gospels don't record Jesus saying that before His death, He does say it after His resurrection. In Revelation 21:5, John the apostle sees Christ upon His throne saying, "Behold, I make all things new" (NKJV).

Some people think that the world is hopelessly winding down, that it's progressively getting worse, "going to hell in a handbasket" as some say. Some think Jesus will return to claim His own any minute now, so why bother trying to make things better? Why not sit back, hunker down, and wait for Armageddon?

Other folks, however, think that while we're waiting for Jesus to return, we should work to restore, refresh, and renew. To rule and subdue and to advance God's kingdom on the earth. They believe that He is all about making things new now, as well as later.

That's what I tend to think, that in the middle of incredible disaster and destruction and the terribleness of life, lives are being changed and made new.

Just like Joan taking a lost and near-hopeless dog, left homeless in a storm, adopting it, and giving it a new name and a new purpose, so God is taking lost and near-hopeless lives and doing the same. No, God does greater things—He gives those He rescues His own Spirit and begins to conform them into His own likeness.

Last week was Easter, but the message of new life doesn't end with the turning of a calendar page. God came to a broken earth to seek and save the lost and restore them to new life. To give them a future and a hope. He still comes; He still makes all things new.

You might even say He makes tails wag and hearts rejoice again.

A Six-Pound Grace Gain

IN THE GRAND SCHEME of things, a six-pound weight gain is so trivial that it doesn't even warrant mentioning. And before you think this is going to be an "Oh, no! My thighs are huge" introspective foray into self-indulgence, it is.

But it's also not. It's a lesson about enduring grace—the grace to endure.

In 2003, through membership in Weight Watchers, I reached my weight loss goal. It took about a year to lose thirty-eight pounds, and truthfully, it was incredibly easy. Even the few times I ate entire layer cakes—and suffered the consequences with stomach-aches—I still lost weight.

That taught me about the grace of God, that those who are His can and most likely will stumble and fall, but His grace enables us to keep going.

Unlike some weight loss plans with strict rules and regulations, with Weight Watchers you don't have to go back to Day One when you mess up. You just keep going, start over from where you are.

Like in life, when I sin and confess, the Bible assures me that God is faithful and just and will forgive and cleanse me from all my sins (1 John 1:9). But that doesn't mean that sin doesn't have consequences. If I shoplift, chances are I'm going to get arrested. Likewise, if I regularly eat too many cookies and stop keeping track of every bite I put in my mouth, chances are I'm going to see the number on the scale go up.

King David wrote, "Keep me safe, O God, for in you I take refuge.... You have assigned me my portion and my cup; you have made my lot secure. The boundary lines have fallen for me in pleasant places" (Psalm 16:1, 5–6).

Grace tells me that I'm accepted by God just as I am, but grace also compels me to want to be better, to stay within the boundaries of the law of God, which are there to protect me.

If there were no boundaries, how would I know what was beneficial? Left to myself, I wouldn't naturally do the right thing. People tend to do what makes sense to them and what feels good for the moment. If that's true, left to myself I would eat cake three times a day. Grace gives a person the power to choose right over wrong, best over good enough.

I chose "good enough" for a while, and it caught up with me, six pounds worth. All along I knew I was overstepping the boundaries set for me, but cake tastes good for the moment.

The beauty of Weight Watchers and the beauty of grace is the freedom to admit you've blown it. There is no condemnation for those who are in Christ, the Bible says. Weight Watchers doesn't make you wear a dunce cap either.

I contacted my Weight Watchers leader and told her that I had strayed. She didn't berate me or call me a failure—she struggles, too—but graciously encouraged me to revisit the boundaries, to make wiser choices, to choose best over good enough, to master my body, not let it be master over me.

So I've been doing the right things for a while, and yet, the numbers on the scale aren't going down.

Life is like that at times. You do right, you sacrifice, you go the narrow way and watch everyone else on the broader way appear to have lots more fun. However, that way, Jesus said, ends in destruction.

I told my Weight Watchers leader that it's frustrating, but there's no better way. It's like what the apostle Peter once said when some of those who had begun following Jesus started turning back because it was getting too difficult. Jesus asked His closest disciples, "Do you want to leave, too?"

Peter answered, "Lord, to whom shall we go? You have the words of eternal life" (John 6:68).

I always come back to that. When following Jesus gets weary and difficult, when doing right seems fruitless and everyone else seems to be having more fun, I remember Peter's words. Same goes for staying with Weight Watchers. For me, it's a way of life. For me, Jesus is the way of life.

How could I choose anything less?

WELCOMING LITTLE BIRDS HOME

*I*T'S BEEN ALMOST two weeks since my nest emptied, although it's not completely empty. My youngest daughter moved her bed, bookcase, TV, and table out of her room and into a house with a bunch of other people (and a cat that makes her sneeze), only fifteen miles from home, but it's a long fifteen miles when it's your last little bird to leave the nest.

She's gone, but not completely. There's still a bunch of her clothes in her room, along with her toy box, although now that she's almost an adult, I should probably call it something other than her "toy box."

Last year we painted it a sophisticated glossy black to go with her black and white and red decor. However, it still has her old toys inside: her stuffed animals, an old Cabbage Patch doll, and some doll clothes. Mementos of little bird days that seem an eternity ago.

It's been weird with her gone. The house stays clean. The door stays locked at night. The phone doesn't ring at midnight. The neighbors are once again enjoying a boom box free existence.

My daughter's gone, but she hasn't left completely. When I come home from work, I find evidence of her having been there—a wet towel, a missing nectarine. Her new place doesn't have a computer, so she stops by to use mine. It doesn't have food, so she stops by to eat mine. Her new place doesn't have privacy, security, or stability, so she stops by to try to recapture what she once had but didn't fully appreciate while she had it.

How well I remember her as a teenager shouting, "I can't wait till I leave home and can do what I want!" Now that she's done just that, she's not so defiant anymore. Doing what you want isn't all it's cracked up to be. After being gone only one day, she said home never looked so good.

I don't know which is more difficult, being the little bird trying to fly or the mama bird back in the comfortable nest watching as her little one falters in the wind. That first night, as I stood in the quiet of her empty room, I wanted to go get her. But I knew if she's going to ever learn to fly, I couldn't. I can't.

Her current living situation isn't ideal, but I'm not sure if anything this side of heaven is ideal. Even as comfortable as I am with my furniture the way I like it and a semi-well-stocked fridge, it's not ideal. I still have a longing for home.

We all have a longing for home. That's the way God made us. He gave each of us a longing for Himself, although we try our hardest to satisfy it with anything and everything but Him. That's why we're alcoholics and gamblers and potheads. That's why we roam the malls with bags of stuff we don't need and work twelve hours a day even if we don't have to.

When my daughter first moved out, she called to say she was homesick. I knew she missed me, but I also knew, even if she didn't, that she was really homesick for her Father. The good news is, no matter where she may go, her Father will never be farther than a breath away.

In the children's classic *The Runaway Bunny*, the little bunny tells his mother he wants to run away. His mother says, "If you run away, I will run after you. For you are my little bunny."

So the little bunny says he'll become a fish in a trout stream and swim away from her or a sailboat and sail away from her. The mother gently, yet persistently, answers that she will become a fisherman and fish for him or the wind and blow where she wants her little one to go.

In my favorite part, the little bunny says, "Then I will be a bird and fly away from you." His mother answers, "If you become a bird and fly away from me, I will be a tree that you come home to."

God is that fisherman. He is the wind that blows His precious ones where He wants them to go. He is that tree, sturdy and strong, welcoming little birds back home.

My little bird is attempting to fly away, to find a new home, and that's as it should be. I want her to fly, to leave the nest. I pray that as she does, she will fly straight into the welcoming arms of her Father, for it's there and there alone that she will find her true home.

JUST ASKING...

HEN I WAS a new Christian, I knew two sisters. One attended the same church I did. That church emphasized obedience and holiness. *Do what God says, and you will be rewarded for your effort.*

Her sister went to a church that swung way the other direction. Her church's philosophy was, "Hey, the Bible says that where sin increases God's grace abounds, so let's revel in our sin!" Her house was a mess because, "Hey, God's grace shines through!"

Her church's basic teaching was this: We are saved by grace alone; therefore, there's nothing we can do to earn more of God's love than we already have, and at the same time, there's nothing God's people can do to make God love them any less.

My church believed that, too, in theory, but we still were instructed that we'd better obey. We were never sure where we stood with God. Our lives looked good on the outside, but most of us were terribly insecure on the inside. At the other church, the people lived like hell, but they were joyful and exuberant. They knew the truth of eternal security in Christ.

That raises questions. On the one hand, we're called to live holy lives. On the other, we're free in Christ. Can we live wild, raucous, and rowdy lives? What about lives that are mildly on the edge? How short can I wear my skirt? How coarse can my language be?

Why shouldn't I bet on the horses, drink tequila shots at Chili's? If grace covers my sin and my debt is paid in full by Christ's death, then what's to keep me from doing whatever I want, "that grace may abound"?

A group of my friends met recently, and our discussion turned to the topic of duty and grace and whether they are mutually exclusive of one another. We had met to talk about studying the Bible and how we, as women in leadership positions, can encourage other women to study. First, however, we had to get honest with ourselves and with each other about our own struggles.

We began with some probing questions: If you examine the amount and depth of your Bible study during the past year, what do you conclude? What, if anything, hinders you from regular, serious Bible study? What will you do about it?

Outside of job-related study or a panicky need for help, my Bible study tends to be shallow and spotty. What hinders me? (Interest in other things.) What do I conclude? (I should be flogged publicly.) What will I do about it? (Thank God that His grace covers my sin—and watch another rerun of *Gilmore Girls*.)

We discussed the thoughts of theologian R. C. Sproul, who stressed our duty to study, whether we want to or not. We agreed that he was right, but...

But guilt is a poor motivator. It works for a while, but only produces resentment and insecurity. Does God want my obedience, to study His Word because I feel I have to? Should I obey His commandments because He said to and, by golly, if I don't, then I should be ashamed to call myself His child?

Is the church that teaches "God said it—grit your teeth and go do it" correct? Or is the one where "grace abounds" correct? Is there such a thing as "too much grace"? King David, who sinned greatly, often wrote about how he loved God's law. Yet he didn't keep it. At my core I, too, love God's law and delight to do it, yet if I'm honest, I have to admit that those times are rare. What does that say about me? About you?

Is there an answer? Is there a balance, a middle road? My friends and I agreed that there must be, but we aren't sure what it is, only that when our hearts need changing, God's the only one who can do it.

Perhaps change begins with asking questions, voicing doubts, confessing need. Maybe our questions are evidence that God is at work in us, making us willing and able to obey Him—with willing being first (Philippians 2:13).

I like that—that means there's hope.

FEEDING GOD'S SHEEP

I MET RUTH Falsetti by accident, except there's no such thing in my opinion. I think we meet the people God wants us to meet.

It was about ten or so years ago, and I had tagged along with my husband, who was fixing something at her house.

Ruth is one of those easy to talk to people. You should meet her—you would like her. She runs the Feed My Sheep program at a local church, serving free hot meals to people who are hungry. Sometimes the food-hunger is only secondary. Ruth says more often it's the soul-hunger that drives people there.

The day I met Ruth, I asked her about her life; that's just what

I do. My kids say I can't have a normal conversation with someone without turning it into an interview.

She told me about being in her fifties and facing homelessness. She had had a good job at the hospital and thought that was God's purpose for her life, but then osteoarthritis nearly crippled her, and she lost her job.

No job and no income plus escalating medical bills plus not being physically able to get another job equaled a desperate situation. She was destined to be a bag lady, she said—a bag lady in a wheelchair.

So she wouldn't be turned out on the street, her landlord graciously wrote off six months' rent, and people from her church paid her utilities bills. A woman who worked at the courthouse brought Ruth food and called several times a day to check on her and stopped by and helped her get in and out of bed—Ruth was in terrible pain back then—and the woman also paid a lot of Ruth's bills for her.

That's what God does for His people. Like a shepherd, He cares for His sheep, using His people to meet the needs of others.

Ruth said that's when God told her, "Feed My sheep."

However, she wasn't exactly in the position to do much of anything at that time, but she knew that God was calling. So she made a bargain with Him: "If You keep me healthy, I will do Your work." Shortly thereafter, she started feeding people three times a week at her church.

Then the doctor discovered a tumor, which turned out to be benign, but she had a hysterectomy anyway. Then five years ago she had breast cancer.

The other day I told her that some people might question her "bargain" with God, saying that He didn't hold up His end. But she said she needed to go through everything and that she has come through every set back even stronger. "Besides," she said, "my spirit has always been healthy."

She's seventy-one now and still has arthritis, but she doesn't take anything for it and gets around quite well. She said everything she's gone through has been a gift from God so that when she sits at the tables and eats with those she feeds and listens to their stories, she understands and knows what they feel—and they know that she knows.

And she knows God and knows how He takes care of His precious sheep.

"We all have a purpose," she said. "It took me a long time to find mine, but I know why I'm here."

Currently, the top-selling book in the nation attempts to answer the question: "What on earth am I here for?" The simple answer is that we were created for God's pleasure, not to be slaves, but sharers in His kingdom work.

Sometimes I envy people like Ruth who do the important work of being God's hands and feet. Not just do it, but love doing it. But God hasn't called me to operate a food kitchen. Instead, He has called me to write about the people who do, which I love doing.

To paraphrase Olympic runner Eric Liddell in the movie *Chariots of Fire*, when I write, I feel God's pleasure. Likewise, when Ruth Falsetti bastes a chicken or pours a glass of iced tea, she also feels God's pleasure.

That's what happens when you find your purpose—you find God's pleasure and it becomes your pleasure as well.

THE LAW ACCORDING *to* GRACE

Y FRIEND Mike loves kitschy stuff, and he loves God. So anything that combines kitsch and God is a slice of heaven to him.

Recently someone gave him a Moses and the Ten Commandments clock with Moses holding a stone tablet in each arm and looking off in the distance, all holylike, with lightning behind him.

Every hour, but not quite on the hour, the clock plays some light piano music, and a voice—could be God, could be Moses—announces a commandment: "Thou shalt not kill" or "Honor your father and mother."

Mike thinks the clock has a light sensor because Moses (or God) only calls out commandments in the daytime. He also wonders if he can program additional commandments into it for his daughter, like: "Thou shalt make thy bed."

Every morning when Mike comes in to work, he tells me about that day's 8 a.m. commandment. "Thou shalt not bear false witness against thy neighbor" seems to come up a lot, which prompted a discussion among several of us one day.

Mike said he wonders why God included that in His Top Ten. Next to murder and stealing and adultery, it seems benign. Besides, what does it even mean, "bear false witness"?

We decided it means gossip and slander and lying, which, if you think about it, are akin to murdering someone's character. The New Testament writer James said the power of life and death is in the tongue. So it appears that not bearing false witness is a biggie after all.

But before I go off on a watch-your-words tangent, what I really want to discuss is the whole body of commandments—all ten on the stone tablets Moses has under his arms.

For starters, it doesn't make sense (in my opinion) for God to have given us rules that are humanly impossible to follow. For example, take just the first one. "Love God first, best, most, highest, only, in everything I do, think, and say" (my paraphrase).

Not even on my best day can I do that. Not only that, the Bible says if I stumble at just one point of the law, I'm guilty of breaking it all (James 2:10). Therefore, I'm defeated before I even try to move on to number two.

My pastor tells a story about a man who came to see him one day, ticked off about the whole concept of becoming a Christian by grace and faith and trust alone. The man said, "Why can't we go to heaven the old-fashioned way—by earning it?"

My pastor told him, "You're right. I hate it when they change the rules. How about this: If you can say you've kept all ten commandments, I'll talk to God and try to get you in."

Then he asked the man how many commandments he'd kept. The man paused and counted. "Seven," he answered.

If this were a game show, the buzzer would sound and the game show host would say, "Oooh, wrong answer. Johnny, what do we have as a consolation prize?"

If you blow one, you've blown them all.

However, that's good news—that's *great* news.

Because God knew I could never keep the commandments, Jesus kept them for me, and because I trust Him, that means I'm "in."

As for the law, that's in the Bible as a model, a standard, and a guide for my life. At the same time, because I can't keep the law perfectly, it's there to show me how badly I need Jesus to do for me what I can't do for myself. (I didn't make this up. See Romans 3 and 7 for yourself.)

The amazing thing is, once I admit that I can't obey the law, once I begin to rest in what Jesus has done and I believe and trust that even on my worst day I'm still His, then I find the law—the

Ten Commandments and beyond—to be a delight. I truly want to obey it. Sometimes I'm actually able to, and sometimes I'm not. When I do, it brings great happiness.

When I don't? It brings even greater grace.

THE POWER *of* WOMEN *in* LOVE

RECENTLY, I attended a women's night of worship at my church. We sang, we prayed. A few women spoke. Afterward we hung out and ate some incredible food.

Toward the end of the worship part of the evening and before the eating part, Angel, our women's ministry leader, asked us to dream big for a moment. She said, "Imagine what our community would look like if women 'got it'—if women truly grasped both the concept and the experience of the gospel, of being loved and forgiven and set free in Christ. What kind of an impact would that have?"

She left the question open-ended and unanswered, allowing us to explore it in our imaginations. To dream big and grand.

She read a prayer from Ephesians 3:14–19 and prayed it for us. Paul's prayer for the Ephesians, which was Angel's prayer for us, was that believers in Christ would be strengthened by God's Spirit—a deep inner strength, a strong conviction, and an unshakable sense of who and *whose* they are. Not wishy-washy or easily swayed. Not doubting or fearful, but strong.

Next, Paul (and Angel) prayed that we who are God's people would know, really know, Christ's love. Paul uses phrases like "deeply rooted" and "far surpasses." His words have the connotation of a love that's great and extravagant, amazingly wonderful, and deeply personal. He urges believers to test this love to see if they can measure its height and width and depth and breadth, knowing that they can't because it's immeasurable.

Angel had asked us, "What would our community look like if women 'got it'?" Not just non-Christian women coming into a new faith in Christ, but long-established believers, longtime church ladies. What would our community look like if that happened?

I've been thinking about that, and here's what I think would happen:

If women knew that their sins are forgiven, if women knew that in Christ they stand before the Father accepted and acceptable, if women knew that they can rest underneath the Father's smile…

If women knew that though they are deeply flawed they are dearly loved, they would go home and love their husbands. Not just putting dinner on the table and washing dirty socks with gritted teeth or an expectation-of-something-in-return kind of love, but love from a deep wellspring, like a fountain overflowing. With such a love, they would stop bickering about the trash not being taken out. They wouldn't rush to the phone to complain about their husbands to their girlfriends. They wouldn't yell and snipe and belittle their husbands in Wal-Mart. They wouldn't flirt with other men, dream of greener pastures.

They would love their husbands, honor and respect and accept them.

When that starts happening, when women start loving their husbands consistently, then their husbands want to love them back. Men would feel that home is a safe place and that their wives are allies and friends. There would be a whole lot of kissing going on, maybe even some dancing in the kitchen. Problems would be faced together. The "twos" all over this community would be "ones," just as God intended.

There would be peace in the home, which would spill out into the schools and the workplaces. The saying "If Mama ain't happy, ain't nobody happy" would work in reverse. Now *because* Mama's happy, Daddy's happy and the kids are happy. Daddy goes to work happy and does his job well because it's all for Mama back at home.

Can you see it? Can you see that happening?

I realize that these thoughts are idealistic and simplistic and Pollyannaish, but is that such a bad thing? Why shouldn't we aim high and dare to dream and imagine what God could do?

What would our community look like if women "got it"?

It's definitely worth dreaming about, praying for, and working toward.

Radical, Delightful Thinking

HERE'S A RADICAL thought: What if you believed—truly, completely, utterly, absolutely believed— that God delights in you? I'll get back to that in a minute; first I want to tell you about my granddaughter.

She used to be a baby, but lately she's turned into a kid. Currently she's two and a half and saying and doing and learning new things hourly. The other day I asked my daughter to send me some Caroline stories. Alison wrote back:

> She does many things that put a smile on my face. She always asks how we're doing. When Daddy comes home, she'll run and say "Heeeey!" and "How doin'?" She'll ask, "Good day?"

She talks to our feet—and calls them "baby." Every morning she'll say, "I wanna talk to Mommy's babies." So I take my feet out from under the covers so she can talk to them and give them kisses. She even tries to feed them. But she'll say, "Babies don't eat poop; they eat dinner." She's very into potty humor already.

When Craig comes home from work, she makes him take off his boots and socks immediately so she can talk to the babies. "Oh, cute baby feet," she'll say.

She wags her little finger and says, "No markers" or "Only one vitamin" or "One pack of goo-gahs (fruit snacks)." That wagging finger always makes me smile.

When she asks for something in a whiny, demanding way, I often tell her she'll be more successful at getting what she wants if she asks nicely and politely. So sometimes when she wants something very badly she'll say, "I have trail mix? Pleeeese, nicely and politely."

When she's in the bathtub she'll say, "I'm all sparkly clean."

When I take out her hair band, she'll say, "I have kooky hair." It's true. She looks like a troll doll.

She likes to look out the window, and if a certain neighbor's car is gone, she gets all bent out of shape. "Where's Maddy's car?" she'll ask. "Where's Mecca's mom's car?" And I'll say, "Maddy's dad took it to work." And then she'll say, "Like Daddy." She says, "Daddy makes money."

She's been singing a lot lately, especially patty-cake. I love to hear her sing to herself.

For some reason, watching her blow up balloons makes me smile. Must be her puffed-out cheeks or something. Oh, and when she wears her pink glittery sunglasses—they're definitely smile inducing.

And this will make Grandpa proud: She played T-ball

the other day. She swung and hit the Wiffle ball right off the tee!

Most of the time she's whining for something, and that's very undelightful. But there's still an awful lot that she does that *is* delightful.

This weekend I am visiting with both of my daughters and my son-in-law—and Caroline. All week I've been shopping for "prizes," like finger paints and M&M's and a Dora the Explorer wristwatch. I picked up a few things for my daughters, too. It's my delight to do so. I'm so delighted that I've been singing all week.

Recently, we had a guest preacher at my church who spoke about the delight God has for His own. He quoted the Old Testament writer Zephaniah, who wrote, "He [God] will take great delight in you, he will quiet you with his love, he will rejoice over you with singing."

Take a minute and get a picture of that in your mind. The God who directs storms and who set the planets in motion takes great delight in those He calls His own. Not just tolerates them, not demands their obedience and allegiance, not constantly reminds them of their human failings, but delights in them.

And when those in whom He delights are agitated and anxious, fretful, fearful, and guilty, He quiets them with His love. And not just quiets them, but sings over them. His delight causes Him to break out in a song! Like a parent who delights in a child, like a man in love with his bride. Got that picture?

This brings me back to my original question. What if you believed—truly, completely, utterly, absolutely believed—that God delights in you? How would your life be different?

What's keeping you from believing it?

Love *for the* One Who Needs It Most

EVEN WHEN YOUR babies are almost twenty, they're still your babies. And when one of your babies cries or is sick, as a mother, you still want to rush in and make everything better.

My youngest was sick this past week. She moved out several months ago, but even before she moved her stuff out, she began to move away from me. I'm not complaining—that's as it should be. It's what I've spent the past almost twenty years preparing her and myself for. But she was sick, and when your baby is sick, no matter how old she is, as a mom you want her with you.

One of the most difficult aspects of parenting almost-adults is restraining yourself from jumping in immediately to do God's job for Him. At her first whimper, I was set to tell her, "Okay, you've been an almost-adult long enough. It's time for you to be my baby once again."

I chomped at the bit to call her workplace for her and say, "Sorry, my baby can't come outside and play or work today." I was all set to move her back in with me, tuck a blanket around her on my couch, and spoon-feed her ice chips. I carried my phone around the house with me all day Sunday, waiting to hear from her and resisting the urge to call her every three minutes, just to see if she needed me.

She needed me, but at almost twenty, she didn't need me running interference for her or backing up a moving van to her door just because she was sick. Even if she secretly wanted me to take care of her like I did when she was five, at almost twenty, she needed me to let her be sick in her own house, in her own bed.

I don't know why, but as I waited for my daughter to feel better, I remembered how, a long, long time ago, she would ask, "Who do you love most?"

That's a tough question to ask a mom.

"Well, of all the people in heaven, I love God most," I would tell her. "Of all the people I'm married to, I love Dad most. Of all my kids age twelve, I love your sister most, and of all my kids age six, I love you most."

We all want to be loved most. Telling her that always seemed to make her feel better. The truth is, my heart beats hardest for the one who needs me most.

Jesus once told a story about a shepherd who had one hundred sheep, including one who'd wandered off. Instead of shrugging it off and saying, "Oh well, what's one sheep? I still have ninety-nine," the shepherd went searching for the lost one, not giving up until he found it. With great joy the shepherd placed the lost lamb around his shoulders and rejoiced all the way home.

I think God loves all His kids equally, but I think His heart beats a bit harder for the one who needs Him most. Just like a mom's heart does for the one who needs her most.

Sometimes God lets His children cry. He lets them hurt and feel their need. Sometimes He lets a mom fret and worry and devise ploys to bring her baby back home. He lets her feel her need, too.

Then, with the heart of a kind shepherd, He reminds them both that He loves them most and that His love for little ones in need, even those who are almost twenty and those who are a lot older, surpasses even the fiercest love of a mom who would move heaven and earth to rush to her baby's side.

That kind of love makes everything better.

The Grace We Hate

I'M GOING to tell you something that will make you crazy. It might make you throw this book down or spit out your coffee. You may send me a scathing e-mail or anonymous letter. You'll definitely question my Christianity.

Here goes: Jeffrey Dahmer, the serial-killing cannibal, might be in heaven.

In 1992, he was sentenced to life in prison and was later beaten to death in 1994 by another inmate. Six months before that, according to the *Milwaukee Sentinel* and other sources, Dahmer reportedly came to faith in Christ and was baptized.

I'm not saying for sure he's in heaven, but if that really happened, if a genuine "by grace are ye saved through faith" transaction took place in his heart, then he is.

He's in heaven, and religious Aunt Louise, who never missed Sunday school in her entire life and who trusted in that to get her through the pearly gates, isn't.

I told you that would make you crazy.

The truth is, although we church people love to sing about "Amazing grace! How sweet the sound, that saved a wretch like me," we really hate grace. Oh, we love it for ourselves, but we hate it for others. We hate it for Jeffrey Dahmer. *He doesn't deserve it.*

We think grace is okay for those who clean themselves up. Or grace is okay for those who are still dirty, yet have potential, like the prostitute with a heart of gold or the alcoholic who isn't such a bad guy when he's not drunk.

But not for serial killers, and certainly not for cannibals.

Sure, the Bible says grace is totally a gift from God and we can't earn our way into heaven and that God gives His gift of salvation to whomever He chooses...

But that doesn't include Jeffrey Dahmer, does it? It can't include him, can it? God's grace surely isn't for people like him! Is it?

A story that church people hate, even though Jesus told it and church people generally like His stories, is about a man who owned a vineyard and went out early in the morning to hire men to work in it. They agreed on the wage offered and set out to work.

Later in the day, the man hired more workers at the same pay. As the day wore on, he kept hiring more workers, all at the same pay.

Finally, he hired the last few, who barely tied their shoes before the foreman called it quitting time. They lined up to be paid, with those who were hired last being paid first. When they opened their pay envelopes, they let out a whoop. Even though they knew they hadn't earned it, they still received a full day's pay.

Then the next group got paid, receiving the same amount as the first. That's when the group that had worked the longest and hardest started talking among themselves.

"Maybe we'll get a bonus," one of them said.

But they didn't. They got the same as everyone else. "No fair!" one guy said, throwing down his hat. "Why should those guys get the same thing we get?"

The vineyard owner replied, "I haven't been unfair to you. I gave you exactly what we agreed on. As for the other guys, it's my money, and I felt like being generous. Don't I have that right? Or are you envious because I'm generous?" (see Matthew 20:1–16).

Murderers and thieves—and people that most respectable folks call "sinners"—love that story, especially when they realize it's about God's grace and how it can't be earned and that He gives it to whomever He chooses and that He usually chooses those who least "deserve" it.

But church folks—who don't smoke, don't drink, don't cuss, and who wag their fingers at people who do and who think that's why God should choose them—hate this story. Funny in a sad sort of way, isn't it?

I don't know if Jeffrey Dahmer is in heaven, but if he is, he's there the only way any of us will get there: not by any good thing we've done, but solely by God's gift of grace.

When it comes to offering His grace, God's playing field is level. That means serial killers and Sunday school teachers are equally undeserving.

That, my friend, is grace. It either makes you crazy or it makes you glad.

WELL, BLESS MY HEART

*I*T WAS A WEEKEND right out of the pages of *Southern Living* magazine. As a guest of an old and traditional Southern Methodist church outside of Birmingham, Alabama, I stayed in a house on the shores of a gorgeous lake.

The dogwoods and wisteria were in bloom; the hand-squeezed lemonade flowed freely. I dined on chilled strawberry soup, shrimp primavera, fresh asparagus, and mandarin orange layer cake.

It's what I call "suffering for Jesus."

Not being a Southerner, I'm fascinated by the culture, so refined, with lovely ladies dressed in pastels, their skin porcelain-smooth, their handshakes warm and inviting.

As I shared with the church women my stories of dyeing my daughter's hair bright orange, stealing Sweet'N Low, my obsession with Bare Minerals cosmetics and shopping on eBay, repeatedly these ladies would purr, "Well, bless your heart." Only they made it more drawn out and melodic: "Blezz yor haahrt."

Later I learned that "Bless your heart" is Southern-speak for "I can't believe what a moron you are."

That may or may not be true. Nevertheless, I came home with my heart blessed beyond containment. At that weekend retreat, as I stood inside the hundred-plus-year-old sanctuary, I was overwhelmed with the goodness of God to me, that He would allow me to travel and to be showered with affection and attention, that He would allow me to speak for Him, to eat fabulous food, to stay in gracious, luxurious homes, and to be loved by equally gracious people.

Yes, my heart is blessed.

In a few weeks, my husband and I will celebrate another wedding anniversary. Our daughters love us; they're stretching and growing, developing strong character, bless their hearts. Our granddaughter sends us kisses over the phone and drawings in the mail. Our son-in-law is a good man who loves his family.

My heart is blessed.

The junipers and succulents that I planted out front haven't died (yet). Weight Watchers just came out with candy that tastes like candy and snack cakes that satisfy my sweetest cravings. My checkbook almost balanced.

My heart is blessed.

I love my job. I love my friends—even better, they love me. I'm forgiven by God, the best heart-blessing of all. Listen to these words penned by hymn writer H. G. Spafford: "My sin, oh, the bliss of this glorious thought! My sin, not in part but the whole, is nailed to the cross, and I bear it no more. Praise the Lord, praise the Lord, O my soul!"

I truly believe that! Oh, how my heart is blessed because I believe that.

My heart is blessed as I watch a friend's faith take root. My heart is blessed to know that God allowed me to have a role in it. My heart is blessed whenever people ask me to pray for them, whenever people say they're praying for me.

I love my church—my heart is blessed. We believe in purity and holiness and the sufficiency of grace. My heart is so very blessed.

When I'm steeped in foolishness, out on a shopping binge, or I've wasted the day watching TV, as my soul cries out, "I'm not satisfied!" my heart is still blessed. Jesus said, "Blessed are the poor in spirit." He said that those who know their desperate need for Him will find the satisfaction of the kingdom and of the King. As I turn my heart to Jesus, it is blessed.

When life doesn't go my way, when my children cry and I can't fix their sorrow, my heart is blessed because God draws near with His comfort. When I've gorged myself on food, yet still hunger and thirst for righteousness, God fills my heart with blessing. I am filled with God Himself, and my heart and my soul are blessedly satisfied.

When I'm misunderstood, when I stomp on toes and offend with the gospel I proclaim, when I suffer persecution for Jesus' sake (not that I've ever truly suffered for Jesus, at least not in the ways some do), I am blessed, for mine is the kingdom of heaven—heaven belongs to me!

I have a place. I have a role. I am known by Jesus. I have a calling and a purpose. There's a breeze blowing through my life, the holy wind of the Spirit.

Well, bless my heart. My heart is blessed indeed.

WHAT CHILDREN BELIEVE

MY GRANDDAUGHTER is fascinated by age these days and wants to know how old everyone and everything is.

The other day she asked my daughter, "How old is Grandma?" When Alison told her that I'm "almost fifty," Caroline said, "Grandma's old!"

Thank you, Caroline. Guess who's not getting any more M&M's?

She told the neighbor that her daddy "lives in the bushes." That's because when Alison points out Craig's work to her from the road, the building is beyond some tall trees. So she naturally concluded that he works (or lives) in the bushes.

She also thinks that "being taller" has magical powers and that she'll be able to do whatever she wants when she's taller. It's always about being taller, even if height isn't the reason she's not allowed to do something.

Oh, the things children believe.

The other day I found a website called "I Used to Believe." People post the crazy things they used to believe about a variety of topics, including God.

Here are some of my favorites:

"I used to believe that Jesus was killed by a guy called The Conscious Pilot, and I was, like, but they didn't have airplanes back then!"

"At school I was taught that God lived 'above' us. I lived in an apartment at the time, and I used to believe the man on the floor above us was God, so I would shout my prayers so he could hear me."

"When I was about five or six, I heard a preacher on the radio talking about how Jesus had died for our sins. I asked my brother how Jesus died and he told me He died in a car wreck. I believed that for years."

"I used to believe God's name was Peter because at the end of Mass we would all say, 'Thanks, Peter God.' Then I learned it's 'Thanks be to God.'"

"My mother always told me, 'God is always watching you,' so while I brushed my teeth I would dance around the bathroom so He wouldn't get bored."

As for me, I used to believe that the devil lived behind the doors of the confessionals at church and that women became nuns because they were disillusioned with life and couldn't find husbands.

I used to believe that God was distant and unknowable. That He mostly frowned and disapproved of everything people did. I used to believe that I could sin too much for God to forgive, that He would reach a breaking point, that I'd cross some arbitrary line and go beyond His mercy. I'm not sure I believed in heaven and hell, just divine retribution, quid pro quo, karma.

I used to believe that people who talked about loving God were loopy at best. I used to believe that I had to be holy to go to church. I used to believe that one day God would run a movie projector and broadcast all my secret, shameful thoughts and deeds for everyone to see.

I used to believe that I wasn't good enough for God to answer my prayers and that He was sorry He saved me because I didn't (and still don't) want to be a missionary in Africa.

I used to believe that God was disappointed in my lack of faith, my prayerlessness, my self-centeredness and self-righteousness. That He extended grace to me because He had to, not because He wanted to.

But what I used to believe is wrong. Now I believe the truth:

I believe that there is "no condemnation for those who are in Christ" (Romans 8:1) and that nothing can separate one of God's own from His love (v. 39). I now believe that God's compassion doesn't depend on one's desire or effort, but solely on His mercy (9:16) and that He will keep even the weakest strong to the end so that all who are His will forever be blameless before Him (1 Corinthians 1:8).

I believe that no matter who sits in the White House, no matter who our enemies are, no matter what the morning headlines say, God is on the throne, and His kingdom reigns—and that His children are quieted when that's what they believe.

THE JERK WITHIN

I'M READING a book about jerks titled *Don't Let the Jerks Get the Best of You*, by Paul Meier, MD. So far, the most interesting thing about the book is the comments I've been getting from the people who see it on my desk.

"Is that about me?" they'll ask.

It seems most people have a gut knowledge that they harbor jerk tendencies.

(The Bible calls it sin.)

When I found the book, the title intrigued me. I thought it might give me some insight into the jerks in my life. Not that I have any, but just in case I ever do. The subtitle promises *Advice for Dealing with Difficult People.*

As I settled down to read, I prepared to take copious notes, again, just in case I recognized anyone I know.

The author defines a jerk as someone whose selfish thoughts or behavior ultimately harms someone else. He said the root cause of jerkiness is a sense of selfish entitlement that is both inborn and learned. He defines entitlement as thinking, "I deserve to act, be, or have what I want." It's good old-fashioned self-centeredness.

Only on page six, and I had already begun to squirm.

Maybe this book isn't so much about others, I thought. *Maybe it's about me.*

The author goes on to describe three categories of jerks: First-, Second-, and Nth-Degree, with Nth being sociopaths like Saddam Hussein and Adolph Hitler.

Everyone, Meier says, is a jerk to some degree because none of us is perfect. The goal is to keep our jerkism under control and reign in our sense of entitlement.

(The Bible calls this sanctification.)

It's amazing how acutely tuned-in we are to the jerkiness of others but are often blinded to our own.

As squirmy as I was reading about the various degrees of jerkiness, I still didn't think mine was any more than a blip on the screen. A pin dot. Microscopic.

Compared to (I won't mention who) I'm not so bad, I thought. *I'm Jerk Lite.*

But then I took the Jerk Quiz. Out of a maximum of seventy-five points, I scored a fifty-nine, which ranked me as a "high-level First-Degree Jerk." Most people are First-Degree Jerks, writes Meier. They're the "good guys" who mean well and try to be honest, fair, and trustworthy. Their jerkiness is usually done unintentionally, and they feel genuine guilt when confronted with their jerky behavior.

Second-Degree Jerks purposefully and willfully manipulate, control, and abuse others. They may feel guilt, but they don't let that stop them from continuing their jerkiness.

I wasn't surprised to learn I was a jerk. I was, however, shocked to learn just how big a jerk I actually am.

(The Bible calls our hearts deceitful and desperately wicked.)

Using the answers "seldom," "sometimes," or "often," the test asked about such things as telling "white lies" to avoid trouble, taking delight in "exchanging news" about people *(the Bible calls that gossip)*, feeling sorry for those in need but not helping them, choosing hobbies and personal interests over people, monopolizing conversations, and blaming others when things go wrong.

Even though I had a lot of "sometimes" answers and one "seldom," I had more "oftens" than I care to count. To paraphrase Pogo, "I have met the Jerk and he is me."

Now that I'm confronted with this knowledge about myself, the big question is: What am I going to do about it? Because I'm a high-level First-Degree Jerk, my first response is to feel guilty and either shrug it off and try ignoring it, or to try atoning for it by vowing to work harder to lower my score.

(The Bible calls that self-righteousness.)

The better response—the biblical, and therefore best, response—is neither. The best response is taking my guilt to the Cross and accepting the forgiveness found there and knowing that in me dwells no good thing. I'll always be a jerk, but through Christ I am progressively getting better. He gives me the "want to" as well as the ability to change.

(The Bible calls that grace.)

LOVING BERNIECE

IF YOU CAN love someone you've only known one hour, then I love Berniece Robertson with all my heart.

She called the newsroom early one Tuesday morning from the hospital. She was dying, and it was her last day in our area. Her son had come from Missouri to take her to his farm to live out her remaining days.

I went to see her, not knowing what to expect, although I should have had a clue when I noticed the sky. Over the newsroom it was dark and gray, but the sky to the east, where Berniece was, was brilliant and bright.

As I entered her hospital room, Berniece greeted me with a raspy voice and a huge smile.

"I'm dying—and this is the happiest time of my life!" she said.

She told me that for the first sixty-four years of her life she lived rough, drinking and smoking. "But I won't go into that," she said.

Fifteen years ago when Jesus changed her life, she asked God to help her stop drinking. "I had a can of beer in my hand and took a drink and spit it out—it tasted like soap!" she said.

Quitting smoking wasn't as easy. "I disobeyed God on that one," she said.

While we talked, her friend Sandy called. Sandy cried and told Berniece that she would pray for her. Berniece yelled into the phone, "Don't you do that, Sandy! Don't you pray for me to be cured. I want to set an example for others that God gave us the ability to accept His will."

When Berniece hung up the phone, she said Sandy loved her and that she loved Sandy. It's hard to say good-bye to someone you love.

"I used to preach and pray for people in front of Big Lots," she said, "but then I got disabled. That made me unhappy, because I couldn't talk to people that really needed it."

One Sunday morning she had a terrible headache and got into her van to go to town. "I was in shorts, a T-shirt, no bra, and sandals, and I didn't have any intention of doing this, but God took my van to the Vineyard church."

She walked in and right up to the front.

"The minister said, 'Do you need help?' I said, 'My head is hurting bad.' He said, 'Do you believe the Lord can heal you?' I said, 'Yes, that's why I'm here!'"

She faced the congregation and said, "People, believe in the Lord because He can heal you and ease your pain, and I need prayer right now!"

They prayed and five minutes later her headache was gone, she said.

"Some say the Christian life is hard to live, and I believe that," she said, "but it's easier to live a Christian life than a sinful one. Going to church doesn't cost anything, but a sinful life costs a lot, your beer and everything else you want."

Although she was sad about leaving her friends and neighbors and the town she loves, she was almost giddy to get on with her death and to see her Savior face-to-face.

"I'm leaving this evil world," she said, "and I hope to be happy while I'm doing it. My son has an eighty-acre farm and has horses. He teaches disabled kids to ride and how to be brave. And I'll be with my grandchildren and great-grandchildren with all the love they can pour out on me. Anyone can come over to see me—it'll be like church!"

When it was time for me to leave, I hugged her for a long time; then I went to my car and wept, although I'm not sure why.

Her joy in the face of dying made me ashamed of how tied I am to this world, how tied I am to things, to money and comfort and TV. She longed to die well; I longed for a grilled cheese sandwich. I also longed to taste what she tasted—the nearness of eternity and the grace to travel there.

Her name is Berniece Robertson, and although I only knew her for one hour on a Tuesday morning, I love her with all my heart.

THE CLEANSING POWER *of* BLOOD

ON MAY 30, 1978, the blood of Jesus cleansed me from all my sin.

Actually, that happened two thousand years before that, but I didn't know it until that day.

As my Jesus-anniversary present this year, I bought myself a CD of old hymns set to new music.

One of my favorite songs is "Let Us Love and Sing and Wonder," written by John "Amazing Grace" Newton in 1774. I don't know how the original tune goes, but I like the new one. It's bouncy and catchy and the refrain is simple:

He has washed us with His blood.
He has washed us with His blood.
He has washed us with His blood.
He presents our souls to God.

I've been going around Wal-Mart and the grocery store and the newsroom singing, "He has washed us with His blood…"

Some of the other songs on the CD use words like: "Love has redeemed His sheep with blood"; "Mercy speaks by Jesus' blood"; "Thy blood alone, O Lamb of God, can give me peace within."

All that blood talk got me thinking about outsiders and aliens, those not familiar with church lingo. Years ago my friend Cheryl Peterson and I were accosted on a Southern California beach by a Bible-wielding man who asked if we'd been "washed in the blood."

We'd been slathered with Coppertone tanning oil, but frankly weren't interested in a bloodbath. We ignored him, and he went on down the beach accosting other sun worshipers.

Now I know about the blood of Jesus cleansing us from all sin (1 John 1:7), but I often wonder what other people think. It's an odd concept—blood as a cleaning agent. If I cut myself and bleed on the carpet, it will leave a stain, not a clean spot. You don't dump a cupful of blood into your washing machine, and if you were to take a tree branch, dip it in blood and shake it out onto a crowd of people, they wouldn't shout "Hooray! Do it again!" They'd shout, but not "Hooray."

But God being God decided that the sins of humans could only be cleansed by blood. "Without the shedding of blood there is no forgiveness" (Hebrews 9:22).

A few years ago, *Christianity Today* ran a story, written by surgeon Paul Brand, about the life-giving power of blood, beginning with its "miracle" cleansing properties. Brand detailed the process of blood traveling throughout the body, simultaneously feeding each cell with oxygen and absorbing waste products (carbon dioxide, urea, and uric acid), then delivering the toxic waste chemicals to organs that can dump them outside the body.

"Blood sustains life by carrying away the chemical by-products that would interfere with it," he wrote. "This then is the [condensed] medical explanation of blood's cleansing property."

He went on to write about sin and forgiveness. He said we tend to think of sin as a "private list of grievances that happen to irk God…but even a casual reading of the Old Testament shows that sin is a blockage, a paralyzing toxin that restricts our realization of full humanity."

Forgiveness, he said, "cleanses the wasteful products, sins, that impede true health, just as blood cleanses harmful metabolites."

He said from a biological, physiological perspective, blood as a cleansing agent makes perfect sense. "The Creator chose a theological symbol with an exact analog in the medical world," he wrote.

That still doesn't explain why God chose blood as the only acceptable sin-cleanser—as offensive and icky as it is—but He did. Maybe Bible scholars and theologians know, but most likely they don't. No one knows why God does anything, and any explanations would only be speculations.

For me, it's enough to know that God is God; therefore, He gets to make the rules. And if He says the answer to "What can wash away my sin?" is "Nothing but the blood of Jesus," then that's the way it is.

I'm just glad that on May 30, 1978, I believed for the first time that it did.

MARRIAGE LIKE DIAMONDS

*B*ACK IN THE early 1970s, the British duo Malcolm and Alwyn were part of the Jesus Movement, singing Jesus songs. In one of their songs, "The World Needs Jesus," they sing about the sad state of the world, the church, themselves, concluding each verse with, "Ahhhhh, the world needs Jesus."

They end the song with, "I need Jesus."

Even though the song itself is more than thirty years old, the message remains timeless. The world needs Jesus. The church needs Jesus. People need Jesus.

Marriages need Jesus.

Lately I've been meeting devastated women trying to work through the grief and feelings of abandonment and loss because their husbands have left them.

One woman, the same age as one of my daughters, hadn't even reached her first wedding anniversary and already her husband decided that he would rather drink and smoke pot and chase other women than stay married.

"He said he was a Christian—we grew up in church together!" she said. She married him for better or for worse and forever. Now he's gone, and she's devastated.

I hear of church pastors leaving their wives and families and marrying others for no better reason than personal happiness. How tragic to see these former wives left behind to grieve and make sense of their feelings of betrayal, sort out their anger, wrestle with forgiveness while the remarried one moves on almost callously.

It's more than not right—it's just plain wrong.

I know it's not only men who do the leaving, but they seem to do a lot of it.

My husband tells me all the time about the people he works with, men and women who are on their second, third, fifth marriages. He says everyone's looking for that greener pasture, but what they're finding is a lot of horse manure. When they discover they were better off with the spouse they left, by then it's too late. The damage has already been done. Lives shattered, families irrevocably destroyed.

The world needs Jesus. The church needs Jesus. Marriages need Jesus.

More than thirty years ago, my husband slipped a plain gold band on my finger. Over the years it became marred and misshapen and lost its luster. Much like our lives. Much like our marriage—like all marriages at times.

But neither of us left.

Then one day as we went out for a drive, a brown velvet ring box fell out of the glove compartment. "That's for you," Barry said.

Inside the box was the most exquisite antique diamond ring I had ever seen, a treasured family heirloom. Except to have it cleaned, I haven't taken it off in all the years since Barry gave it to me.

Sometimes, when I'm outside, the diamond will catch a beam of light and scatter into a burst of colors. When that happens, I'm drawn to its beauty and brilliance. That's when I remember how a diamond is created: It starts as a particle of carbon, one of the most common elements in the universe, deep in the mantle of the earth. Through years of extreme heat and intense pressure, the carbon is crystallized into a diamond. It eventually reaches the earth's crust through molten rock, exploded through a volcano.

It's the process that turns the common and ordinary into the toughest and most precious of gems. Just think of the beauty we would miss out on if the process were thwarted.

To me, that's a picture of marriage, and of life itself. We're in process of becoming precious and durable and strong, but only if we stay put—even through the times of extreme heat and pressure—holding on to Jesus as He holds on to us.

If there's a "secret" to not leaving, maybe that's it.

For those who are suffering through a divorce, I am truly sorry for your pain. But even though your marriage will never be a diamond, if you hold fast to Jesus as you go through the heat and pressure, you yourself will emerge on the other side, a brilliant diamond, a durable gem, a precious jewel.

Oh, how we all need Jesus!

AS I WAVE GOOD-BYE

*T*HIS IS AN *open letter to my daughter.*

Dear Laura,

After twenty years of you being my baby, it's difficult to believe that you are a young woman on your own. As I said good-bye to you in Georgia just a week ago and watched you drive away to your new life in Charlotte, North Carolina, I felt a piece of my heart rip. It was the same ripping that I felt when your sister left home for good, too.

I remember your tears. You didn't see me, but I cried as soon as you drove away. (Then I went and bought towels to replace the ones you took with you from home!)

For a long time, you and I didn't get along. But in this past year, we've become sushi-eating and mall-crawling buddies. You've shared things with me about your life that have shocked me, but at the same time have endeared yourself to me even more than I could imagine possible. Thank you for trusting me with your secrets, with who you are as a person and as a young woman. I will always treasure that.

Now you're on your own, in a strange city filled with strange people—and you do seem to attract some strange ones. That's because you're strange yourself, and I mean that in the best way. You're different; you stand out. That's always been your strength as well as your downfall. You evoke strong emotions in people. Folks either love or hate Laura Kennedy.

I hope you meet more who love you than hate you, wherever you go.

When you first talked about moving to Charlotte, you wondered if God was answering your prayer. I smiled when you added that you don't make a habit of praying, even though I think you do. Deep in your heart, I think you've always prayed.

So even though this opportunity seemed to come from nowhere, I know God chose it for you. He's been leading you, and your sister, ever since before you each were born.

On my drive back from our trip to Georgia, where we said good-bye, I played a new CD. One of the songs was about "everywhere I go, I see [God]." The singer sang about God going before him as a "cloud by day and fire by night." That's an Old Testament reference to God leading the children of Israel during their exodus from Egypt. He went ahead of them in a pillar of clouds during the day to guide them and a pillar of fire at night to give them light. The Bible says God never left them. He will never leave you either.

I know that now that you're young and on your own and five hundred miles away from your mom and dad, the last thing you want is to be reminded of God's constant presence. But even if you don't think so now, it's a good thing.

It's good to know that you can never go farther than His arm can reach and that He will be with you with every step you take. He will be with you with every decision you make, good or bad. He will pick you up when you fall, hold you when you cry, and carry you when you think you can't go on.

Expect good times, but expect hard times, too. In all your

times, He will be with you. So wait for Him, and look for Him. Everywhere you go, you will see Him.

Again, that's a good thing.

Remember, too, that I am forever praying for you, just as I pray for your sister. I'm not your mommy anymore, but I'll always be your mother. (And that's a good thing, too, most of the time.)

Laura and Alison, I am infinitely proud of you both. I'm thankful that God chose the two of you to be my daughters. My hope is that someday you'll have daughters who are just like you. I guarantee that if and when you do, you will be glad that God is with you.

Laura, you know that I can't conclude a "God talk" without reminding you that "whether you turn to the right or to the left, your ears will hear a voice behind you, saying, 'This is the way; walk in it'" (Isaiah 30:21).

Walk with God, my sweet daughter. He's already walking with you.

GOD NEVER LEAVES US STRANDED

*A*S I WRITE this I'm sitting in the Tampa airport waiting for my husband to arrive from Baltimore. I came early to work on this column, having planned to write about turning fifty this week and how excited I am to have my own AARP card and finally be eligible for the senior discount at Bealls Outlet.

I had wanted to write about how, in the Bible, the fiftieth year is called the "year of jubilee," when the land lies fallow and debts are canceled and how it is to be a time of fresh starts and new beginnings.

However, those fiftyish thoughts aren't flowing. Instead, I'm thinking about my husband and why he's coming in from Baltimore.

Ten days ago, our oldest daughter, Alison, and granddaughter, Caroline, came for a visit from Maryland. Because Caroline is terribly squirmy and overly friendly to strangers, likes to escape, and is fast as lightning when she does escape, my daughter (who could make big bucks if worrying were a career option) was worried that Caroline might escape at the airport and get on a plane to Australia or Minnesota and go home with someone else.

To ease my daughter's fears, my husband devised a detailed and elaborate itinerary. First, he flew from Jacksonville, Florida, where he currently works, to Baltimore. When he got there, he helped my daughter load up the car seat and the snacks and the junior-sized backpack and two suitcases and all the rest of the toddler paraphernalia, then flew with them to Tampa, where I met them at the airport. Then he flew back to Jacksonville, only to drive home a few days later for an extended visit during Thanksgiving, and then back again.

This morning he flew in again from Jacksonville to Tampa to meet Alison and Caroline at the airport, flew with them to Baltimore, put them in a taxi, then went back into the airport to catch a return flight to Tampa. He arrives in about an hour.

We'll spend the weekend in Tampa celebrating my fiftieth birthday a week early, and then he'll fly back to Jacksonville Sunday night.

My daughters and I talk a lot about my husband, their dad, about how he does these strange and wonderful things for us, rearranges his life for us, goes out of his way for us, saves the day for us.

And he loves doing it. Like Batman, he loves to swoop in and take charge. Nothing makes him happier than to be with his girls, keeping us safe.

It's actually totally nuts and probably looks insane to anyone who doesn't know him. I mean, who flies all the way to Baltimore and turns around and comes back? Not only that, he never holds it over our heads or uses it to say, "I did this for you, so you have to do this for me." If you try to pay him back—as if you could— it's almost as if it takes away his whole joy in doing what he does.

So as I'm sitting here in the airport waiting for my husband's flight to arrive, I'm thinking about how this thing that compels him to do what he does might be a tiny glimpse of what compels God to do what He does for those He loves.

I'm thinking that when life gets scary and difficult and confusing sometimes, when I need to know that I'm not alone even when I feel that I am, when I start to wonder if God really does care, sometimes He sends flesh and blood glimpses of who He is and reminds me that He's so much more.

And right at this moment, I need to know. I need to know that God is so much more and that He goes out of His way to bring those He loves safely home.

I might tell that to my husband sometime this weekend, but maybe I won't. Maybe I'll just spend the weekend feeling safe, feeling loved, feeling secure and thanking God that He never leaves the ones He loves without a reminder that He is our help and strength—and so much more.

That's a pretty good birthday present, don't you think?

WHO CAN FIX THIS BROKEN WORLD?

*O*UR WORLD is broken. As I write this, the news of the beheading of the young American in Iraq—somebody's son, somebody's brother!—has me reeling with sick-to-my-stomach disbelief. I can't seem to put my brain around this one. It doesn't make sense. How can we humans do this to each other?

Muslim fundamentalists in Nigeria killed eight pastors and fifteen hundred Christians, while destroying 173 churches. The violence there in one month displaced twenty-five thousand people.

Our world is so very broken.

My husband tells me about the soap opera lives of people he works with. Never mind the guests on *Jerry Springer*, who may or may not be telling the truth about the bizarre goings-on in their lives. The people my husband tells me about are real and breathing, bleeding and terribly, terribly broken.

The other day I sat in a restaurant and overheard snippets of conversations going on around me. At the same time, the images of Nick Berg, the man who was beheaded, flashed on the television screen nearby.

Conversations drifted from politics to local sports to rising gas prices. "It's all the president's fault," someone offered. "They're all a bunch of crooks," said someone else.

One man got up to leave, and although I can't be sure, he appeared to be drunk. Someone announced that he had been doing this "every day for twelve years—his car automatically knows how to get home."

I wanted to stop him; I probably should have. I wanted to tell him that we're all broken, that I'm broken, too, but that Jesus can fix us.

Earlier this week I got a call from a woman who has a dear elderly friend who lives alone and is facing eviction. How can this be? How can someone not let a woman in her eighties have a place to live? How broken is that?

Another friend called crying. She said she's haunted by memories and regrets from a stupid mistake she made a lifetime ago that refuse to go away. Just when she thinks the memories are dead and buried, her husband brings her indiscretion up again.

My friend is broken; her husband is broken; their marriage is broken.

We are all so very broken.

On television we vote people off the island, cheer when "The Donald" says, "You're fired." We revel in public humiliation. We are coarse and rude. We put dog collars on naked Iraqi prisoners and pose for the camera.

We give birth to babies, put them in plastic bags, and toss them in trash cans. We strap bombs to our children and send them into crowded cafés.

We are alcoholics and porn-, food-, and drug addicts. We steal because we want to, not because we're in need. We lie to protect ourselves. We keep score; we are cold and unfeeling, self-centered and unforgiving.

We need a constitutional amendment to protect the concept of marriage between a man and a woman. We march to save the whales and the rain forests, and we scream to let us continue killing our unborn children.

We are broken, so very, very broken.

On my desk sits a grease board on which I used to keep a record of stories that I am scheduled to write. One day I became overwhelmed, erased the board altogether, and wrote, "Dear God, I need help!" Someone came by and added, "Me, too!"

I haven't erased the messages, and I don't think I will. Not that I need to be reminded of my brokenness, but that I have a God to whom I can bring all my brokenness and He will fix it. Not that He will necessarily fix everything in this life, but He will *ultimately*. He's all about making everything fresh and new again. That's our hope, often our only hope for some of our broken situations.

Near the end of the Bible, the apostle John wrote these words of ultimate hope:

> "He will remove all of their sorrows, and there will be no more death or sorrow or crying or pain…." And the one sitting on the throne said, "Look, I am making all things new!"

Oh, may we all have eyes to see and hearts to grasp these words of hope in this broken, broken world!

GRACE *in the* DARKNESS

IF YOU DON'T KNOW my husband, then you should. When your life falls apart, next to God, he's who you want on your side. This past week, my awe of him was renewed.

For the past few years, Barry has worked and lived out of town. Just one week ago, Sam, his buddy, coworker, and part-time roommate, died of a heart attack.

Sam's wife, who lives in South Carolina, had just found out

that she has cancer, and because Sam was focused on caring for her, he ignored his own chest pains.

Barry and Sam had made a pact. Because their wives and families live elsewhere, during their remaining months at Jacksonville Naval Air Station, they agreed to be each other's buddy and to care for each other. They were going to retire on the same day and walk out the gate together.

I'm in awe of Barry because he's a rock in a crisis. Upon hearing the news about Sam, he immediately went to work, gathering the guys in their shop, arranging for a caravan to South Carolina for the funeral, and contacting the base personnel office about Sam's life insurance and pension so his widow would have one less thing to worry about.

At Sam's funeral, Barry served as a pallbearer. That's what he does best; he bears the pall and the overshadowing and oppressive darkness of others. He has broad shoulders, capable of carrying great weight. I am in awe and so terribly proud of him.

But he is human. Years ago, surprising those of us who know him best, he fell into darkness. My always up, always even, beloved husband became depressed. He wouldn't and couldn't say so then, but he will and does talk about it now.

In *God Works the Night Shift*, author Ron Mehl calls darkness "God's anesthesia." He says, "The God who works the night shift sometimes brings numbing darkness into our lives before He begins certain surgical procedures. He gets us alone, He brings us to vulnerability, He removes outward distractions, and He then goes to work."

That was true of my husband during that time. For the first time in his life, he couldn't carry anyone and could barely carry himself. Only after he came out of the darkness a year and a half later did he discover that, through the prayers of those who love him, God carried him. Now he's the same old Barry again, only different.

When you emerge from darkness, you can't help but be different—either bitter or better. Barry's better. His strength is a more gentle strength. His shoulders, still broad, are more flexible. He's still stiff-necked and stubborn, but not like he was.

When he called to tell me about Sam, he asked me to pray—for Sam's wife and for Sam's children. I'll also be praying for him, Sam's friend and my beloved, maybe more than I ever have before. Losing a friend is one of life's darkest moments. I fear he'll go back into the darkness.

Next week, Barry and I are going away someplace. It's a surprise. Not a surprise that we're going, but where we're going. He has it all planned—that's another thing he does best. All I have to do is show up with my suitcase. (That's what I do best.)

Next week, when I see my husband, I plan to hold him until my arms fall off and trace my finger across the creases around his eyes caused from years of smiling. I'll ask him to make a muscle so I can punch it, just for fun. I plan not to notice the things that drive me crazy and instead concentrate on the evidences of God's hand upon his life.

Someday death will separate us. One of the things Barry and I are going to do next week is talk about the bank accounts and life insurance and what to do if one of us should go before the other. It's something I've avoided dealing with, as if talking about it will make it so. I'm not ready to be the one left behind. The years we've had together haven't been long enough.

But God gives grace. In life, in death, in darkness, and in light, God always has and always will give grace.

GLADNESS *and* GLUE *and* GRACE

S I WRITE THIS, I'm sitting in the back of my church, way over on the far right side where I never sit. I walked in late, and there's a can of spray adhesive in my purse—not that that has anything to do with anything, other than it's one of the reasons why I'm late.

The glue is for a project I'm working on at home. I'm gluing burlap onto the flat surfaces of a wooden footlocker, and then I'm going to paint it shiny black. Not that you asked.

I stopped at Wal-Mart on my way to church and bought the glue and brought it into church inside my purse because I didn't want it to explode in the heat of my car. Again, not that you asked.

However, if you had asked, I would tell you that, glue in my purse or not, I'm so very glad to be here, sitting where I never sit. I'm glad because it's been a struggle to get here, beginning when I got dressed for church last week and then didn't go. No reason. No crisis of faith. I wasn't even busy doing anything. I just didn't go.

But I came today, although I almost didn't. *Again.* On my way here, I stopped at Wal-Mart just for a minute, which ended up as many minutes. Then the checkout line was slow, and by the time I got to my car it was 10:58. Church starts at eleven, and oh, well, maybe I just won't go.

Then I did the squirrel thing, like how squirrels will start to dart across a street then stop and dance back and forth, debating. *Should I go? Should I not?*

Sometimes squirrels go when they shouldn't and become road-kill, but I highly doubted that if I chose to go to church, albeit late, I would end up as roadkill. And I'm not saying I'd experience a type of roadkill of the soul if I didn't go, because that's just dumb, but maybe I would.

Anyway, I went on to church and walked in late. I missed the opening song, but that's okay. I'm here.

The pastor's message—I'm listening to it as I write this—is about security, in Christ and in the gospel, security in the love and grace of God. On the overhead video screen is one of my favorite Bible verses about if God begins a good work in you, He will finish it.

Earlier we sang, "Nothing in my hand I bring, simply to the cross I cling; naked, come to Thee for dress; helpless look to Thee for grace; foul, I to the fountain fly; wash me, Savior, or I die."

When I sing that, when I sing, "or I die," I sing *die* with great emphasis. I believe it that strongly, that unless Jesus washes me, I will die in my dirt and sin.

Later we're going to have Communion, although I sense that I'm already experiencing communion. I'm thinking about the can of spray adhesive in my purse and how much this holy place and the gospel and even the people sitting around me are like glue.

The songs and the sermon remind me that God has adhered me to Himself and that I am forever stuck to Him, but in the best sense of the word.

Please forgive me, I usually hate inane similes and metaphors and wordplays, and I'm tempted not to write about glue in this way, but I will because I believe it's true. I am bonded with Christ, secured to the Father, the Holy Spirit and I held fast to one another.

I don't know how the burlap on the footlocker thing will work out, but I do know that I will never be separated from God. I know that I might have thought of all of this even if I hadn't come to church, but I did and I'm glad.

I'm glad I'm here. I'm glad there's security in the gospel and that I can sneak into church late, a can of spray adhesive in my purse, and be welcome. Always and forever welcome.

WHOSE GOD IS TOO SMALL?

*R*ECENTLY I met a woman who titles her upcoming years. She decides what she wants to accomplish or see happen in the coming year and then assigns a theme to it. This year's theme is: "Your God is too small."

She said she had been telling a friend about all the things she doubts will ever happen—her parents coming to faith in Christ, her son returning to his faith. She doubts her life will ever make a great—or any—impact in people's lives.

There truly is nothing new under the sun, as King Solomon once said. I have similar doubts.

The woman's friend told her, "Your God is too small."

Not that God, the Maker of heaven and earth, is too small, but that her perception of Him and what He is willing and able to do is.

When I heard about her theme and that she planned to increase her perception and expectation of God, I thought I heard God say, "Listen up, child. Your God is too small, too."

As I thought of all the ways I've made God small, I immediately thought about how little I trust Him to care for my family. If I don't do it for them, if I don't fix things when they're broken, or at least give it my all trying, then nothing will get done. Nobody, not even God, loves my family more or better than I do, or so I think.

I thought about all the ways I've browbeaten people with the gospel, not allowing the Spirit of God to do His work as they mull over spiritual concepts and ideas, not allowing them to respond in God's time.

I've tried desperately to nag, cajole, and wheedle people into the kingdom—or at least into church—but it never works. My God is too small when I think it's up to me to do His heart-work for Him.

I'm most guilty of making God small when I expect too little from Him, as if He's a miser, unwilling to part with blessings from His hand.

Most recently I'm reminded of my shoulder, which I injured more than a year ago. A muscle knotted and I've walked around with a pain in my neck for months. I've gone to the doctor and all that, and it has been slowly getting better, but not really.

Then about a week ago I decided to ask my wee, small, little God if maybe He would, you know, help my neck to, sort of, um, feel better—if it's not too much to ask.

As I've said before, I always know that God, in His immense awesomeness, is all-powerful and big enough to do anything. It's my trust in His willingness that shrinks Him down to the size of a dried pea.

Not immediately, but darn close to it, the knot in my shoulder muscle started to relax and my neck is feeling significantly better.

Yeah, yeah. It might've happened anyway even if I hadn't asked, but I did ask, and God grew bigger.

In *Prince Caspian*, one of the Chronicles of Narnia books, C. S. Lewis writes about a reunion between Lucy, one of the children who discovered the magical land of Narnia, and Aslan, the lion who is the Christ figure in the series.

Time had passed since Lucy had seen Aslan, and as she "gazed into his large, wise face," she said, "Aslan—you're bigger."

"That's because you are older, little one."

"Oh, not because you are?"

"I am not," Aslan said. "But every year you grow, you will find me bigger."

I love that, don't you? God never changes. He stays immense and huge, majestic and almighty. He spoke creation into being, and it was.

However, God having spoken the universe and all that's in it into existence doesn't get my attention nearly as much as when He humbles Himself to grant one of my faithless requests. To me, that's the bigness of God—that He would make Himself small just for me.

In many ways, my God is still way too small, but every year as I grow, with every tentative step I take, I believe that I will find Him bigger.

I'M (NOT) *the* GREATEST!

SOMETIMES I think I understand men, but mostly I don't. I do, however, find them entertaining.

I grew up with two brothers who, for the most part, were aliens. They used to pound the daylights out of each other, get up from the floor, and then go in the kitchen and fix themselves a sandwich.

The guys here in the newsroom are the same way, only they pound each other with words in red-faced, teeth-baring debates and then walk out the door laughing on their way to lunch with each other.

That's so different from girls, who snip and snipe and backstab and hold snooty little grudges for days and make snarky comments while smiling sweetly. That I understand, having a sister and two daughters and being a girl myself. But the whole macho, chest-thumping, beating each other to a bloody pulp, territorial boy stuff is foreign.

But, as I said, it is entertaining.

A man I knew in California used to have arm-hair-pulling

contests with his dad. They would sit at a table and yank on each other's arm hair. Whoever flinched first lost the competition.

Like I said, aliens.

One of the things I've observed about men is their aversion to being last or least. Even men who love to serve others seem to do it with a sense of chest thumping. Maybe not so much with a "look at me" attitude, but with an "I'll be a servant, but on my own terms" thing, which, frankly, contradicts the whole concept of servanthood. Servants don't get to be the boss.

Last week I visited a church where the pastor talked about the time Christ's disciples were doing some chest thumping of their own, arguing among themselves about which of them was the greatest.

"What were you arguing about?" Jesus asked them, although He already knew because next He called them over and said, "If anyone wants to be first, he must be the very last, and the servant of all" (Mark 9:33–35).

As the pastor was telling the story, I had a mental picture of men pulling each other's arm hair and pounding each other, and I felt quite smug in a girly, "I'm so glad I'm not a boy" way. *Girls are naturals at being last and servants of all*, I thought.

Then I imagined myself walking with the disciples, overhearing their conversation and the pearls of wisdom that would spring from my lips. But then I got sideswiped by truth and realized that if I had been there, I would not have said anything, but not because of anything virtuous in me.

I would've kept quiet, all the while thinking, *You dolts. When Jesus turns around and sees all of you arguing and that I'm not a part of your testosterone party, He's going to make a mental note to put me at the head of the line. By being quiet, does that not prove that I am the greatest?*

That's when I realized that wanting to be first and greatest isn't a gender thing, but a human thing, and that I didn't know squat about being last or least.

When it comes to being a servant, I don't think many of us ever truly get it right, not completely and not consistently anyway. I think it's more natural to fight for first place and against being last, either by outward boasting or inward self-righteousness.

Jesus said the greatest is the servant of all, and as far as I know, He's the only one who fits that description.

But the hope for us is that, by the power of the Holy Spirit, we are increasingly being made more like Jesus, inside and out, and that even with all our unservantlike posturing, Jesus continues to love us, chest-thumping, silent sniping, and all.

PANTS *of* GRACE

FOR NEARLY twenty years, my friend Lorrie Bridges in California has held the title of Keeper of the Red Wool Pants.

They originally belonged to Raquel Diaz, who got them at a thrift store. They're gorgeous—a rich red, like a fine red wine, 100 percent wool, fully lined.

Raquel is tall and medium build, and I am short. Even so, the pants fit us both, which was always a mystery to us.

Although I hardly ever wear red, I wore these pants. It was cold where we lived, on the Monterey Bay, but when we moved to Florida, where it's rarely cold enough for wool pants, I gave them to Lorrie. It's like the *Sisterhood of the Traveling Pants*, only for middle-aged women.

Of all my friends in California, Lorrie is the one I've kept in contact with most regularly. Last time she and her family came to Orlando on vacation, I went to see her, although I forgot to ask her about the red pants.

As we caught up on news from California, Lorrie told me that she's been thinking about writing a book on parenting, but she doesn't think her story is valid. First of all, she grew up in a happy family and has loved the Lord all her life. She once told me a funny story about singing in church when she was little. Everyone would be singing, "And we sing glory, glory, glory to the Lord," but she thought they were singing about her—"Lorrie, Lorrie, Lorrie to the Lord."

She grew up happy, and then she married a good man who also loved the Lord. They led worship together in church for probably twenty years. They're still married; she's still happy.

They've raised three children, all who have excelled academically and athletically. They're decent and well-adjusted. No drugs, no drinking, no promiscuity. The kids love going to church. They love to be with their parents.

Years ago, Lorrie's husband, a triathlete, broke his neck riding his bicycle, but he's recovered now. Lorrie has some health problems, but her eyes still sparkle when she laughs.

For years, other parents have come to her for her parenting "secrets," asking, "Why have *your* kids turned out so well?" She told me nothing she does is secret. She follows the Bible and uses common sense. Still, she said, she could list about a dozen questions she's asked most often and the answers she gives. I told her that's a book right there. Each question could be a chapter.

But beyond a book's structure, Lorrie's afraid that her story isn't valid. She said sometimes people laugh and call them the "Stepford" family, as if doing well is somehow not normal or not a valid testimony of God's grace.

"Who would listen to what I have to say?" she asked, as if her family's wellness and wholeness and functionality are somehow a handicap. But is that true?

Sure, dysfunctions and messes and mistakes and how God

rescues and redeems make compelling stories—great drama. Everyone likes to hear ashes to diamonds stories. People like to hear stories from those who have it worse than them. It's comforting to know that you're not the only screwup out there.

But what about those who do things right? What about those who follow God's laws and commands—with delight, not grumbling—and who reap the benefits of living right? Why should they be dismissed or be made to think their lives don't reflect reality?

At age thirteen, my youngest daughter bemoaned not having an interesting testimony. "What am I going say—that I've been to church every Sunday since I was two weeks old and a Christian since I was three?" she asked.

I told her that that's a good testimony. That, too, is a testimony of God's grace.

Grace fits everyone's story. It's not just for the lawless, but also for the law-abiding, not just for the hedonist, but for the self-controlled and temperate as well.

It's a little bit like the red wool pants that fit the tall Raquel, the not-at-all-tall me, and the medium-tall Lorrie. Different body types, same pants. Different life stories, same grace.

It's really quite amazing.

BRINGING MY ANGER *to* CHURCH

*I*T'S PROBABLY not a good thing to go to church angry at God, but a few weeks ago, although I tried not to, that's what I did.

Have you ever done that? Try not to be angry when that's what you are? Have you ever forced yourself to think pleasant, nonangry thoughts when what you're really thinking would cause any mind readers sitting near you to move away to avoid the lightning bolt that is sure to strike any moment?

I don't remember what set me off. Probably I wanted to control the universe and couldn't. Probably I thought something should've happened that didn't or shouldn't have happened but did. Maybe I thought that if I could be good for a day or prayed long enough or hard enough about who knows what, God would give in and grant me my heart's desire, but He didn't.

Like I said, I don't remember what triggered my anger, but I do remember the anger itself because it scared me. I had come to church angry at God. I had marched into His house on His day, ready to duke it out with Him.

"Come on, give me Your best shot," my attitude taunted.

At the same time, that scared me, because who am I to raise my fist to the One who made my fist or challenge the One who has the power to drop-kick me all the way to kingdom come and back again? But I couldn't switch my anger off. I didn't know how to be un-angry, didn't know how to leave it in the car, so I brought it into church with me.

At one point I thought seriously about leaving—this was long after I had taken my seat and fake-smiled my way through greeting friends. I thought about gathering up my things and running out and never coming back.

That'll teach You, God, for being mean! I won't ever come to Your house again. So there. As if my running out, as if my anger, would cause Him to lose sleep.

I swear, sometimes I don't know why God doesn't just sell me to traveling gypsies or turn my skin green or smite me with boils on my backside.

But I was angry and had come to church, and since I was already there I figured I could suck it up and then continue my mad fest once the service ended. While everyone else sang about how good God is, I would think about how not good I thought He was.

Then the soloist sang not about "God is good," but about "When anger fills your heart." She sang about being doubtful and feeling like life is unjust and how when these thoughts come and you don't give in and give up, when you bless instead of curse, that's when the kingdom comes.

As she sang, it was as if God peeled back a curtain revealing eternity. It lasted only a brief fraction of a moment, but long enough for Him to remind me that I see life with blinders on, one slice of history unfolding at a time, and that He sees it all, from eternity past to eternity future, and that every confusion, every dashed dream, everything that appears to go wrong isn't wrong at all, but eternally, ultimately right.

I don't understand God. I had come to church angry at Him, wanting a fight, and instead I got a glimpse of eternity through the lens of His mercy and grace.

Sometimes I feel sorry for God, having to deal with morons like me. But maybe that's all part of Him being God and me not being Him.

Maybe the best thing you can do when you're angry at God is to come to church, bring your anger with you into His house, into His presence. The apostle Peter says to cast all your cares upon God, for He cares for His own (1 Peter 5:7). I'm guessing that means your anger and venom, too, not just your worries and concerns about paying your rent on time.

I don't have a neat, tidy way of summing this up. No "and now I'm no longer angry at God and never will be again" happily-ever-after conclusion. The truth is, I left church still angry, but not nearly as angry as when I had arrived.

Maybe sometimes that's all we can hope for.

FOLLY IS *as* FOLLY DOES

*T*HERE'S A PROVERB that goes: "As a dog returns to its vomit, so a fool repeats his folly." I think about this proverb a lot, especially when I find I'm falling into the same sin pattern, "repeating my folly."

For me, it's always about my youngest daughter. She's off on her own, making her own way—mistakes and all—slaying her own dragons, battling her own demons, learning her own life lessons.

God has His hand firmly and securely on her life, which is part of the problem, at least from my point of view.

When things are going well with her, then I thank God for His gracious hand of mercy. A stranger at a gas station paid to have her tank filled, and the day before she found twenty-six dollars on the ground. Sometimes she comes home to find groceries on her doorstep.

Way to go, God! He loves my kid. He's treating her nicely. She thinks He's cool.

Cool stuff like that happens to her all the time, and when it does, I lift my hands and say "Amen!" and vow never to worry about her ever again. Once I told a friend, "God doesn't need me—I can relax. Finally. He'll take care of her. I believe. I truly believe."

Not twenty-four hours later I was crying to another friend about being scared and worried—I can't even remember what it was about—and how badly I wanted to rush to her side and take care of things.

My vomit (my folly) is not trusting that God knows exactly what He's doing in my daughter's life and that whatever hardships she goes through are ultimately for her own good.

I know with every fiber of my being that God is infinitely more kind and more loving toward her than I am or could ever hope to be, but I don't *know* it. I believe it in theory but not in practice, which means I don't really believe it.

So, God and I go round and round, usually until I'm exhausted from trying to box with Him. Or maybe wrestle is a more accurate term. Either way, it's not a sport with me.

This is my kid we're dealing with, and I'm sorry, God, but if You think I'm going to give her up without a fight… then I'm in for a shel-lacking, as my husband would say.

Sometimes I bypass God and go right to my daughter, which rarely turns out the way I want it to. Actually, I get hurt less from being shellacked by God than by her. But you have to give me credit for trying, right?

I'll call her with my mom-nag of the moment, all with the intention of keeping her safe and happy and wholesome and whole. She'll listen and then ask (before she hangs up on me), "How old am I, Mom?"

To which I'll answer, if only in my head, "Twelve."

She's twenty-three.

To her credit, she has become a lot more polite at hanging up. Last time she said, "I'm hanging up the phone now, Mom. Love you." *Click.*

I know she'll be okay, that she is okay, although I don't see how that's possible without my steady, unrelenting, neverending, non-stop, continuous input. I still don't understand why I can't just hand her a list of everything I think she should do and not do, and then she could just do what's on the list and then we'll both be happy.

It makes so much sense to me…

A few weeks ago, after a hang-uppance that I admit I deserved, I couldn't sleep. I was worried and scared, conjuring up grisly what-ifs, accusing God of being unfeeling and uncaring and cruel.

When I couldn't think of any more adjectives to hurl at

Him—and trust me, I can think of many—He reminded me that I have never had to watch my kid be tortured, beaten, and mocked, crowned with thorns, crucified.

I knew He was right.

But then He said softly, "I know how you feel."

And, if only for the briefest of moments, I knew that He did.

EVERYBODY'S WATCHING EVERYBODY

ONE OF MY daughters is a "secret shopper." Companies pay her to go into restaurants or clothing stores and shop. As she eats or shops, she's paid to observe the store's employees, all the while behaving like any other average customer. After she leaves the store, she writes a report of her observations: "The salespeople seemed too busy talking to each other to pay attention to customers." "The waiter disappeared as soon as he brought the food and failed to suggest dessert."

She also notes good service: "The salesperson was helpful by retrieving pants in a different size when asked."

Although not many of us get paid to people watch, we all do it. It's human nature to observe others and to make judgments based on what we see.

Before I had children, whenever I'd see a dirty-faced toddler, I'd think, *Surely that child's mother is unfit as a parent.* And then I had a toddler and discovered that no matter how immaculate the child may be when you leave home, by the time you get to where you're going, half the dirt in your county will have made its way to your child's person like a heat-seeking missile.

But most of us don't see the clean child; we only see the dirty one and think, *Tsk, tsk, tsk. Bad parenting.*

My point is, everybody's watching everybody else and taking notes, especially when it comes to other people's lives of faith. Announce that you're a Christian, and stand back as people pull out their notebooks—"Last Tuesday you didn't pay for a grape you ate at the market" or "Wasn't that you I saw coming out of Sleazy's Bar the other night?"

When I started having my picture in the paper every week, I told my daughters, "Now I can't slug you in public." Not that I ever did, but just in case I ever wanted to, that would be the moment someone would see and think, *And she calls herself a Christian!*

On the one hand, knowing that others are watching can be a good thing. It makes you think twice before doing something wrong. Knowing that I have an "Enjoying God" bumper sticker (with the name of my church) on my car often keeps me from speeding or showing my impatience with other idiot drivers on the road.

Even non-Christians watch their behavior if they think someone may see.

On the other hand, hiding sin from the eyes of other people doesn't remove it because sin is a heart issue. I can do everything correctly and uprightly on the outside but be rotten on the inside and no one will know. But even though I may fool you—I may even fool myself—I'm still guilty.

Take last Friday. I had just come from my weekly Weight Watchers meeting, feeling good. I'd been steadily losing weight, shrinking out of my clothes. But no sooner had I left the meeting than I had an overwhelming urge to hit every fast-food place on my way home and then eat an entire seven-layer cake.

I didn't, of course, but I thought about it. I thought about ways I could eat everything in my path and still show a weight loss the following week so no one would know.

Sin is that devious and that mind corrupting.

It makes you think that who you are on the outside, the person others see, is who you really are. But it's who you are when no one's watching that's the real you, and the real you often isn't real pretty.

That's what makes the gospel so incredible. "God demonstrates his own love for us in this: While we were still sinners, Christ died for us," writes the apostle Paul.

More and more, as I'm daily confronted by my utterly sinful heart, I'm at the same time captured by the depth and breadth of God's love for sinners like me.

So for those who are taking notes, write this: Christ died for sinners, and He lives to change them from the inside out, little by little, day by day.

That's what I hope people see when they see me.

Psalm *of* Foot-Stompin' Thanksgiving

DEAR GOD,

As I ponder the past year and attempt to put a theme to it, more than anything else this has been a year of foot-stompin' fun.

The chief end of man is to "glorify God and enjoy Him forever," and this year I have experienced that enjoyment. Thank You,

Lord, for fun and laughter. Thank You for cake with buttercream icing, stretch boot-cut jeans, mugs of steamy chai latte, and the book *Blue Like Jazz*.

Thank You for the moonlight that shines on the lake, first stars to wish upon, *The March of the Penguins*, and daughters who make me smile. Thank You for towels hot from the dryer, kisses at midnight, and the scratchiness of my husband's unshaven face early in the morning.

Thank You, Lord, for laughter so hearty it hurts—and for cleansing tears. Thank You that Your grip is sure and Your arms underneath me are strong. Thank You, Lord, for Bare Minerals cosmetics and fat black pens.

At times this year Your grace to me in the face of my ungrace to others has caused me to come undone. To look skyward and ask, "Who are You, Lord, that You would lavish Your kindness on someone such as me?"

This year I've tasted goodness undeserved. I've feasted on Your mercy, gorged myself on Your love. I've also run from You—in many ways I'm still running. But even as I run, my spirit cries, "Catch me, Lord!"

Oh, thank You, Lord, for Your sure and steadfast grip that will not let me go no matter how fast and far I try to run.

This year I've wrestled with doubt and unbelief and plain old laziness. I've wrestled with pride and greed and wanting just one more bracelet or pair of shoes. I've wrestled with unkind thoughts and attitudes that shame me to my core, and I've welcomed Your mercy and soaked in Your forgiveness that washes me clean.

Thank You, Lord, for inner stirrings that nudge me out of myself and for tears shed for others. Thank You for breezes that blow against my face and for Your holy wind that blows through my life. Thank You for friends who pray and for bitter tears and boisterous laughter that we share with each other.

Thank You for awe and wonder, for curiosity and the longing to know You more.

Thank You for answered prayer that ignites my faith and unanswered prayer that tests it. Thank You for grilled cheese sandwiches on sourdough bread, for faithful pastors and wise mentors, for digital photography, a goofy-grinned granddaughter, and thunder so loud it shakes the house.

Thank You, too, Lord, for dissatisfaction and discomfort, insecurity and failure, because they point me to You, the One who alone satisfies and comforts, brings security, and redeems even the most humiliating failures.

I have wandered far and You have brought me back, flirted with sin and You've exposed my heart—yet always, always, *always* with an overwhelming, everlasting love. Thank You!

In a world gone mad, You are and always will be a rock on which I can stand, a shield I can hide behind, a fortress to keep me safe from my enemies.

Lord, as I write this, my heart and spirit soar. Aware of Your majesty and greatness, I'm humbled before You. You who are King, You who created the ocean and the stars and who designed Labrador retrievers and fuzzy pink pigs, You stoop from Your highest heaven and invite sinners like me to join Your great party.

Thank You, Lord, for calling me to Your party, for the gifts of repentance and faith, for eyes to see, ears to hear, and feet eager to dance with You.

The psalmist said, "Let everything that has breath" give You thanks and praise, and so I do. With all my heart, my mind, and my strength, thank You.

Thank You, Father, for Your watchful care. Thank You, Jesus, for Your passionate sacrifice. Thank You, Spirit, for breathing life into every cell of my being.

To the One who has rescued and redeemed me, given me purpose and hope, and who fills my life with delight, with a heart filled with foot-stompin' gratitude, I give You thanks.

GOD MAKES ALL THINGS BEST

*T*HERE'S A BED in my bathroom, a tree in my dining room, and a fuzzy miniature penguin in my freezer, which can only mean one thing: My husband is home.

After working (and living) in Jacksonville, Florida, for seven years, he finally retired and moved back home full-time. Since he's still young and not one to be idle, he plans on finding a midlife career. Eventually.

For now he's doing what he loves best—tearing the house apart and putting it back together, although I haven't yet figured out what the penguin in the freezer is all about. It does, however, make me laugh.

I love my husband. I love how he can take a house or a machine apart and restore it. But I also love order—and there's a bed in my bathroom, a thirty-gallon trash can in the living room, a bed frame out on the screened porch, and books stacked everywhere.

We've only been in this house for three and a half years, and I lived in it alone for two and a half, so it's not like the house has had a chance to deteriorate. But there was a microscopic (in my opinion) mark on the wall of the front bedroom I use as a writing room, and I made the mistake of pointing it out to Barry.

The next thing I knew, there was a bed in my bathroom—and four fingertip-sized holes poked into the bedroom ceiling. As Barry explained, the builder didn't drive the nails into the ceiling drywall properly, and the protruding nails created rust spots, which needed to be fixed.

That was a week ago, and the holes are filled, the walls are primed and ready to be repainted, and I hope by the time you read this the bed will be out of the bathroom and back in the bedroom and I can have order in my house again.

Except…my husband's home and he's not satisfied to fix just one thing. I know him well enough to know that he's already thinking about the next thing that needs his attention. The tile in the shower is high on his hit list.

If you ask me, I'd rather cover up the imperfections with a plant or a picture and keep the lights dim; disorder makes me nuts. But Barry has this thing about fixing things that need fixing, and he doesn't stop until everything is right. Not just "good enough," but the way it should be.

That's how God is, too.

He takes a person, content with things the way things are, who likes his favorite sins, who likes her pet faults, and who doesn't want things messed up, and then He moves in and razes and rearranges everything.

I've been on the razing and rearranging end enough times to know that the process is often messy and disorderly—like my house right now. It can be unpleasant and downright painful, too.

But I also know that I've been on the fixed end of God's improvement projects, such as being able to forgive someone I thought I never could—and not only forgive, but have genuine affection for.

God makes people better.

Likewise, whenever Barry tears a room apart, he always puts it back better, even if he does take his sweet time doing it.

And whenever I start fretting about the mess—did I mention how much I hate disorder?—he'll say, "This won't take forever, I promise. And you know that it'll be done right."

That's also what God says.

"He who began a good work in you," wrote the apostle Paul, "will carry it on to completion until the day of Christ Jesus" (Philippians 1:6). Another translation says, "He'll be faithful to complete it in you."

When God starts something in you, He might make a mess and you might chafe at the disorder, but He's doing something better—something best. And He gives grace along the way.

Maybe that's what the penguin in the freezer is all about. It reminds me that my husband is home, that he loves me, that he's working on my behalf, and that in the middle of all the chaos that makes me so nuts, he adds moments of delight that make the process bearably sweet.

HOPE WHISPERS ITS SURE PROMISE

URING THE Christmas season, I play a CD called *The Promise* by Michael Card. Card is a troubadour, a storyteller in song, and he sings about the story of Jesus, from His prophesied birth to the fulfillment of the promise that He came to earth as "Immanuel, God with us," to bring hope to those who desperately need it.

Even when my Christmas tree is packed away and the CD is back in its case, Card's Christmas message continues to echo through my mind and my heart: "His wounds are for our healing." "The just and gentle Promised One would triumph o'er the fall." "Tired eyes at last can see You; longing lips can speak Your name." "If God is with us, who can stand against us?"

Card's words are soft and gentle, yet full of power—and hope. They make me think of hope as a whisper, a warm sweater, the color aquamarine with a hint of gray, muted and soothing. Hope as a warm breeze, the smell of fresh bread, hot from the oven; the giggle of a three-year-old as she grabs her daddy's knee and holds on tight.

We need hope, don't we?

I got an e-mail today, an urgent prayer request for two women—one whose child died, the other with a child "in a bad place." Earlier this week I learned that a dear man, who always greeted me with, "Hey, Kennedy," died unexpectedly.

"Don't leave off hoping, or it's of no use doing anything. Hope, hope to the last," wrote Charles Dickens in *Nicholas Nickleby*.

We need hope.

In the movie of *The Lion, the Witch and the Wardrobe*, the land of Narnia, where it's forever winter but never Christmas, is controlled by the White Witch. According to the Deep Magic, written on the Table of Stone and put there by the Emperor-Beyond-the-Sea, every traitor belongs to the White Witch, and with every treachery she has a "right to a kill."

Of the four human children who find Narnia, one of them, Edmund, turns traitor, and his life becomes forfeit to the witch. "His blood is my property," she says. And unless the traitor dies as the Law says, all of Narnia will be overturned and will perish in fire and water.

The lion of Narnia, Aslan, takes Edmund's place upon the Stone Table and allows himself to be slain. A battle ensues between the creatures of the kingdom and those who follow the witch, which ends when Aslan comes back to life. With the Deep Magic satisfied, the White Witch loses her control over Narnia, and the children are brought into the kingdom to reign with Aslan, in fulfillment of the prophesy.

As I watched the movie, I took notes. One of the things I wrote—"Hope weakens the witch's power."

Even before the climactic battle, hope melted the snow. As the children journeyed toward Aslan's kingdom, the closer they got, the more winter turned to spring. It was subtle at first; the trees started dripping, buds appeared, patches of grass poked through the snow-covered ground, and the ice on the rivers started to crack.

"Winter is almost over," and "Long live Aslan!" someone in

the movie said as hope was about to triumph.

Oh, how we need hope.

Recently, I went back and read some old columns I've written, and I noticed that I have recurring themes: worry, worship, wanting to be in control, unfulfilled longings—and hope. I write a lot about hope, mostly because we all need it so desperately.

But the thing about hope that is most disconcerting is its bite. Hope isn't hope unless it's preceded by pain or grief or sorrow or worry. Hope isn't hope unless it's all you have left. Not only that, it's often merely a whisper, a distant promise, but a promise nonetheless, that one day God will wipe away your tears, make sense of your confusion, and melt away your winter.

It's distant, but it's also sure and certain, because it comes from the One who sits upon the throne, who has promised He will makes all things new, and who never lies.

If God is with us, who can stand against us? That's our hope.

Winter is almost over!

HOME *for* CHRISTMAS

I CAN'T WAIT! Even though I know I'll be facing a messy house, maybe even a few crayon scribbles on the walls, this year—the first time in seven years—my two daughters, son-in-law, and granddaughter will all be home for Christmas.

I already have nose prints on my front window from pressing my face against it, eagerly awaiting their arrival home.

Unlike many families, we don't have any holiday traditions.

Two years in a row, because my husband had to work on Christmas Day, my daughter Laura and I drove to Tampa to eat sushi, but I don't think that counts as a tradition.

I used to decorate the Christmas tree with dated ornaments, adding one each year since our first Kennedy Christmas in 1975, but one year I stopped. Now my tree's not decorated with dated, mumbo jumbo ornaments. Now each year I put up a small artificial tree on an end table and decorate it with fake fruit and white lights.

I also don't cook anything well enough to have people clamoring and salivating over it in eager anticipation every year. I can't make a roast that isn't dry; my lasagna tends to be runny. My cakes bake lopsided and gooey in the middle. I do make great homemade tamales, but they're a lot of work.

Even so, despite a lack of family traditions, my family is coming home for Christmas.

From as far back as I can remember, I've always wanted a *Leave It to Beaver* home. The Cleavers weren't perfect, but they came darn close, at least in my opinion. But my home isn't and never has been like the Cleavers. We're not quite the Simpsons, but we come darn close at times.

Mostly we're just a mishmash of odd characters who, through genetics and the providence of God, wound up together as a family. None of us "fit," yet strangely we do. We're exactly who God placed together to create a home.

I think the story of Christmas is the story of home.

We all want to go home, but not necessarily to the ones we have here on earth. Not the homes where the dad is cruel or distant or gone. Not the homes where the mom drinks secretly, even though everybody knows it.

Not the homes where everybody fights about things that should've been forgiven and forgotten years ago. Not the homes where grudges are stronger than affection, where everyone feels inadequate and unappreciated, or just left out.

Not the homes made up of flawed human beings.

I think we all have an image of an ideal home, and rarely is it the one we grew up in or live in now. But deep inside, we know such a home exists. We just don't know how to get there.

That's the story of Christmas: Jesus left His perfect home to enter our dysfunctional, mishmash ones. Not to make them perfect, but to provide a way that we could be part of His home, His family. Forever.

In the melancholy Christmas song "I'll Be Home for Christmas," the singer lists all the things that would make it "home"—snow, mistletoe, and "presents 'neath the tree." The punch line is: "I'll be home for Christmas, *if only in my dreams.*"

Some people say that the Christmas story of Jesus coming to earth to seek and save lost souls who are longing for home is nothing but a dream, that it's too good to be true. Or else they say it's hogwash.

But it isn't hogwash or a dream. Deep inside, the longing we feel for "home" tells us that it's true, that we were made for home.

The best part is, as much as we might long for home, God's the One who wants it more. Not just at Christmas, but even today, God's the One with His face pressed against the front window eagerly awaiting His children coming home.

Follow Your Bliss

Bliss is a line of delightful, true-to-life books fashioned for the busy woman seeking a momentary escape...a slice of heaven just for herself.

MORE BLISS BOOKS...

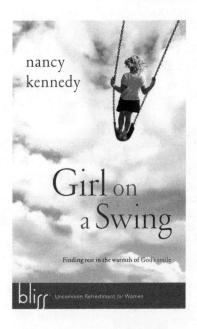

God's grace proclaims that you are His and He is glad He chose you. Delight in His love and learn to soar—like a girl on a swing.

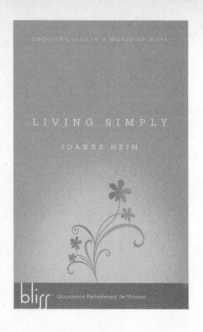

You yearn for something more …not on your to-do list, but in the heart of daily living. Choose simplicity to gain the riches of God's abundant life!

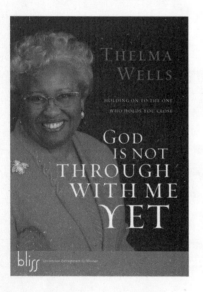

God is working every day to help you more deeply trust in Him. Popular Women of Faith speaker Thelma Wells shows the way to a more intimate walk with God.

 Uncommon Refreshment *for* Women